Starring
Miss Barbara Stanwyck

Starring

Miss Barbara Stanwyck

By Ella Smith

Crown Publishers, Inc.
New York

Grateful acknowledgement is made to the following for copyrighted material:

Doubleday & Company, Inc. *To a Lonely Boy* by Arthur Hopkins, copyright 1937 by Arthur Hopkins. Reprinted by permission of Doubleday & Company, Inc., and of David J. Hopkins and his Agent, James Brown Associates, Inc.

Alfred A. Knopf, Inc. *Willa Cather: A Critical Biography* by E. K. Brown, completed by Leon Edel. Copyright 1953 by Leon Edel. Reprinted by permission of Alfred A. Knopf, Inc.

Little, Brown and Co. *The Dress Doctor* by Edith Head and Jane Kesner Ardmore. Copyright © 1959, by Edith Head. Reprinted by permission of Little, Brown and Co. and of William Morris Agency, Inc.

The Macmillan Company. *The Name Above the Title* (referred to in text as NT) by Frank Capra. Copyright © 1971 by Frank Capra. Reprinted with permission of The Macmillan Company and of W. H. Allen & Co. Ltd.

Movie Digest. "This Was My Favorite Role" by Barbara Stanwyck. Copyright © 1972 by *Movie Digest*. Reprinted with permission of *Movie Digest*.

Prentice-Hall, Inc. *The Autobiography of Cecil B. DeMille* by Cecil B. DeMille, edited by Donald Hayne. Copyright 1959 by Cecil B. DeMille Trust. Reprinted with permission of Prentice-Hall, Inc.

All photographs from *The Noose* and *Burlesque*, except Edward Steichen's, are reproduced by permission of the Theatre Collection of The New York Public Library at Lincoln Center—Astor, Lenox and Tilden Foundations.

Steichen photograph courtesy Edward Steichen.

Frontispiece and other Engstead photographs courtesy John Engstead.

Inquiries should be addressed to Crown Publishers, Inc., 419 Park Avenue South, New York, N.Y. 10016.

Printed in the United States of America

Published simultaneously in Canada by General Publishing Company Limited

Designed by the author

ACKNOWLEDGEMENTS

The author is deeply grateful to the following for their generous assistance:

John Alton
Anne Baxter
Albert Beich
Ralph Bellamy
Curtis Bernhardt
Lyle Bettger
Joan Blondell
Scott Brady
Frank Capra
William Castle
Nancy Coleman
Ricardo Cortez
John Cromwell
Bob Cummings
Delmer Daves
Joe DeSantis
Andre de Toth
William Dieterle
Allan Dwan
Robert Florey
George Folsey
Henry Fonda

John Ford
Samuel Fuller
Michael Gordon
James Gregory
Laurence Harvey
Sidney Hickox
William Holden
Paul Ivano
Leigh Jason
Joe Kane
Fritz Lang
Mitchell Leisen
Anatole Litvak
Joel McCrea
David Manners
Fletcher Markle
George Marshall
Lewis Milestone
John Llewellyn Moxey
Barbara O'Neil
Gerd Oswald
Irving Rapper

Governor Ronald Reagan
Ray Rennahan
Roy Rowland
Joseph Ruttenberg
Alfred Santell
John Seitz
Anne Shirley
Robert Siodmak
Harold E. Stine
John Sturges
Barry Sullivan
Regis Toomey
Jacques Tourneur
King Vidor
Virgil Vogel
Robert Wagner
Joseph Walker
Charles Marquis Warren
Billy Wilder
Robert Wise

John E. Allen, Inc.; The American Broadcasting Company; The American Film Institute—David Shepard; Spencer Berger; David Chierichetti; The Columbia Broadcasting System; Columbia Pictures Corp.; The George Eastman House—James Card, George Pratt; John Engstead; William K. Everson; Films, Inc.—Allen J. Green; Four Star International, Inc.; Guy Giampapa; Gerald Haber; Bill Hahn; Larry Kleno; Richard Lawton; The Library of Congress; The Lincoln Center Theatre Collection—Dr. Rod Bladel; Leonard Maltin; Metro-Goldwyn-Mayer, Inc.; The Museum of Modern Art; The National Broadcasting Company; The New York Public Library; Paramount Pictures, Inc.; *Photoplay* Magazine; RKO Radio Pictures; *The San Francisco Chronicle* —John Stanley; Edward Steichen; Charles L. Turner; Twentieth Century-Fox Film Corp.; United Artists Corp.; United Press International; Universal International Films, Inc.; Warner Brothers–Seven Arts, Inc.; Franciene Watkins; WBZ-TV; WJAR-TV; WKBG-TV; WMUR-TV; WNAC-TV; WNEW-TV; WPRI-TV; WSBK-TV; WTEV-TV.

The author is a director and, for this book, has seen all of Barbara Stanwyck's films and television work.

*Ella Smith has written a love song
about a gutsy lady of Quality. A
woman who, as a person or an actress,
never gave anything less than her best
shots, no matter how rough and major
the circumstance or how tough and minor
the role.*

*And all her peers in Hollywood chorus
"Hosanna!" in this joyous chorale to
the First Lady of the Screen—Barbara
Stanwyck.*

—Frank Capra

CONTENTS

Part I   The Merry-Go-Round   XI

Part II   The Brass Ring   97

Part III   Three-Ring Circus   179

Part IV   The Bandwagon   269

Awards and Honors   321

Filmography   324

Index   334

Part I

The Merry-Go-Round

Yes, she does look wonderful—but I feel we are losing something. I think she is potentially a great actress, a unique personality, but we are not getting it on the screen. I want to shoot the sequence over with no make-up, no glamorous portraits—just show her as she really is and I think she will be great.

—Frank Capra to Joseph Walker
Ladies of Leisure—1930

They did and she was. Four decades later she still is—because Barbara Stanwyck's appeal on the screen lies not in illusion but in the sincerity and naturalness of her acting. As Capra says, when she "turned it on everything else on the stage stopped."

Since Capra's discovery of her talent, Stanwyck has acquired a thorough knowledge of how to project it—through make-up, glamorous portraits, and all the other technicalities of film making that once hindered her. Her flawless mastery of her craft has made her a delight to all who have worked with her. But her greatest asset remains that ability to move an audience. Combined with the skills she has learned, it has made her what Samuel Fuller calls a "happy pertinence of professionalism and emotion."

There is another side to Barbara Stanwyck—as satisfying as her talent and professionalism. She is as gifted in the art of living as she is in the art of acting. In his autobiography, *The Name Above the Title*, Frank Capra states that Stanwyck was "destined to be beloved by all directors, actors, crews, and extras. In a Hollywood popularity contest, she would win first prize hands down." It seems she has done just that. The author did not interview those who have worked with Stanwyck in order to conduct such a contest. But the admiration that poured forth from these people was so overwhelming that—as their comments will show—one can only conclude that Barbara Stanwyck is, as Capra says, a "rare individual."

Stanwyck was born in Brooklyn July 16, 1907—the fifth child of Byron and Catherine McGee Stevens. She was named Ruby. Orphaned at four, she was looked after by her sister Millie—a show girl who paid foster homes for keeping her. This situation has been served up Oliver Twist style by Hollywood for years. But, as Stanwyck has put it: "It was not as bad as it's been made out to be; foster homes in those days weren't cruel—they were just impersonal."

As a child, she was strongly drawn to things she would love all her life. In *Portrait: Barbara Stanwyck*, a special filmed on the set of *The Big Valley* in 1968, she told director-interviewer Ralph Nelson:

When I was a kid I was so crazy about Westerns. This was the Pearl White era, and she was my idol. I always swore when I became an actress ('cuz I knew I was going to be an actress —nobody told me—I just knew) that I was going to do that.

After watching *The Perils of Pauline* or *The Exploits of Elaine*, she would act out her "own version of Pearl White" in Prospect Park. And the resulting passion for stunt work—which Stanwyck has indulged fully throughout her career—has produced some glorious footage and some nervous directors.

Dancing in the streets to the music of the hurdy-gurdy, she discovered the other area of the entertainment world that appealed to her. She has said: "All the kids danced in the streets in those days" but added "I loved dancing and knew I wanted to do more of it."

It all pointed toward show business—and actual contact with this was the deciding factor. Her sister often played in road shows and, occasionally, took the young Stanwyck with her. Here—watching from the wings, living and traveling with show people— Stanwyck developed her great fondness for the profession and realized she wanted to be a part of it.

At 14 she graduated from grammar school and took her first job—that of "a package girl at the Condé Nast outfit." (A number of early jobs have been erroneously listed for Stanwyck, including one as a telephone operator—which she wasn't.) Her stay with the Condé Nast organization ended when "I said I knew how to cut from a pattern. I didn't know what the hell I was doing and I was fired." An ad which she answered from the Remick Music Publishing Company led her, at 15, to a chorus call at the Strand Roof and what she had wanted in the first place: show business.

The Strand Roof was a nightclub over the Strand Theatre on Times Square. And its dance director, Earl Lindsay, hired her as a floor-show chorine at $35 a week. Lindsay was a serious worker and gave the self-taught Stanwyck her first professional training. She learned fast and pleased him—so much so that, later, when he was staging dances and ensembles for Broadway revues, he cast her in a couple.

The first of these was a summer show called *Keep*

In stroller, with brother Byron. UPI

The Noose, *with Rex Cherryman
and Helen Flint*

Kool; it starred Hazel Dawn, Charles King and Johnny Dooley and opened May 22, 1924 at the Morosco. Stanwyck danced as one of sixteen "Keep Kool Cuties" and appeared as Agnes in the sketch "A Room Adjoining a Boudoir (Apologies to Avery Hopwood)."

Lindsay's work was singled out by several, including *Variety*, which said it was

> . . . the hoofiest chorus seen in ages. The 16 girls are pips, lookers and dancers. They pop over a ballet that would make Tiller [Lawrence Tiller, whose art graced the *Ziegfeld Follies* at the time] turn green, kick like steers and look like why-men-leave-home in their many costume flashes.

The sketch in which Stanwyck appeared was part of a satire showing how George M. Cohan, Avery Hopwood and Eugene O'Neill might each treat the same plot. And its success led her to another engagement. *Keep Kool* moved to the Globe in early July and closed there August 30th. Shortly after that, some of its material was incorporated into the touring company of the *Ziegfeld Follies.* Stanwyck repeated her role in the Hopwood sketch, sang and danced in two numbers, and was part of a third—the famous "Ziegfeld Shadowgraph"—which she described in 1953 to Hedda Hopper:

> Three-dimension is nothing new—just a revival of an old stunt and perhaps an improvement or two. We had a three-dimension stunt when I was a chorus girl with *Ziegfeld Follies.* I did a strip tease behind a white screen and tossed my clothes out into the audience. They were given polaroid glasses and saw me in third dimension.

When asked what happened if they didn't use the glasses, she replied: "Then they didn't see anything."

Her tour with the *Follies* ended in 1925 and, by the fall of that year, she was appearing in a Shubert revue, *Gay Paree.* Winnie Lightner, Billy Van and Ruth Gillette headed this one. Dances were again staged by Earl Lindsay, and Stanwyck was billed as one of the "Ladies of the Ensemble."

Mae Clarke, who went on to film work too, was in the chorus with her. And Stanwyck was now rooming with Clarke and Walda Mansfield—another chorus girl, who later became the wife of songwriter Walter Donaldson. The three were good friends and shared their "prosperity" when it existed, and their stretches "at liberty" when it didn't.

In January of 1926, Stanwyck and Clarke secured spots at the Everglades Café and combined these with their work in *Gay Paree* in a nightly race between club and theatre. As Stanwyck has recalled the experience, she and Clarke ran back and forth in little but coats and shoes "in freezing weather. And the coats were not so hot either. But we worked like dogs, were strong as horses."

Gay Paree closed at the end of the month and a period of being "at liberty" set in. Whenever this happened, Stanwyck and her roommates (along with any other out-of-work performers who came to him) survived through the kindness of Billy LaHiff, owner of The Tavern, a restaurant on 48th Street where show people and other celebrities congregated. Billy LaHiff's generosity provided on-the-cuff meals. And his concern for those he was helping led to the combination of luck and timing that would give Stanwyck her first big break. Learning that Willard Mack—leading producer, director, playwright and actor of the day—was casting a play called *The Noose,* LaHiff introduced Stanwyck to him. She was hired as a chorus girl. Mack needed four of these and Stanwyck volunteered: "I got two others so you don't have to look!" Clarke and Mansfield were hired too.

The Noose bombed in its tryouts and Mack did some rewriting. The play concerns a young man who has been condemned to death and a society girl whom he loves. Stanwyck was playing a cabaret dancer who loves the man but goes unnoticed by him. An emotional scene in the third act was to have found the society girl pleading for the body of the hanged man. Mack decided it should be the dancer who pleads. This meant that Stanwyck—who had had only a few lines—was given an entire scene to carry. A look at the original synopsis will show what a fitting one it was for her at the time:

> They are startled when Dot [Stanwyck] begs an audience with the Governor. She probably can furnish the clue [to a mysterious telephone message which has delayed the hanging]. Dot is almost too dazed at first to speak—the Governor kindly helps her. Last night, after the performance was over, they all sat round—talking about Nickie. Only a few hours more now—then he would be gone. It was terrible watching the minutes tick by. They took up a collection—all they could raise. For Nickie. His body, you

know. No, he didn't love her—another girl. But she thought now that he was dead, she could take him to a little cemetery that she knew—and there tell his deaf ears the things she would not dare say while he was alive. Deeply affected, the Governor tells her that Nickie is not dead. There can be no doubt of the girl's sincerity—she had no knowledge of the telephone message. Almost hysterical with the knowledge that Nickie is still living, she goes—begging passionately that he never be told of her visit.*

Willard Mack prepared Stanwyck thoroughly for her dramatic debut. It was, naturally, an overwhelming experience for her. As she has described it:

Only through Willard Mack's kindness in coaching me, showing me all the tricks, how to sell myself by entrances and exits, did I get by.

It was Willard Mack who completely disarranged my mental make-up. The process—like all processes of birth and rebirth, I guess—was pretty damn painful. Especially for him. I got temperamental. The truth is, I was scared. I'd storm and yell that I couldn't act—couldn't, and what's more, wouldn't. I think I can honestly say that this was my first and last flare-up of temperament, because Mr. Mack—who had flattered and encouraged me—shrewdly reversed his tactics.

One day, right before the entire company, he screamed back at me that I was right. I was dead right. I was a chorus girl, would always be a chorus girl, would live and die a chorus girl, so to hell with me. It worked. I yelled back that I could act, would act, was not a chorus girl—was Bernhardt, Fiske, and all the Booths and Barrymores rolled into one.

From there they could go somewhere and they did. Mack continued to coach her and she continued to improve. Further tryouts brought applause and satisfaction.

In the course of his work with her, Mack also decided that Ruby Stevens was not a very good name for a dramatic actress. Looking at some old programs in the Belasco Theatre, he came across one reading: "Jane Stanwyck appearing in *Barbara Frietchie*." Avoiding a second Jane (because of Jane Cowl) he

arrived at "Barbara Stanwyck"—and presented his protégé with a name as strong as the actress she would become.

The Noose opened at the Hudson on October 20, 1926. It was a hit—and so was Barbara Stanwyck. The *New York Sun* said: "Miss Barbara Stanwyck . . . had a moving scene in the last act and played it well enough to make first nighters wipe tears from their eyes." The *Billboard*, a Cincinnati newspaper, announced: "Barbara Stanwyck . . . is splendid as the leader of the little chorus. She achieves real heights in her brief emotional scene." And the *New York Telegram* was beside itself:

There is an uncommonly fine performance by Barbara Stanwyck, who not only does the Charleston steps of a dance hall girl gracefully, but knows how to act, a feature which somehow, with her comely looks, seems kind of superfluous. After this girl breaks down and sobs out her unrequited love for the young bootlegger in that genuinely moving scene in the last act, of course, there was nothing for the Governor to do but reprieve the boy. If he hadn't the weeping audience would probably have yelled at him till he did.

Willard Mack not only discovered Barbara Stanwyck's talent; he helped her develop it all he could. Throughout the run of the show (197 performances) she took approximately a play a week and studied it. She has said: "Mr. Mack was a busy man and he couldn't work with me constantly. But he did when time permitted—and I had the advantage of working with him two or three times a week."

While still in *The Noose*, Stanwyck was brought by an agent to the old Cosmopolitan studio at 125th Street and Second Avenue to make a screen test for producer Bob Kane. Wilbur Morse Jr.—a press agent for Kane at the time—gave an account of the proceedings some years later:

Everyone in the studio was nuts about the girl except the cameraman who photographed her screen test. He wanted to make her, he said, and she wasn't in the market for cameramen, producers *or* press agents.

She was handicapped further that day because the scene that she was asked to play called for her to cry. The director had the old-standby methods of starting the tears to trickle—an onion, a rasping violin, and a cracked piano.

---

* This was to be the substance not only of Stanwyck's first success on Broadway, but of the screen test which would bring her to Frank Capra's attention for *Ladies of Leisure*.

6

Burlesque

Burlesque. *Improvisation with Hal Skelly.*
Photo by Edward Steichen

Burlesque, *with Hal Skelly* ▷

Ruth Chatterton came on the set while Barbara was doing her best to emote. The Henry Miller star was accompanied by a Negress, her maid. The white woman and the black one watched the director's efforts with the onion and the music.

Then Ruth Chatterton tittered and in a voice that would have frozen a Boston butler began talking to her maid—asking her to imagine anyone on the stage resorting to onions and audibly wondering if all cinema persons had to do that sort of thing.

I walked over to where Miss Chatterton sat with her maid. Barbara had already hissed a "shut up" between sobs.

"You are probably so busy with your own show," I suggested to Miss Chatterton, "that you may not know this girl is Barbara Stanwyck, whose crying scene in *The Noose*—when she asks for the body of the man she loves, after he is hanged—is bringing the critics back night after night just to have a good cry!"

There were no more titters and la-de-dah accents thrown around the set until Miss Chatterton herself started a screen test. (P.S. Ruth Chatterton did not get a job—at the Cosmopolitan studio.)

The picture for which Stanwyck was testing was *Broadway Nights*—a silent—in which she subsequently played a small role as a dancer and sweetheart to the producer of a show. Morse added:

> It took Hollywood and motion pictures three years to learn that Barbara Stanwyck was an actress. That she would have been ideal for the cabaret dancer [the lead] in *Broadway Nights* was the contention of everyone on the set that day, except the rebuffed cameraman, who photographed her badly, and the director, who was busy paying his respects to a chorus girl between takes of the test.

Broadway Nights, starring Lois Wilson and Sam Hardy, was released by First National in May of 1927. Stanwyck does not regard it as one of her films. Her screen debut is generally considered to have been in *The Locked Door,* and it is of little consequence in a study of her work that the negative of *Broadway Nights* has crumbled.

The unfortunate experience of her first screen test was soon counteracted by the interest in her expressed by producer-director-playwright Arthur Hopkins.

George Manker Watters' first play, *Burlesque*—whose second act Hopkins had rewritten—needed two versatile players for the lead roles. In his autobiography, *To a Lonely Boy,* Hopkins recalled that he wanted

> . . . actors who could play comedy and pathos and sing and dance. For the man I engaged Hal Skelly, a musical-comedy comedian. He had had little experience in plays but he had an engaging, lovable quality which was essential to the part of the burlesque comic. After some search for the girl I interviewed a night-club dancer who had just scored in a small emotional part in a play that did not run. She seemed to have the quality I wanted, a sort of rough poignancy. I engaged her. She at once displayed more sensitive, easily expressed emotion than I had encountered since Pauline Lord.

Following a tour that caused excitement, *Burlesque* opened the New York season at the Plymouth on September 1, 1927, and was an overnight hit. Its second performance broke house records.

The play—staged by Hopkins—focuses on comedian Skelly and his dancer wife Stanwyck in drama behind the scenes. They are playing a hick town in the mid-west when Skelly gets a chance at the big time: an offer of a star spot in New York. Stanwyck encourages him to accept, although it will separate them and place him near a feminine rival. When he takes up with the other woman, Stanwyck files for divorce and plans to marry a butter-and-egg man. But she learns that Skelly is drinking himself to death without her and returns to him instead. They are together at the play's end—hoofing in a small-time show, and making up with each other as they dance.

The appeal of the play lies in the heart of its characters and the colorful vernacular which they speak. There are a number of touching scenes—two of which are outstanding. These were well described by reviewer Gilbert Gabriel in the *New York Sun:*

> The reconciliation of the hoofers is exquisitely playful. You are watching the actual burlesque show. The two young ones—nimble, funny, shabby, creatures of loose ankles and chapped souls—are dancing dutifully on. And while they dance—in broken, breathless asides—they patch their cheap little quarrel up. A last crazy twirl, like powerless marionettes—and that's all of their amen.

Burlesque

Burlesque

There is another such dance scene, though, even more stabbing. It comes at the ragged end of the second act. The drunken comedian is faced by his wife and her nice new man. He has only two weapons, song and dance. He does a terrible, heart-gnawing mimicry of the wedding march—as sickening to himself as to them—and dances himself futilely, incoherently out, a pagliaccio rigid in the wires of jazz.

Some years later, Mae Clarke told an interviewer how moving the latter scene had been when Stanwyck could take this no longer:

> Suddenly Barbara began beating her hands on the piano and screaming, "Stop it! Stop it, I tell you!" I have never heard one person get as many vibrations into her voice as Barbara got into hers then. It was like a symphony chorus in the Hollywood Bowl instead of just one person speaking.

Critics did not all accept the play or its direction. But they were loud in their praise of its stars. Brooks Atkinson in *The New York Times* said:

> Hal Skelly's high spirited performance of the slap-dash comic and Barbara Stanwyck's quietly sincere interpretation of the music hall wife are joys to behold.

And Alexander Woollcott in the *World* felt:

> Miss Stanwyck's performance was touching and true and she brought much to those little aching silences in a performance of which Mr. Hopkins knows so well the secret and the sorcery.

Today—some forty-five years after *Burlesque*—theatre and film people who saw Barbara Stanwyck play Bonny remember this as one of *the* outstanding experiences in theatre, and have vivid recollections of what she brought to the role.

During the run of the play, Oscar Levant—who was also scoring in it—introduced top vaudeville-star Frank Fay to Stanwyck. Fay, billed as "Broadway's Favorite Son," had been in show business since childhood. When he met Stanwyck he was at his peak, having set a record of twelve straight weeks at the Palace in 1926. On August 26, 1928 they were married in St. Louis, where Fay was appearing as M.C. at the Missouri Theatre. Stanwyck returned east to tour with *Burlesque,* and Fay continued with his engagement. She left the show a few months later and joined him in New York.

Continuing his statement in *To a Lonely Boy,* Arthur Hopkins wrote:

> She and Skelly were the perfect team, and they made the play a great success. I had great plans for her, but the Hollywood offers kept coming. There was no competing with them.

And, shortly before his death, Hopkins told an interviewer: "Barbara Stanwyck is the greatest *natural* actress of our time."

James Hargis Connelly, Chicago

The Hollywood offer Barbara Stanwyck accepted came from Joseph Schenck—then head of United Artists—who had seen her on Broadway and wanted to feature her in *The Locked Door*. But the film that would have been better for her was *The Dance of Life* (the first film version of *Burlesque*) which John Cromwell and A. Edward Sutherland were directing for Paramount.

Cromwell had begun his career in the New York theatre, just before sound took over on the screen. He had seen Stanwyck in *The Noose* and, as he tells it: "was terribly attracted to her but didn't have anything [a property] for her then." In 1928 he went to Hollywood to direct pictures. *The Dance of Life* was set to roll in February of 1929, and Cromwell wanted Stanwyck to play Bonny. Paramount tried to get her but, unfortunately, it could not be worked out. As a result, the richly praised teamwork of Stanwyck and Skelly was lost forever, and she was destined to begin her film career with a couple of scripts that would do little for either her reputation or her spirits. It's true she might have had some difficulty with any first film. But—as with her stage debut—a fitting role and good direction would have helped.

At any rate, she did *The Locked Door*—a sound remake of Channing Pollock's play *The Sign on the Door*. Since the "movies" had just become "talkies" the handicaps were many, and they were particularly hard on a natural actress. Stanwyck's stage training had taught her to project to the balcony, a larger-than-life technique. The proximity of a mike was in direct opposition to this. And she could not scale her performance down convincingly because the film was directed with slow, precise speech—in deference to crude recording techniques. In short, she couldn't win.

Nobody did in this film. And the primary reason was the script: a masterpiece of pitfalls for an early talkie. As a stage vehicle, it had gotten by in 1919. But it was less impressive in 1921 as a silent starring Norma Talmadge. And by 1929 it was worn out. What it offered was contrived, archaic and cinematically dull.

Briefly—it shows Stanwyck suspected of murdering a man who has, instead, been killed by her husband. In a lengthy police investigation, the husband confesses to save her—and a "deus ex machina" saves them both. It seems the murdered man is not dead after all. He still has a few moments—just long enough to tell "whodunit." In a deathbed scene which lacks only Little Eva ascending to heaven, he reveals their

Columbia. General publicity—1930

innocence. He was shot by the husband—but it was an accident.

With *unbelievable* kindness, critics shot the film down but defended the actors. The *New York Herald Tribune*'s comment was typical:

> Miss Barbara Stanwyck gives an honest and moving picture as the distraught wife. . . . It is in every way an excellent piece of work. [William Boyd, the stage actor] is just about right as the husband, and Rod La Rocque plays the villain as well as could be expected. . . . But you always feel that they should be playing *The Locked Door* in powdered wigs and crinoline.

The film looks terrible today, and application of the term "excellent" to Stanwyck's performance is hard to understand. However, her intensity draws—even through the discomforts that hinder it—and it may have been this that blinded the critics.

In 1958, Stanwyck herself gave a much better description of *The Locked Door* when she told the *Los Angeles Times*: "They never should've unlocked the damned thing."

Her next, *Mexicali Rose*, was even worse. This one has her playing a woman of easy virtue—married to Sam Hardy and faithful to no one. Hardy finds she has been deceiving him and divorces her. To get even, she marries his young ward and tries to corrupt him. Hardy and his henchmen do her in.

Stanwyck has called the film "an abortion" and said she "didn't even know how to make an entrance and exit." That she was in trouble and unhelped is apparent.

No matter how much ability an actress has, she cannot go from one medium to another without instruction. On the stage, Stanwyck had been able to shape a performance—to work it through in sequence and build it. And since *The Locked Door* was really a filmed stage play, it had allowed her, at times, to use what she had learned. In the loosely constructed and confusing *Mexicali Rose*, she was faced with less control over the final product. And without knowledge of how to key in in her scenes, she was working blindly. The director—or someone—should have guided her and taught her the tricks that would make her secure.

Because she lacked this security, her timing was off and sometimes even her vitality disappeared because she was so uncertain. To make things worse, she was miscast. She had too much class for the cheap tart she was playing, and she was not yet proper material for a heavy. In trying to make her into something aesthetically wrong for her, director Erle C. Kenton resorted to externals. She was forced to keep her hands on her hips and slink a lot, and the camera focused more on her bottom than her acting. All in all, it was a sad experience for the girl who had proved herself in *Burlesque*.

And so, with two dogs to her credit, Stanwyck found herself without further film offers. Her sensitive nature felt alienated by Hollywood, which worshipped success and overlooked anything less. And, as she faded further into the background, she developed an impregnable shell for protection. Hollywood mistook this for sullenness, and the director who was to discover and guide her talent to striking heights for them both was almost fooled by it too.

Along with her two films, Stanwyck had been making tests. About all these did for her was to develop an aversion toward what she still looks upon as an unfair practice. But one was to give her the break she needed. And, although the making of it was grim, the experience did foreshadow what was to come. As Stanwyck has told it, after her "two horrible films":

Nobody in Hollywood wanted any part of me. I sat around idle for six months, working myself up into a panic of self-doubt. My confidence had almost been destroyed. Finally, it happened.

A studio was to test me. It was a night test and I guess they figured they'd get the kid in and out in a hurry. There was no director, no make-up man and no script.

A man came in and said "I've been asked to do a test—can you suggest something?"

It's a cruel moment when you know you're being given the brush-off. But I couldn't blow up at this man. He was in a spot too and he was just too nice. I told him that I could do a scene from *The Noose* without a script. He set the light and gave me some pointers. I knew it was wasted motion but I thought, what the hell, and gave it my best.

When it was over, I was amazed to find tears in his eyes. He seemed to be searching for words. At last he said, "I want to apologize for the way this studio has treated you tonight. It doesn't mean anything coming from me. I'm leaving Hollywood a failure. But I want you to know it's been a privilege to make this test with a real actress—a privilege I won't forget."

And he kissed my hand as if I'd been Sarah Bernhardt. I will always be grateful to that man for those words and that gesture because they sent belief in myself back to me. Incidentally, that "failure" was the man who was to win a knighthood for his great screen achievements— Sir Alexander Korda.

A sequel to the evening is related by Ray Rennahan (later, cinematographer for Stanwyck's first color film, *California*) who photographed the test. Rennahan explains that, on the day of the test, he was shooting

A Technicolor picture for Warner Brothers [when] the production manager came on the set and said:

"The front office has a foreign director and a young girl, from New York, that they want a test of in color to see if they have any motion picture potential."

A few days later when [he returned] I asked him how the test came out. He said: "The front office ran the test, and said neither the director nor the girl had anything to offer for motion pictures."

The test was soon shown to a more discerning audience. Columbia had an option on Stanwyck's services, and Harry Cohn suggested her to Frank Capra for *Ladies of Leisure*. Capra had other ideas for the leading role in this film, but agreed to interview Barbara Stanwyck. In his autobiography, he describes their meeting:

She came into my office, sullen, plainly dressed, no make-up. Obviously hating the whole idea of an interview, she sat on the edge of her chair and answered in curt monosyllables. I didn't want her before she came in, and what I saw of this drip now made me sure of it. After about thirty seconds of the usual inane questions—"What plays have you been in?" . . . "Have you made any movies?" . . . "Would you make a test?"—she jumped to her feet and snapped, "Oh, hell, you don't want any *part* of me," and ran out.

I phoned Cohn. "Harry, forget Stanwyck. She's not an actress, she's a porcupine."

A half-hour later, Frank Fay, her sarcastic, comedian husband was on the phone.

"Look, fella, what the hell did you do to my wife?"

The Locked Door, *with Rod La Rocque*

The Locked Door, *with Harry Mestayer and William Boyd*

Columbia. General publicity—1930

"Do to her? I couldn't even talk to her."

"Well, she came home crying and upset. Nobody can do that to *my* wife."

"Listen, funny man. I don't want any part of your wife, or of *you.* She came in here with a chip on her shoulder, and went out with an ax on it."

"Frank, she's young, and shy, and she's been kicked around out here. Let me show you a test she made at Warner's."

"A test?"

"Yeah, a scene from *The Noose.* About three minutes long. You gotta see it before you turn her down. I'm coming right down with it . . ."

The test flashed on the screen. Nothing in the world was going to make me like it. After only thirty seconds I got a lump in my throat as big as an egg. She was pleading with the governor to pardon her convicted husband. Never had I seen or heard such emotional sincerity. When it was over, I had tears in my eyes. I was stunned.

"Wait in my office," I said to Fay and rushed off to see Cohn.

"Harry! Harry! We've got to sign Stanwyck for the part . . ."

"What're you, nuts? Half-hour ago you told me she's a kook."

"Yeah, yeah—but I just saw a test of her. She'll be terrific. Frank Fay's in my office. Sign her up. Don't let her get *away* . . ."

Barbara Stanwyck was lucky: the right role, right time, right director, others pulling for her. But she was also capable. Once in, she had to produce. And Capra was to discover what Mack, Hopkins and Korda had found—or as he puts it:

Underneath her sullen shyness smoldered the emotional fires of a young Duse, or a Bernhardt. Naive, unsophisticated, caring nothing about make-up, clothes, or hairdos, this chorus girl could grab your heart and tear it to pieces. She knew nothing about camera tricks: how to "cheat" her looks so her face could be seen, how to restrict her body movements in close shots. She just turned it on—and everything else on the stage stopped. (NT)

Stanwyck was, and still is—despite the flawless technical proficiency she has acquired—a *natural* actress.

As different as night from day is her work in *Ladies of Leisure* from what she had done previously. In fact, *Ladies* contains a couple of scenes that rank with the best she has ever played. Capra attributes this to her "pristine quality." Maybe lack of instruction on her first two films did her a favor, because it allowed her to fall into Capra's hands untouched. She acted by instinct, and Capra was just the right person to recognize the importance of preserving this.

Cinematographer Joseph Walker, who would photograph all four of Stanwyck's early films with Capra—creating as much enchantment for her with his lenses as the director did with his understanding—tells how it began:

When Miss Stanwyck was signed by Columbia Pictures for *Ladies of Leisure,* Harry Cohn said he thought she would be hard to photograph and wanted me to do everything possible to make her look glamorous. This was the day of the glamorous stars and his request was in line with studio policy.

So I told Frank Capra I must take time to make many tests and do everything I knew to get the results Harry Cohn expected of me.

Capra said, "I would rather do a sequence from the picture instead of a test. You can take your time and do anything you want to." We had a rush print made so we could see the result the next morning.

Barbara looked beautiful. I had put in several big close-ups and the result was gorgeous. I knew Cohn would be happy. Capra seemed pleased, but I knew him well enough to know that something was bothering him. So I said, as we left the projection room, "I've done my best—I think she looks wonderful—what's the trouble?"

"Yes, she does look wonderful" he said, "but I feel we are losing something. I think she is potentially a great actress, a unique personality, but we are not getting it on the screen. I want to shoot the sequence over with no make-up, no glamorous portraits—just show her as she really is and I think she will be great."

I said, "OK, but when Harry Cohn sees it I'll be right out on Gower Street looking for a job." Capra replied, "Well Joe, I'll be right out there with you if that happens." That was good enough for me, and we now know just how right Frank Capra was.

And so, aware of her potential, Capra says:

When we started to work, I attempted only one thing—to preserve the intense honesty of the

Mexicali Rose, *with William Janney*

Mexicali Rose, *with Sam Hardy*

Mexicali Rose

Noose scene. I insisted that Barbara show how really deeply she felt things. In that way she was encouraged to develop a dramatic personality which, if it hadn't been real, might have been melodramatic. But it *was* real.

In his attempt to preserve her genuineness, however, Capra soon hit a couple of snags. The first occurred when he learned that her gift carried with it some unique demands:

> . . . after a few scenes, I discovered a *vital* technical lack—one that shook us all up: Stanwyck gave her all the *first time she tried* a scene. . . . All subsequent repetitions, in rehearsals or retakes, were but pale *copies* of her original performance. (NT)

This, he explains, is because

> Stanwyck doesn't act a scene. She *lives* it. Her emotions are so genuine that they must be captured in their first expression. Her best work is the result—not of timing and rehearsing and study—but of pure feminine reaction. She gives everything she has, and its great sincerity and strength must be caught at fever heat.

Capra found this

> . . . a new phenomenon—and a new challenge; not only to me, but to the actors and crews. I had to rehearse the cast without her; work out the physical movements without her. The actors grumbled. Not fair to them, they said. Who ever heard of an actress not rehearsing?
>
> And the crews had problems. I had to take the "heart" of the scene—the vital close-ups of Barbara—first, and with multiple cameras so she would only have to do the scene once. Multiple cameras aggravate the difficulties of lighting and recording in geometrical progression, i.e., four times as complex with two cameras, eight times with three cameras.
>
> On the set I would never let Stanwyck utter one word of the scene until the cameras were rolling. Before that I talked to her in her dressing room, told her the meaning of the scene, the points of emphasis, the pauses. Her hairdresser Helen had become her confidante. I let Helen give her the cues from the other actors. I talked softly, not wishing to fan the smoldering fires that lurked beneath that somber silence. She

remembered every word I said—and she never blew a line. My parting admonition was usually this: "Remember, Barbara. No matter what the other actors do, whether they stop or blow their lines—you continue your scene right to the end. Understand? Good girl." (NT)

The second snag was easier to handle. As Stanwyck has told it:

> Things went well for two weeks, until I decided I ought to look at the rushes. I was sick. My gestures seemed abrupt. My hands looked awkward. And I pulled my mouth to one side when I talked fast.
>
> The next day I waved my hands around in elaborate gestures and delivered my lines very carefully. Capra let it pass, but the following morning he said, "Want to see the rushes again?"
>
> I was embarrassed by how bad they were.
>
> "See what you're doing?" he said. "You're trying to look beautiful. And in doing that you're losing the wonderful thing you had—complete naturalness. If you lose that, you're sunk. I want you to promise me not to look at the rushes again."

Stanwyck has avoided the rushes ever since.

Frank Capra's careful work paid off with one of the most exciting director-actress combinations ever to hit the screen. It would be repeated in four more films and remain complementary. (Capra cast Stanwyck more frequently than any other actress.) A look at his philosophy as a director will show why he was so pleased with her.

Capra likes to move his audience. He places emotional appeal above intellectual. And, for this, he wants real people on the screen—people with whom the audience can identify, and for whom they can care. He feels a film director should "convince actors that they are real flesh and blood human beings living a story."(NT) He makes the actor—not the camera or director—the star. And so he needs actors who can run with the ball when he gives it to them.

He often uses spectacle to enhance his approach, but it is to support—not replace. Music and the elements add excitement; they overwhelm, humble, uplift. But actors (or, as he would say, "people") remain his primary concern and he keeps them with him in the climb, making the final product theirs.

Stanwyck's intensity guaranteed that she could reach any heights he asked of her. She never dropped the ball, and she scored. She is able to believe in any logically motivated situation and—more important—she has the equipment with which to put it across. Her physical, mental and emotional make-up allow her to become absolutely transparent—revealing whatever she thinks or feels. Her eyes mirror this; her voice and movements do the same. She is the most "human" material a director could want.

Ladies of Leisure was an excellent script for Stanwyck, because it permitted Capra to use what he had seen in her. She plays a "party" girl who is hired by artist Ralph Graves to pose for a portrait which he titles "Hope"—because he has glimpsed this beneath her tough exterior. In time she falls for him, and her true nature abandons the make-up and wisecracks that have protected it.

But this is one of those two-sides-of-the-tracks stories. And Graves' business tycoon father—who has had enough trouble with his son's impractical interest in "art"—draws the line at welcoming a party girl for a daughter-in-law. Stanwyck runs off on a pleasure cruise to drown her sorrows—and herself. Graves finds out and radios the ship just as she jumps overboard. She is rescued and they are reunited.

The plot outline may not be great reading (are they ever?) but its treatment was something else. Jo Swerling had taken the original script (a dull rendering of the 1924 play *Ladies of the Evening*) and given it a transfusion. As Capra puts it, it became "human, witty, poignant."(NT) Capra supplied the same touch with his direction, and his actors gave performances to match.

Stanwyck shone handsomely in those two areas which were to become her trademark—areas out of which she has built the major part of her career: toughness and suffering. Within each, she was capable and comfortable. As a tough cookie, she masks her feelings with a steady stream of flip remarks—never missing a trick. And when she falls for Graves and loses her ability to "take it," her mask comes off—showing "Hope" as "the thing with feathers" that hurts when they are pulled out.

The heart of *Ladies of Leisure* is a twenty-one-minute love scene of exquisite sensitivity. It is really two scenes, with an interruption that serves to bring the second to its conclusion.

Despite his reverence for them, Capra says he finds love scenes difficult to do. "Love is desire—an intangible thing." He "usually approached them obliquely through argument, idle talk, or complete silence. The idea was to charge the minds and atmosphere with hot desire, stringing out the fulfillment as long as possible. . . . the bringing together of two people in love can be as suspenseful as a Hitchcock thriller." (NT) It certainly is in *Ladies.*

Capra sets his scene carefully. It is 1:15 in the morning and it is raining. He states: "In practically every picture I've ever made there are scenes in the rain—especially love scenes. It's a personal touch. Rain, for me, is an exciting stimulant, an aphrodisiac." (NT)

As he uses it, it is also poetry. The studio closes in on two people alone in the world. Light from the fireplace draws them closer. A skylight slants inward, and rain patterns it with reflections from the terrace.

Stanwyck, who has posed for four hours, passes out—and Graves carries her to a chair and revives her. Because of the hour and the rain, he suggests she stay overnight. She agrees, but her disappointment is profound because she misinterprets his offer. She loves him and wants him to be different from the other men she has known.

As the two make up the studio couch, Capra places her between this and the rain-jeweled skylight—making her more helpless, and contrasting the homely image of the bed that runs through her mind with the beautiful one of her that Graves fails to notice.

Graves goes to his room, and Capra builds the scene by cutting back and forth to their awareness of each other as they undress. Back lighting from the terrace frames Stanwyck, and an impressionistic shot from the other side of the window heightens the intensity of the rain and the desire. In Graves' room there is no poetry; but there is strong attraction to what is in the studio.

After Stanwyck has gone to bed, the scene is filmed entirely from her viewpoint, showing what she sees and hears. There is a shot of a doorknob turning and of Graves' feet crossing the floor. Because she pretends to be asleep, she does not see the blanket he is carrying. When he puts it over her and leaves, it becomes as large in her mind as the doorknob and footsteps—and it restores her faith in him. The climax of the scene must be a silent one, so she brings the blanket to her mouth. The way in which she does this provides the outlet for her discovery and her joy.

Scene two opens with a shot of eggs frying, as a cheerful Stanwyck fixes breakfast. Sunshine and "Hope" fill the kitchen. Graves enters, cross as a bear,

Ladies of Leisure, *with Ralph Graves*

Ladies of Leisure, *with Ralph Graves and Lowell Sherman*

Ladies of Leisure, *with Marie Provost*

and fails to appreciate her efforts. She knocks herself out trying to please him, but he hides behind the morning paper. She reaches across the table to bring the rose she has cut for him to his attention. His newspaper knocks it over. Irritated, he puts the vase on the floor. She begins to cry, and tries to cover her hurt with a futile display. Tossing toast into the air in one of the most pathetic moments a human being could hope to survive, Stanwyck reaches a peak equal to any she has ever played. Capra gives her the scene, and she is able to give him exactly what he knows will make it. Emotion, real and unrestrained, pulls the audience apart.

It gets through to Graves too. But he has beaten her too badly. Their relationship is now awkward, and pity is no substitute for love. The scene could not be expected to make it from here. So Graves' father arrives unexpectedly, and serves as a catalyst. Trying to break them apart, he drives them closer.

When the father insults Stanwyck and leaves, Graves—in his rough way—defends her. Rough treatment is hardly what she needs, and the physicalization inevitable in their feeling for each other occurs by accident when her hands touch his mouth to stop his words. They kiss, and he realizes she is not the tramp he thought. Capra lifts the scene to its climax by having Stanwyck jump into Graves' arms—be picked up by him and carried to the sofa.

Because he has slapped her down for so long, Capra now handles his heroine with infinite gentleness. He keeps the camera close to absorb the softness and warmth with which he envelops her. He has Graves cradle her on his lap, or on the sofa, or with her head over his shoulder. He sets up the camera to photograph her where she is going to be and has her fall

into the position. Actors and director trust each other, and the work is completely natural.

With a few careful choices, Capra thus concludes a love scene whose structure and impact can hold their own with any ever filmed. Study actually enhances its value, and it can teach a prospective film maker more in twenty-one minutes than he might ever learn by himself.

Because Capra's "oblique" approach in the beginning of the scene is largely one of "complete silence" (except for the rain, and there is something to be said for silent rain) it might be argued that the silent version of this is the most beautiful. It leaves more to the imagination. However, both versions have their magic.

Stanwyck's work in *Ladies of Leisure* is perfection. If she had never made another film, she would be remembered for this one.

Reviewers were enchanted and praised her without restraint. The *New York Review* said the picture "gives Barbara Stanwyck an excellent opportunity to show that she is as good an actress in the talkies as she is on the stage." *The New York Times* announced: "MISS STANWYCK TRIUMPHS." And the *New York Herald Tribune* called her work "assured and frequently brilliant."

Hollywood at last recognized the gift it had in her. Fan magazines were at her feet with tributes such as *Photoplay*'s:

> . . . it is a really fine picture because of the astonishing performance of a little tap-dancing beauty who has in her the spirit of a great artist.
> Her name is Barbara Stanwyck.
> . . . go and be amazed by this Barbara girl.

Ladies of Leisure

After the successful *Ladies of Leisure*, Barbara Stanwyck found herself in a very different position in Hollywood. Her value had shot up overnight. Non-exclusive contracts with Columbia and Warner Brothers followed, as did publicity build-ups, and she was on her way.

Her first film under this arrangement was Warners' *Illicit*—a chic mounting of arguments for and against free love. Done up in fancy gowns and wigs, Stanwyck is happily carrying on an affair with James Rennie and putting off marriage which she feels will kill the fun. When she gives in and becomes his wife, the glamour vanishes and—as predicted—they become petty, dependent and suspicious. She finds him seeking diversion with a former sweetheart and walks out. But when it looks as though he will go off with the diversion, the realization that she would rather be married to him than lose him hits her and they are reconciled.

Illicit is of no great consequence, but it is sincere. A light approach saves it from being clinical or dull. Comic relief is provided by two of the supporting characters (Joan Blondell and Charles Butterworth) and Stanwyck's spirit keeps things bubbling.

It was on *Illicit* that Stanwyck and Joan Blondell met and worked for the first time. Blondell was one of the many who had seen *Burlesque* and been deeply impressed. As she tells it, "I was never so overcome in my life." Referring to the team of Stanwyck and Skelly she says, "What they did to an audience we should be so lucky to have today. Never again have I experienced anything like it." Stanwyck "made me cry—laugh—want to hug her." She and Skelly were "two consummate artists."

Blondell feels that it is Stanwyck who was the major reason for *Illicit*'s success. ("What she did, she did on her own.") This is because director Archie Mayo knew Stanwyck could give him what he wanted and let her. Mayo once said that he had no interest in the mechanical end of things, and knew nothing about camera, sound or acting technique. He worked instead through an understanding of cameramen, sound engineers, and actors and depended upon them to know their jobs. His approach would result in two more fine Stanwyck performances—one of them (in *Ever In My Heart*) very special. Her work in *Illicit* is charming and effortless. Critics thought so too, and the film did well.

Illicit was the first film in which Stanwyck received star billing. And, in their local publicity, Warners

went all out and referred to her as "Miss" Barbara Stanwyck—an honor they were according only two other stars: Mr. John Barrymore and Mr. George Arliss.

Returning to Columbia, Stanwyck did *Ten Cents a Dance*. It was at first called *Roseland*, and then *Anybody's Girl*, but was finally named for the popular song by Lorenz Hart and Richard Rodgers upon which —the credits say—it was based. Plot and dialogue were by Jo Swerling.

In this one, Stanwyck is a disenchanted taxi dancer in a dime dance hall who marries a young clerk, Monroe Owsley. He turns out to be a weakling, a cad and a total loss—who steals money to pay debts he has incurred behind her back. Ricardo Cortez, a wealthy sophisticate who has met Stanwyck in the dance hall, lends her $5000 to clear him. When she tries to dance with Owsley to celebrate, he accuses her of having been unfaithful to obtain the money—and offers the final insult in the form of a dime, saying: "That's what you charge for a dance, isn't it?" She sees what she has married—"You're not a man; you're not even a good sample"—and leaves him. Later, she agrees to divorce him and marry Cortez.

The film starts off with promise in the "Palais de Dance" where Barbara Stanwyck's first line to a particularly repulsive customer who asks, "What's a guy gotta do to dance with you gals?" is a classic of Stanwyck cool: "All ya need is a ticket and some courage." She follows this with her flair for hitting right between the eyes—in looks, words and actions. The role would seem to be a fitting one for her. And it is. But there was so much against the film's realizing its potential that it's surprising things look as good as they do. There was a lot of hard luck.

To begin with, Stanwyck had a fall on the set which gave her a bad time. As she has put it: "Backing away from Monroe Owsley, in my desire to be vehement— overacting, I think people would call it—I fell down the stairs." Her performance gives no hint of her subsequent discomfort, but probably wasn't helped by it.

Then, Lionel Barrymore (the picture's director) was suffering from arthritis and taking medication. Of the direction, Ricardo Cortez says: "There wasn't any. It was very trying. You'd start a scene and look around and find he'd fallen asleep." Cortez makes it clear that Barrymore was "a charming man" and that none of this was his fault. It was the effect of the medication. (And Stanwyck has said: "He tried his best. As a performer, you just had to try harder.") But

Illicit

the situation created problems and Cortez says he was amazed in the light of Harry Cohn's temperament that he didn't take Barrymore off the picture.

Ten Cents a Dance is not as bad as this may make it sound. But it could have been better. Much of the time it is unsure of itself. Scenes drag or lack directorial decisions that would have made them jell, and it's poorly put together. It clearly shows how helpless actors can be without guidance. However, they gave what they could. Cortez recalls how hard they tried and says of Stanwyck:

> I never knew her terribly well, but I enjoyed working with her. She was my type of person. No nonsense. She came to the studio to work. I admired her for her dignity and professionalism. She was a perfect lady at all times. Perfect.

Night Nurse, at Warners, was Barbara Stanwyck's first film with William Wellman. She was to do five for him in all and become—as with Capra—the leading lady he cast the most.

"Wild Bill" Wellman—referred to by his actors as everything from "a sadistic director when it came to realism in action scenes" to "a ballsy guy, and damn fun to work with"—made some delightfully crazy pictures with Stanwyck. He was not timid with a gag and—while Stanwyck did some moving work for him in *So Big* and *The Great Man's Lady*—their other three films together can best be described as "no holds barred."

Night Nurse shook everybody up. It was taken from a novel by Dora Macy which the author said was true, based on the experiences of a night nurse she had known. And one reviewer called it "lurid, hysterical melodrama, unpleasant in theme, yet well presented" and went on to say:

> Imagine, if you will, a nurse whose first assignment is on a case where a dope fiend doctor and a murderous chauffeur—who slugs youth and age indiscriminately—conspire to slowly starve two darling children in order to thieve their inheritance from a dipsomaniac mother.

Obviously, the film was ahead of its time.

Stanwyck trains in a hospital where the only bright spot is her wisecracking roommate, Joan Blondell. There are a number of gags pulled by a fresh interne—including the placing of a skeleton in Stanwyck's bed. And a young bootlegger, whom she tends in the hospital, becomes her boyfriend.

When she graduates and goes to her first case, she finds the children starving and their mother spending her time with a bottle and the chauffeur (Clark Gable). A reputable doctor has been taken off the case and replaced by an unknown. A drunken housekeeper keeps her eyes closed and her mouth shut. And wild parties prevail.

Stanwyck straightens out the mess and saves the children, whose trust fund Gable was after. And the film ends with Gable "getting his" from her bootlegger friend who has him "taken care of." The couple ride off together—not into the sunset, but into the car parked behind them—as Wellman pulls the last of his stunts to cheer up a grim melodrama.

Wellman was the first to make use of the effect that could be achieved by roughing up his small but resilient leading lady. (Capra tried it soon after in *Forbidden*—probably a coincidence.) What makes it work is the fact that Stanwyck can give it as well as take it—and her revenge is always gorgeous.

In *Night Nurse* she takes a couple of crashing falls across the floor. Especially sadistic is the sock on the jaw given her by Gable (who beats up anybody in the film who gets in his way). And while she doesn't get to punch Gable back (nobody does, and lives) she does have a great time taking it out on another of her attackers.

Trying to drag the children's stoned mother to them, Stanwyck is interrupted by a drunken hanger-on who had assaulted her earlier. With no hesitation, she slugs him—knocking him to the floor. He crawls behind the bar like a wounded dog. And when he makes the mistake of looking out from behind it as she tries to revive the mother with a bucket of water, she lets him have it with the bucket.

Critics had trouble believing their eyes, and called the picture "far-fetched and exaggerated." The nursing profession couldn't be like that. At the same time, they admitted they didn't understand a lot because they were put off by the candor. Those who got the point found the use of humor effective.

Reaction to Stanwyck's work was favorable from all. And, while she still had some distance to go, the hard-boiled side of her image was shaping up nicely—to the delight of those who liked her as much for her guts as her tears.

Clark Gable didn't do badly either. Critics singled him out—as well they might. Joan Blondell remembers that, when she and Stanwyck first saw Gable, they grabbed each other's pinkies in awe. And Stanwyck

Ten Cents a Dance, *with Phyllis Crane*

◁ Ten Cents a Dance

Ten Cents a Dance, *with Ricardo Cortez*

has said, "We all knew he was a striking personality. He commanded attention."

Her next film for Columbia took her back to Capra-land and some very productive pampering. Barbara Stanwyck has worked with many top directors, and given excellent performances under their guidance. But there remains something special about her early work with Capra. It is the result not only of their talents, but of the indulgence she needed—at the time—which he went out of his way to give her.

It has been explained that, as a natural actress, Stanwyck acts more by instinct than by calculation. She lives a part, as opposed to portraying it. And it has been noted that Capra discovered her finest work was thus done on the first take. To preserve freshness and strength, he used multiple cameras and tried to work things out so she would only have to do a scene once. (Sometimes a technical fluff prevented it, but most of his takes of her are first takes.)

Now this may have given the impression that—unless allowed to function this way—Stanwyck has never been at her best. Nothing could be further from the truth. It was true when Capra discovered it, but it did not stay that way long.

Faced, during her early pictures, with directors who were either unaware of her needs or unindulgent, she was forced to learn the tricks that would help her. She taught herself to work under any conditions—to give on the first take or the tenth, and be equally effective. She developed an uncanny ability to turn emotion on and off—to whatever degree she was asked, and as often as necessary. And, actually, her ability to make it on the first take is an asset—particularly in the medium of television, where time is at a premium. Directors who have been associated with her say she makes their work incredibly easy—and give the impression that all you have to do to direct her is wind her up and let her go.

However, in 1931—still under Capra's wing—she could "turn it on" without having to think about restraint or how to keep a scene even. The result was one of those "special" performances that his care with her generated.

If Capra had made the film of ideas he had envisioned, *The Miracle Woman* would be a masterpiece. The screenplay was fashioned by Jo Swerling from *Bless You Sister*—a John Meehan–Robert Riskin vehicle suggested by the antics of Aimee Semple McPherson, who was cashing in at the time. But what started out as dynamite did not—ultimately—follow

in the mark of Mrs. McPherson's French heels.

Stanwyck opens the picture with a fiery sermon to the congregation that has replaced her aging pastor father with a younger, more exciting man. She tells them her father has just died in her arms, and they are to blame because he had to preach to "empty hearts" in "a meeting place for hypocrites." Capra volunteers:

> From here this bitter, disillusioned young lady should have decided *on her own* to give the stupid unwashed the religion they "want": a potpourri of happy sermons, brotherhood, sisterhood, and sex—all in the glittering trappings of "Xmas" paper and musical comedy. She wows them. She gets rich. *Variety* reports her weekly "take" in its show-biz columns. Then the Miracle—and her return to God. One woman's life in three acts: disillusion, venality, conversion.
>
> Is this what we did in the film—after that opening scene of great promise? No. I turned chicken. The thought of a wicked evangelist deliberately milking poor, adoring suckers for money in the name of Christ was just too much for my orthodox stomach. I weaseled. I insisted on a "heavy" to take the heat off Stanwyck the evangelist. *He* cons her into it. *He* gets wealthy. She becomes his flamboyant stooge. Did she or did she not herself believe those "inspiring" sermons delivered in diaphanous robes, with live lions at her side? I didn't know, Stanwyck didn't know, and neither did the audience. (NT)

And so, teamed with the heavy (Sam Hardy) Stanwyck preaches somewhat tentatively from the cage of lions. Her performances are garnished with flowers, music and sensuous costumes. Into this wanders David Manners, a blind ex-aviator who has taken courage from her radio sermons and abandoned a suicide attempt. When she asks for a volunteer, he joins her in the cage.

They meet further and fall in love. The jealous Hardy pulls a number of rotten tricks to separate them and then—to keep Stanwyck from exposing these—sets fire to the tabernacle while she is preaching. Manners rescues her and, at the film's end, she has been "saved" by the Salvation Army—which she's joined, and marriage to Manners—which is planned.

Despite its lack of "ideas," the film is impressive. Joseph Walker (who had become A.S.C. by then—and who remembers the picture as "a lot of hard night work, made particularly difficult by the slow film of

Warners. General publicity—1931.
Photo by Bert Longworth

that period") creates fine atmosphere—such as his firelight shots of the lovers reading a book in Braille. Stanwyck, except for her unhappy experience in the lions' cage, is magic. And *The Miracle Woman* is richly endowed with Frank Capra's genius.

Capra may find love scenes difficult to do, but he never fails with them. This time his "oblique" approach involves toys, improvisation, and a ventriloquist's dummy through which Manners can express what he is too shy to say himself. And a most fragile moment is created at a birthday party for Stanwyck when Manners tries to tell her—through the dummy—that he loves her, loses his courage, and helplessly flaps the mouth of the dummy in silence. Her reaction—as Capra brings them together—and the slow fade to what follows, will always move audiences.

Manners' blindness also helps oblique love scenes. He underplays convincingly. And Stanwyck is able to play on two levels at the same time: one in her words to him, and the other in the expression on her face—which he cannot see—as she says them. When these are at variance, she does particularly beautiful work.

Worth noting for Stanwyck, too, is a scene which shows her looking into a mirror and weeping as she applies make-up. The focus remains on her as she reacts to Hardy and his shills—mirrored behind her—rushing to set up the farewell appearance that will separate her from Manners. She stays very still as she watches, powders and cries. It is an exciting use of counterpoint on Capra's part, and only emotion of the strength Stanwyck can give would have provided the balance necessary to make it work.

If the tough side of Stanwyck's screen image was not getting a workout, her own endurance was. The scenes in the tabernacle carried with them some hazards. Manners recalls, "The lions were only an invisible netting away from us. I could smell their breath. Barbara's cool made me brave!" Capra says underneath her cool "she was scared to death."

He adds, however, that that was the way they were working in those days. There were no process screens. If a director wanted lions, he used lions. And nobody—except maybe the actors—worried very much. (He remembers, in fact, that—when he wanted a few extra roars for the sound track—a trainer obliged by walking up to a lion and slapping it on the nose. It roared. The trainer extracted several more roars and calmly turned his back on the animal to ask if that was enough.)

Equally unnerving for Stanwyck was the fire. The tabernacle burns to the ground in a realistic and spectacular blaze. Capra told Stanwyck to stay in the scene until he came and got her. With timbers falling and smoke encircling her, Capra let her stay there until the very last minute. He remembers how her heart was pounding as he carried her out—and that she would have stayed no matter what.

David Manners speaks of working with Stanwyck and Capra:

> My recollections of Barbara Stanwyck are all excellent, and this is rare for me as I have forgotten most of the people of those days. Barbara stands out as, also, does Frank Capra. They are both dedicated people.
>
> The last time I saw Barbara was at a Writers Guild shindig—an annual affair. She looked marvelous and I approached her wondering if she would remember the blind man of the lions' den. She welcomed me as an old friend, warmly. I had not seen her before at a social function and I can tell you it was a different woman. On the set Barbara was tremendously centered in her work, much too much so for any social chit chat like so many other actresses. I see her sitting alone in a studio chair—almost in meditation. I had the sense to leave her alone.
>
> On the set when we were in action together she was a different person. I have acted with few women who gave me as much as she. Eva Le Gallienne gave much to her fellow actors and maybe one other. But Barbara was *great*. She helped me believe in the character I was playing. And Capra is a *real actor's director*. The three of us were in great harmony and I never had another director like Capra. He was a giant to me. Nor did I ever have a leading lady of the quality of Barbara.

If *The Miracle Woman* did not succeed with its story, it was applauded for everything else. And, although it ultimately lost money—mainly because it was "banned in the British Empire . . . for irreverence" (NT)—it was far from a hindrance to Stanwyck's popularity at the box office.

This had risen to such a degree that she felt justified in asking Harry Cohn for $50,000 for her next film, *Forbidden*. Cohn refused and—angry at the way she was being treated—she refused to make the picture. He took her to court, won, and *then* saw to it that she got more money.

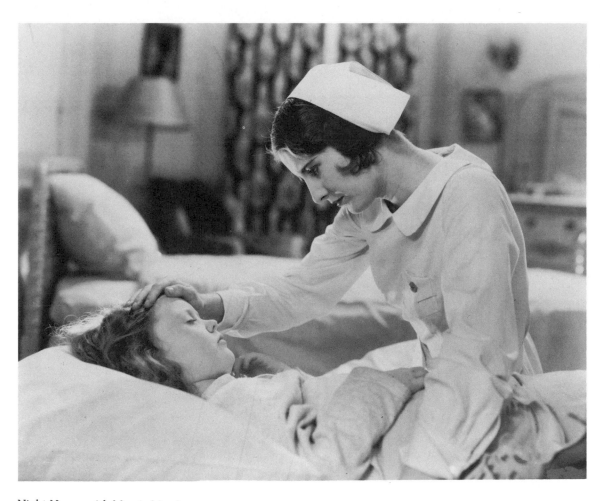

Night Nurse, with Marcia Mae Jones

Night Nurse

The Miracle Woman, *with Sam Hardy and David Manners*

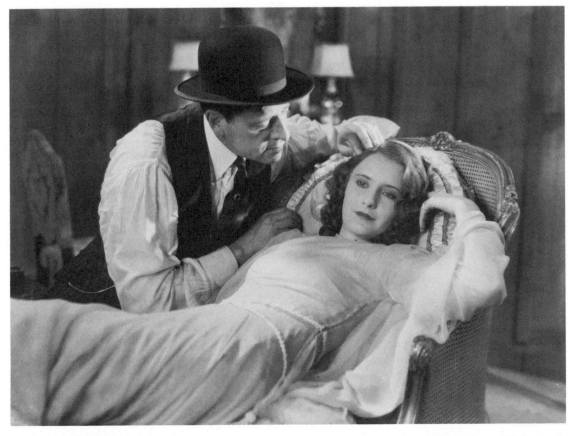

◄ The Miracle Woman, *with David Manners*

The Miracle Woman, *with Sam Hardy*

Forbidden, *with Myrna Fresholt*

Forbidden, *with Adolphe Menjou*

With *Forbidden*, Frank Capra struck out again—if you can believe it. This time he had written the story himself "with a very large assist from Fannie Hurst's *Back Street* [but] in spite of scriptwriter Jo Swerling's valiant efforts to write in some 'bones,' *Forbidden* ended up as two hours of soggy, 99.44% pure soap opera."(NT)

Its lack of potential did not stop Capra from giving it—or Stanwyck—his usual fine treatment. And while—today—he wishes he'd never made the film, it's nice to have it around for the two things even he admits it has: superb performances by its leads (Stanwyck, Adolphe Menjou and Ralph Bellamy) and "one or two directorial 'gems' (sic)"(NT) that will be disclosed shortly.

In *Forbidden*, Stanwyck and Menjou are unable to marry because he feels responsible to a wife, injured in the car he was driving. Stanwyck bears him a child—whom he pretends to have adopted—and spends her life in the background as the woman responsible for his successful political career. To help him, she marries Bellamy—whom she does not love, kills Bellamy when he becomes a threat to Menjou's career, spends time in prison, and destroys the will in which Menjou acknowledges her as his wife.

Soap it is, but it does have something of value. A new dimension comes through for Stanwyck in this film. There is a deepening—a fragile dignity and maturity beyond her years—which the script calls for, and gets.

Barbara Stanwyck's nature contains a pretty equal balance of child and woman. It is one of her most charming qualities and contributes much to her versatility as an actress. It often seems that she was born old and that she will always be young. Capra uses this in two ways. He shows his heroine aging over a period of twenty years, and—within this framework—makes her ageless because of the child-woman balance.

In the first of the "two directorial 'gems' " he places her on a boat bound for Havana. Here, in her cabin (66) she meets Menjou—who mistook it through a mist of liquor for his own (99). The mist clears, and they sweep through Havana in high gear: gambling, dancing and riding horseback against a sparkling surf.

The second gem is the most oblique of scenes—combining mime, improvisation and Halloween masks. Back in the States, Stanwyck is preparing dinner for Menjou when he arrives—wearing a crazy mask and bringing her one. They lark around: play-acting with them on, and being serious with them off. But the device gets away from them when Bellamy phones and Menjou—saddened by the proposal of marriage he hears, and unable to offer her this himself—hides behind his mask, trying to figure out how to tell her he has a wife. They have been carefree, giddy nuts. And it is a master stroke when the games fall apart, and the children age ten years in a single line.

The climax of the film is a tour de force for Stanwyck. Bellamy learns he has been duped and produces evidence that will expose her relationship with Menjou. When she tries to interfere, he knocks her against a chair and to the floor. A melodramatic score begins ticking off the seconds. She gets a gun and threatens him. As the music swells, he runs outside the door and she shoots him through it. He clutches at some window curtains and crashes to the floor with them. Wild with hate, she continues to shoot. The radio blares Menjou's election victory and people pound on the door as she burns the evidence—her eyes staring and her body shaking with fear. It is the most startling scene she has ever played.

An accident occurred on this picture during the shooting of the horseback-riding scene, which was being filmed at Malibu. It's a little hard to believe now, but Stanwyck was then afraid of horses. A double had done the riding, and Capra was preparing for a close-up of Stanwyck on the animal. He thought he had taken every precaution, but when the reflectors caught the light, they bounced it into the horse's eyes and scared him. He reared, threw her, and—because his feet were in wet sand—lost his balance and fell back on her. The soft sand saved her, but not from injury.

Stanwyck's work was highly praised in *Forbidden*. And if she was getting tired of reading about her "directness and sincerity"—always true, but becoming a bit of a bore—she was treated to statements such as the *New York World Telegram*'s "she is one of the few really fine and intelligent actresses on the screen" and the London *Film Weekly*'s "her emotional scenes with Menjou show that she can hold her own with any other actress on the screen today."

Her next film would not give her scenes like this to play. In fact, it would give her a very routine assignment. It's a good thing she was making more money, because *Shopworn* offered her little else—in either script *or* direction.

Joseph Walker, who photographed it, says: "It was a very low budget affair."

Regis Toomey, who played opposite her, calls it "an

Shopworn

undistinguished little effort." He adds:

> I seem to recall that Barbara was not too happy about it from the beginning, whether [because of] the script, the director—who was known as a "B" picture director, I believe—or her leading man. I suppose that is the reason I remember she was unhappy, because I was concerned that I might be the fly in the ointment.

The script of *Shopworn* was what Stanwyck disliked. She has described it as "one of those terrible pictures they sandwiched in when you started." It shows her as a girl from the wrong side of the tracks with whom a socially prominent Toomey falls in love. Their marriage is opposed by his mother who has Stanwyck railroaded to the workhouse on a morals charge. When Stanwyck checks out, it is with vengeance in her heart and no illusions to her name.

She turns to show business and rises to stardom in her own company. Toomey catches up with her and, thinking him responsible for her stay in the workhouse, she tries to strip him of *his* illusions, hinting at the reasons for her success—most of them married. He still loves her. The mother loses ground and confronts Stanwyck with a gun. Stanwyck stares her down and takes it away—and the mother has one of those changes of heart that bring about happy endings.

Sarah Y. Mason's story didn't have a fresh idea anywhere, and Nick Grinde's direction made that clear. Jo Swerling and Robert Riskin were wasted on the dialogue. Joseph Walker had little chance to be creative. And the actors were capable but colorless, because the direction produced no involvement.

The London *Times* called *Shopworn* "a dull and characterless study" and said Stanwyck "does what she can with a thankless part." And the *New York Herald Tribune*'s estimate of the situation was typical:

> There is something about the simple, straightforward sincerity of Miss Stanwyck which makes almost everything she does upon either stage or screen seem credible and rather poignant. I fear, however, that *Shopworn* is a trifle too much for her. It happens, you see, that the film is not *Shopworn* in name only. That unfortunate, but descriptive, title provides, among other things, a pretty good critical estimate of the work. In dialogue, situations and general manner the picture most earnestly lives up to its name and, in such antique surroundings, the work of the star is virtually ineffective.

Stanwyck's popularity with the public was strong enough to make *Shopworn* do well at the box office. But a few more pictures of this calibre could have done her serious harm. So it was encouraging when Warners came to the rescue with the more suitable *So Big* and William Wellman. The venture had every chance for success: a fine role, script and director.

Edna Ferber's Pulitzer Prize–winning novel has been filmed three times: in 1925 with Colleen Moore, in 1932 with Stanwyck, and in 1953 with Jane Wyman.

In Wellman's *So Big*, Stanwyck is a woman of strength, sensitivity and ideals whose philosophy grows from what her father taught her: "I want you to realize this whole thing called life is just a grand adventure. The trick is to act in it and look on at the same time. And remember, no matter what happens—good or bad—it's just so much velvet."

As a result of what he has instilled, she meets his unexpected death with courage and dignity and—in her need—takes a position as schoolteacher in Illinois farm country. She finds a crude and difficult life there—but she accepts this, sees the beauty in it, and gives it all she can. Her attitude is especially influential on a young artistically inclined boy.

Marriage to a farmer, who dies from battling with worn-out soil and old-fashioned methods, leaves her with a small son ("So Big," played by Dickie Moore). With determination and back-breaking sacrifice, she makes the land pay and educates him.

But the grown son disappoints her. He prefers easy money to hard work. And her satisfaction comes—not through him—but through the artistic boy who left the farm and put her teachings to use. He returns to her a successful sculptor—in every way the personification of what she has upheld. And their pride in each other closes the film.

There is a great deal of beauty in this picture: part in the philosophy, part in the direction of a good cast, and much in Stanwyck's approach to her role. The film misses in some of its technical aspects: most noticeably, too short a time (80 minutes) in which to cover the life-span of Stanwyck's character properly. But its strengths are solid.

Probably the most moving scenes are the final ones in which George Brent, as the successful sculptor, returns to Stanwyck. When she comes in from the fields where she has been working, he quietly picks her up and carries her into the house. As they stand by the window admiring each other's achievements, he tells her she is the reason for his. Another character, observing them, speaks of what she sees in Stanwyck:

> A fine splendid face—all lit up with a light that comes from inside. Her jaw line like that of the women that came over on the Mayflower or crossed the continent in a covered wagon. And her eyes. And that gorgeous battered old hat of hers. And her hands. She's beautiful.

Brent kisses Stanwyck's rough hands. And her eyes fill with tears as she responds—ever the lady—with a curtsy.

While they were not sold on the film, most reviewers liked Stanwyck's work. William Boehnel in the *New York World Telegram* announced:

> By her performance in *So Big* Barbara Stanwyck definitely establishes herself with this writer as being a brilliant emotional actress.
>
> No matter what one may think about the picture, the final conviction of anyone who sees Miss Stanwyck's Selina Peake will be that she herself contributes a fine and stirring performance, making of it a characterization which is direct and eloquent all the way.

Shopworn

Shopworn, *with Regis Toomey*

So Big, *with Dickie Moore*

So Big

So Big

Although Barbara Stanwyck's films were varying in their degree of success, she herself continued to gain. In January of 1932, London's *Film Weekly* wrote:

Barbara Stanwyck, who is at present entertaining film-goers in *Night Nurse*, is the third most popular actress in America. The number of her English admirers is increasing rapidly. [In 1933 *Variety* would list her as Columbia's number-three box-office leader for the previous year.]

Her next picture (for Warners) was William Wellman's *The Purchase Price*. Melodramatic to the core—with villains, mortgages, and saloon fights—this one gets away with a lot because of Wellman's tricks.

It opens with Stanwyck as a torch singer in New York who is "fed up with it all"—including her racketeer lover, Lyle Talbot—and yearns for some fresh air. To get it, she goes just about as far from credibility as possible—all the way to Elks Crossing, North Dakota, where she becomes the mail-order bride of farmer George Brent.

The rest of the film shows them trying to adjust to each other, and cope with the land and their neighbors. Brent has never had a bride before, and he is a little heavy-handed. On their wedding night—which occurs only a few hours after they have met—he attacks her, and finds himself sleeping in the barn—alone. When she gets to know him better and calms down, he cannot forget that first night. And it takes the entire film, and a lot of bizarre events, to bring them together.

Among these, there is a wild shivaree, a villainous neighbor who covets Stanwyck and the farm, a snowstorm through which she rides to help a neighbor with a new baby, the appearance of Talbot who has tracked her down, a saloon fight between the two men with Stanwyck caught in the middle, the harvesting of a prize crop of wheat, and a fire—set by the jealous neighbor—which Stanwyck and Brent beat out with blankets.

Of the fire, cinematographer Sidney Hickox (who also photographed Stanwyck in *So Big*, *A Lost Lady* and *Blowing Wild*) says:

We had a double for Miss Stanwyck but after the first take, when the double did not show enough action, Miss Stanwyck said she would do the scene herself, which she did, and she was burned around the legs, resulting in blisters—painful but not serious burns.

Anne Shirley (whose name was still Dawn O'Day and who had appeared, too, in *So Big*—although not with Stanwyck) played the daughter of the neighbor with the new baby. Because Wellman was no slouch on saving time, she recalls that she went to work at 9 a.m. and was finished by noon. This wasn't so helpful to *her* budget, but it was fine for the film. She remembers that she had to hold the baby in the scene and "I'd never seen a baby before." Wellman's words to her were: "If you drop that . . ."

The Purchase Price is dressed up with rough humor and crazy characters. There is, for instance, the wedding ceremony. It begins with the purchase of a ring and Brent's sharp haggling with the jeweler to get the price down. The ring is too big for Stanwyck, but it is the smallest Elks Crossing carries.

At the home of the Justice of the Peace, witnesses are supplied in the form of his wife—who brings a bowl of cake batter with her—and a half-wit who works for them. While the Justice marries the couple, with little interest and less tact, his wife stirs the batter and the half-wit eyes Stanwyck—until he is distracted by a couple of dogs fighting outside.

At the completion of the ceremony, Stanwyck's ring falls off. The wife goes to retrieve it and winds up submerging it in cake batter, bumping into the stove behind her, and bringing a large stovepipe down on them all. When Stanwyck is finally in possession of the "battered" ring, it's pretty apparent the marriage has not been made in heaven.

This is the way most of the scenes are handled, and the approach makes the film entertaining. While it produces no more than reasonable acceptance of the couple's problems, to ask any more of this script would have been pushing it. Wisely, Wellman didn't.

Critical reaction is best summed up by the observer who found the film "worth watching, principally because of" Stanwyck who "as always, is as real as the girl next door—and much easier to look at." She does do a fine job. It's a good role for her and allows her to use her sense of humor (one of Hollywood's best) to advantage. Stanwyck and George Brent work well off each other in comedy that is based on awkward or ludicrous situations. The combination would continue to be complementary in *Baby Face*, *The Gay Sisters*, and *My Reputation*.

Stanwyck's final film for Columbia caused some comment. It is one of her most unusual—not in what it asked of her—but in how it used what she had to give. In *The Bitter Tea of General Yen*, Frank Capra had

Warners. General publicity—1934

The Purchase Price

The Purchase Price, *with George Brent*

The Purchase Price

decided to show "Art with a capital 'A' "(NT)—and he did.

Playing an American missionary who has come to Shanghai to wed another, Stanwyck is captured by Nils Asther—a magnetic Chinese warlord—and imprisoned in his sumptuous summer palace. Although she and Asther clash in their beliefs, she soon finds herself attracted to him. Betrayal by Asther's mistress brings about the loss of his soldiers, his provinces and his money—and Stanwyck decides to abandon her principles and stay with him. But he sees the pain this will cause her and drinks poisoned tea. A stronger and wiser Stanwyck returns to Shanghai.

Critics didn't seem to understand what Stanwyck's function was in this picture. *The New York Times* said: "Barbara Stanwyck fails to be convincing in her role. Her powerful voice is scarcely what is needed to carry out the theme of this tale of a romance between a handsome Chinese General . . . and Megan Davis"—and completely missed the point. Since the film is photographed in a poetic manner, it is removed from reality. Barbara Stanwyck is *always* real, and Capra knew what he was doing when he cast her. While the camera may blend her into her surroundings, her speech and actions will fight this. And she is *supposed* to offer contrast. She is an American in China, and the story's theme requires a battle between two cultures and points of view.

Bitter Tea is the only art film Stanwyck has ever made, and it's interesting to see how her presence fits into one. The picture is "Art" in its execution as well as in its experimental theme. It is visually a tapestry. And Capra and Joseph Walker weave her into it by bathing her in sensuous lighting, ritual and music. As an *objet d'art* she is most satisfying.

The height of her glorification is the dream sequence —a shimmering fusion of the melodramatic and the lyrical. It begins with a close-up which frames her against a chair on her balcony. She is watching lovers—inspired by the "cherry blossom moon"—chasing each other in the garden below. Shots of them show the moon through the trees, glowing paper lanterns, shadows and merriment. There is laughter and music, and a breeze blows her hair. She settles back in the chair and goes to sleep. As she starts to dream the music changes and the shot becomes a double exposure—surrounding her face with panels from the door to her room. It is very Freudian, very Dali and very lovely.

Asther breaks through the door and starts toward her. She is shown recoiling on the bed, framed by grotesque fingernails. A rescuer appears and destroys the attacker. But the rescuer—when she removes his mask—is Asther too. Against a whirling abstract background, she succumbs, and they are brought together in soft close-ups.

Joseph Walker states:

> *The Bitter Tea of General Yen* was my favorite picture with Barbara. The story was ahead of its time [with] some fine writing [including] some of the more romantic scenes by Capra himself. It had more pictorial possibilities and, for the first time, I used a Variable Diffusion device that I invented. . . . I also had the opportunity to use some special portrait lenses I had designed. [One of these, a four-inch, Capra explains, was used for the beautiful close-ups of Stanwyck in which the background goes hazy and a halo of light surrounds her hair.]

Of his association with Stanwyck and Capra on their four films together, Walker says:

> Barbara Stanwyck always came on the set on time and always knew her lines, and was an inspiration to all of us. There is sometimes a certain empathy between the crew and the star, and everyone does his very best to make the picture as good as possible. This was very much in evidence on a Stanwyck picture.
>
> Frank Capra's work speaks for itself. His intelligence and a fine technical education enabled him to easily master the technical problems of Motion Picture Production, but it was his wonderful warmth and understanding that made him a great director. So many people, including myself, can say that their best work was done while working for Frank Capra.
>
> When you think of the slow film, the cumbersome blimped cameras and the problems of sound, it is a wonder the pictures were as good as they were. I guess a lot of the success was due to "Miracle Woman" Barbara Stanwyck and "Miracle Man" Frank Capra.

The beauty of *Bitter Tea* was cited by critics. And it was the first film to play at Radio City Music Hall (in January of 1933). Capra says that, while it didn't win the Academy Award he was pushing for, it "will remain forever as one of *my* pet pictures."(NT) Still, he points out, it became the second of his films to lose

The Bitter Tea of General Yen,
with Nils Asther

◄ The Bitter Tea of General Yen

money, mainly because it was "banned in the British Empire . . . for miscegenation."(NT)

Along these lines it—or at least Stanwyck—found some discontent on these shores too. Fans wanted to know what she was doing "falling in love with a Chinaman." It didn't seem to make much difference that the "Chinaman" was played by a Swedish actor—and was damned attractive besides. (Well, when *Double Indemnity* was released, there were those who complained at her portraying a cold-blooded murderess. You can't win 'em all.)

In late 1932, Stanwyck—now under contract solely to Warners—did *Ladies They Talk About.* It's no *Bitter Tea*, but—as a vehicle for a tough, wisecracking, fist-swinging Stanwyck—it's a ball. She plays a hard case—complete with slang, sneer and chip on shoulder. Even Gable would have had to watch out for her in this one.

The picture was the first for its two directors: William Keighley—a theatrical director who was engaged for the dialogue, and Howard Bretherton—a film editor who was given the action. Cinematographer John Seitz—who would also photograph Stanwyck in *Double Indemnity*—says:

> [*Ladies*] was started without any preliminary tests. I had been borrowed from Fox by Darryl Zanuck, then head of production at Warners, and it's ordinary practice to make a test of the leading lady. Mr. Zanuck's recommendation was good enough for Barbara and we began shooting right away.
>
> It was a short schedule [24 days] but the picture was most enjoyable.

The story concentrates on life in the women's quarters of San Quentin. Stanwyck plays a slick bank bandit who is given a jail sentence by Preston Foster, a vigorous evangelist-reformer. It seems that, as children, these two lived in the same town. But then her father was a deacon in the church and Foster's was the town drunkard. "Too much deaconing took all the sweetness out of" her and she ended up in reform school. From there it was an easy step to her present position. Foster's penchant for the straight and narrow is shaken by Stanwyck's curves and—although he has her convicted—he keeps in touch with letters, visits and promise of parole.

Most of the story is laid in the prison, where Stanwyck takes over with her first entrance. In time, she tries to help the men involved in the holdup with her. Their plan for escape is discovered and the men are

killed. Believing Foster responsible, she goes gunning for him when she is released. She bawls him out and shoots him. Then she is sorry. He forgives. They decide to get married. And, if these two live happily ever after, it'll be a miracle.

The film's dialogue is probably its greatest asset. It is always sharp and often amusing. For example:

> Stanwyck and Susie (a rival) at their first meeting:
> Susie: Say, there isn't any punishment bad enough for you.
> Stanwyck: Yeah, well being penned up here with a daffodil like you comes awful close.
> Linda (a friend) showing Stanwyck the prison's layout:
> Linda: And here we find the dining room—connected with the morgue.
> Stanwyck: Is the food that bad?
> Linda: Well, it's cooked by three dames up here for poisoning.
> Stanwyck: Whadda they use on ya?
> Linda: Beans mostly.

Further comedy for an otherwise drab situation is provided by the characters themselves. The most colorful is Maude Eburne who used to run what she called a "beauty parlor"—until a detective sergeant came there "to get a manicure from one of my girls."

While it may not sound like it, the film was attempting to make a serious statement. These women were not having the "jolly time of it" that reviewers thought. They were trying to keep from going nuts. Denied the two things they wanted most—"freedom and men"—they used laughs defensively. And the treatment was authentic.

Warners had been guided by a check of San Quentin's conditions and practices—and by the technical advisement of a woman who had served time there. The attitude of the film's characters—as well as the fancied-up décor of the cells that nobody believed either—was meant to give a true picture of prison life.

Critics wouldn't buy this. But they did like Stanwyck's work. The *New York Herald Tribune* said:

> She plays her role with shrewd insight and should command increasing attention from discriminating picture-goers for individual style and the admirable honesty of her acting.

Not too crazy about her next film, *Baby Face*, Stanwyck had accepted it because the studio told her she needed glamour. "Everyone else has glamour but me" she told the *New York Sun* in 1933, "so I played in *Baby Face*. Anything for glamour."

The need had arisen because fans were again making themselves heard. They disapproved of all the "gingham" and "flannel" roles she had been playing and wanted her "to go back to her evening gowns." (In the fine-clothes-do-not-a-fine-actress-determine department, it might be pointed out that Stanwyck gave one of her greatest performances—as Stella Dallas—in the most hideous costumes of her career.)

In *Baby Face*, she is wrapped like a bonbon by Orry-Kelly: in ruffles, laces, velvets and furs. Her large wardrobe of blonde wigs runs from curls and fluff to sleekness and sophistication. Heavy make-up and lingering close-ups complete the effect. Glamour she has. She looks like a million dollars. And it's very nice. But the film is worth less.

Baby Face offers its star little room for variety or growth. Stanwyck's role is a repetitious one and the plot must have been twenty years old. Yet here is an instance where she takes flimsy material and gives it the lift of its life. Forced to back up deceit with phony charm, she plays her scenes on two levels—what she says, and how she feels about this and those who fall for it—and she handles the style superbly.

Ads for the film promised "Barbara Stanwyck and thirteen men in *Baby Face*"—and the customers got their money's worth. The story shows the beautiful young woman in the sordid environment who has been wronged by men. She is determined to make them pay and achieves wealth and power through their weakness for her. Fortunately, enough fun is poked at the situation to carry it neatly in Stanwyck's capable hands. She slings the sharp dialogue around with skill, never missing a laugh. As William Boehnel put it, "*Baby Face* is Rescued by Its Star."

Stanwyck is shown working and fighting off revolting characters in her father's speakeasy in a shabby mill town. Her contempt is gorgeous:

The Father: Say, whadda ya think we're runnin' here?
Stanwyck: It looks ta me like a zoo!

When the father sells her to a politician in exchange for the joint's protection—and the man approaches her and puts his hand on her knee—she calmly spills coffee on him and exits.

She gets a break when the father's still blows up—killing him and freeing her. The one man she trusts advises her to go to the big city where she will find opportunity. As a beautiful woman, she can get anything she wants. But there is a right and a wrong way. Understanding everything but the last sentence, she hops a freight for New York and is next seen walking on Wall Street.

Stanwyck begins her climb, flashing smiles and meaningful looks at whoever is in charge of what she wants. Starting with the personnel manager of a bank, she proves to him she's had "plenty" of experience, and obtains a job in the filing department. In no time she has advanced to a posh apartment, paid for by the vice president of the bank who comes with it—too often. Her fortune has grown, but her satisfaction has not. When—many men later—she falls for one of her victims and realizes what the words "right" and "wrong" mean, she reforms—in one of the most unlikely endings ever tacked onto a film.

Critics took the story with plenty of salt but liked Stanwyck. The *New York Evening Post* said:

In the hands of Miss Barbara Stanwyck the character of Lily Powers assumes a formidable aspect. A cold, relentless creature, she plays her game with a cunning hand and reserves her heel to grind down her victims. You may not always believe in Lily's felicitous fortune, but that is the fault of the story; you cannot escape the belief that Lily is a vixen of the lowest order and that the men who play with her are doomed to perish in the flames.

The *New York Herald Tribune* observed that:

. . . despite [the story's] commonplaces and its hokum there is originality in the characterization of Lily and strength and experience in her transfer to the screen. She is not a cheap, stupid girl. [And] it took insight and intelligence to realize the intrinsic idealism within her.

William Boehnel—who had recognized Stanwyck's potential in *So Big*—added:

I can only repeat that she is ammunition for larger and more powerful guns than this, but she never ceases to be the magnificent and intelligent trouper she is.

Interestingly, something of Lily Powers would one day return to the screen in a vehicle that *was* worthy of Barbara Stanwyck's talent: *Double Indemnity*.

Ladies They Talk About

Happily for Stanwyck, her next role was a more challenging and honest one than she had had in a while. And she was enthusiastic about it. *Ever In My Heart* gave her her first chance to play tragedy—with hauntingly beautiful results.

Archie Mayo had a serious story for his second picture with Stanwyck. Its unhappy theme was romantically handled and—in lifting it to tragedy—he was able to show man as more than himself, not less. It was a step forward—and a refreshing change from phony happy endings.

It is 1909 and Stanwyck plays a young girl from a rigid New England family whose cousin has just returned from abroad, bringing with him a German friend—Otto Kruger. For Stanwyck and Kruger, it is love at first sight. In a delicately staged scene, Kruger plays the piano—teaching her a German song: "Du du liegst mir in Herzen."

> You are ever in my heart.
> You are ever in my thoughts.
> You make me many sorrows.
> You will never know how much I love you.

The song becomes the fabric of the film and a shattering experience in the final scene.

Against the wishes of her family, Stanwyck becomes Kruger's bride—and a number of gentle scenes illustrate their contentment. With the sinking of the Lusitania, however, war hysteria takes over. Kruger is dismissed from his job and refused others; their "friends" desert them; denial by Stanwyck's family causes their son to die; and even their dachschund is stoned to death, because he is "a German dog." When poverty threatens Stanwyck's health, Kruger sends her back to her parents, promising to join her. But it will mean changing his name, and he cannot sacrifice his proud ancestry. He goes, instead, to Germany to fight for his people.

Working in a canteen in France a year later, Stanwyck finds Kruger spying and saves him from discovery. When he then shows up at her quarters, she realizes she must turn him in because his information will kill thousands of men—but doing so means he will be shot. They spend a last night together and—with dawn approaching—play out the inevitable tragic ending.

Unseen by Kruger, Stanwyck places poison in some wine and they drink "Brüderschaft." She begs him to wait until it is light before he leaves, and—with pain and dignity—keeps knowledge of what she

has done from him, holding him until he dies. Then she sinks back on the bed in her own death. "You will never know how much I love you."

To describe outstanding scenes in *Ever In My Heart*, it would be necessary to discuss the whole film. There are so many fine ones: Kruger singing a lullaby on a hot summer night as their son lies near death. Stanwyck in the next room, trying to get sleep that will not come. Her reaction as she hears Kruger stop singing. The look on her face as she comes to the doorway and sees him bent over the dead child.

The film's idealism and the performances of Stanwyck and Kruger make the material real and important. It is not a brilliant film—not always even a good one. But it is reaching for something. And, if limitations imposed by program film making are overlooked, it succeeds.

Stanwyck and Kruger are finely attuned to each other and to the script. It is their strength and simplicity—and the great maturity with which they play—that give the film its power. The *Romeo and Juliet* death scene is an achievement—too fragile for further description—but one of Barbara Stanwyck's most valuable screen moments.

Critics reacted violently to *Ever In My Heart*. They contradicted themselves and each other. Some respected the tragic ending. Others would rather have been entertained. But all were drawn to Stanwyck's and Kruger's portrayals. Typical reaction was the *New York American*'s:

> Slow-paced romance is the distinguishing feature of this long-suffering theme which brings us Barbara Stanwyck in a new sort of characterization but, unfortunately, in a picture that is pretty poor as screen entertainment.

and the *New York Mirror*'s "Miss Stanwyck never has made a picture like it, nor has any other star. . . . The story is bitterly real."

The *New York World Telegram*—which understood what the film was trying to do—said:

> Barbara Stanwyck demonstrates that she is one of the first—the very first—actresses among the more exalted leading ladies in Hollywood. She gives a fine, dignified performance.
>
> Earnest and real and rather terrifying in its unhappiness is this portrayal.
>
> I think it is one of the most searching and authentic characterizations [she] has yet offered.

Baby Face

60

Baby Face, *with George Brent*

Baby Face ▷

Baby Face, *with Henry Kolker*

Gambling Lady was Stanwyck's next picture—the first of several she would do in which she exhibits luck and skill with cards. Chic and sophisticated in tone, it was directed by Archie Mayo—who really had to move to cram it into 66 minutes. Fortunately a fast pace was right for the film, and he strengthened this with quick cutting, wipes and similar tricks. Its slick style is typical of the period and the subject matter.

One of the best things *Gambling Lady* did was to pair Stanwyck with Joel McCrea—who was to work with her more often than any other leading man—and who says, right from the start, "Stanwyck was great—as a person and actress."

Playing the daughter of an honest gambler who kills himself rather than compromise his code of ethics when luck fails him, Stanwyck takes up his profession to make a living and also plays straight. Working for the syndicate at ten percent, she cleans up night after night. At the gaming table she meets McCrea—and wins him too. But their subsequent marriage is threatened by a former love interest of each (Claire Dodd and Pat O'Brien) and this leads to murder, blackmail, and more than enough to fill that 66 minutes before it is untangled and wrapped up with a happy ending.

Gambling Lady is entertaining and went over well with reviewers. Stanwyck's most effective scenes are those in which she flips cards and self-assurance around. Especially well handled is a game of twenty-one in which she calmly strips Claire Dodd of every jewel she is wearing. Stanwyck and McCrea are well teamed, and it's not hard to see that the combination will be worth repeating.

Although she was not yet fighting to the extent that she would, Stanwyck was beginning to be concerned about scripts offered her. She said at the time:

> I worry day and night over stories. Right now I'm in the doghouse at the studio because I turned down several stories they wanted me to do which I didn't feel were right for me.
> Then they wanted me to do *British Agent* with Leslie Howard. I'd read the book twice, because I found it so absorbing, but it's a man's story. Howard was made to order for the part, but I turned it down because I saw no reason why I should play second fiddle to anyone. I've worked too hard to get to the top to give up top billing for no good reason. I don't mean the actual

billing, because that's unimportant. I mean the top spot in the picture. In a few years, I suppose, I'll have to resign myself to leads and supporting parts—we all come to that eventually—but I don't feel I've reached that point yet.

That an actress who had nine-tenths of her best performances ahead of her should be reduced to feeling this way says little for the front office.

And their lack of judgement on her next film doesn't say much for them either. This time they took a property of quality, removed the stuffing, and gave it such clumsy execution that it bore no resemblance to its source. Why First National even wanted to purchase *A Lost Lady* from Willa Cather remains a mystery—because that is not what they filmed.

In Willa Cather's Pulitzer Prize–winning novel, the heroine is a gay, complex creature whose seeming refinement is marred by the fact, as the author says, that she "preferred life on any terms." Her story is set in the late 19th century, and the terms she chooses—through both circumstance and desire—mark her for an irreversible decline in society, and in the eyes of the young man who observes her descent. It is a novel of great maturity, with a tenor of tragedy throughout. And, in the light of what Stanwyck had shown in *Ever In My Heart*, it's impossible not to wonder what would have resulted from sensitive direction of what Willa Cather wrote.

But the script went Hollywood, and the director was Alfred E. Green of *Baby Face*. And, of Gene Markey and Kathryn Scola's screenplay, *The New York Times* said aptly: "Change the title, remove Miss Cather's name from the credit line, and you have a made-to-order program film." As such it must be considered—and as such it does not impress.

A Lost Lady shows Stanwyck in a marriage of gratitude to a successful middle-aged lawyer (Frank Morgan) who has restored her will to live. She pretends no love but they have every other happiness. Because they have agreed to be honest with each other, when she falls in love with Ricardo Cortez she tells Morgan and prepares to leave him. Morgan's distress brings on a heart attack and she decides to stay with him until he is well. Now *he* has nothing to live for. He shuts her out and she turns to drink and confusion. Thinking he is dying, he asks her forgiveness. She realizes she does care for him. And a tacked-on ending shows that this has restored him.

If you can forgive the script, there is some merit in the work. The relationship between Stanwyck and

Ever In My Heart

Ever In My Heart, *with Otto Kruger*

Ever In My Heart, *with Otto Kruger*

Gambling Lady

A Lost Lady

A Lost Lady

Morgan is well played, and she has one scene which allows her to impress. It is a two-level affair in which she confesses her unhappiness to Morgan's partner, Lyle Talbot—first by making an attempt at pretense and then by abandoning it. But, other than this, the film is lifeless—and the actors were as victimized by it as was Willa Cather.

Cather, however, got even. Speaking of her subsequent relationship with Hollywood, Willa Cather's biographer states:

> . . . every now and again some movie-producer would discover her novels and want to film them. One producer dreamed of a great panoramic *Death Comes for the Archbishop* (doubtless in technicolor) and another sought to obtain rights to *The Song of the Lark.* . . . As for the dazzling offers from Hollywood, she had had her one experience with the Warner production of *A Lost Lady* and that sufficed; in her will she expressly prohibited theatrical or cinematic treatment of her fiction. Her artistic integrity was not for sale to the highest bidder to be turned into "supercolossal" films, and her reason was simple: she did not want her name attached to dialogue written by some person whose name and ability she did not know and to a product that would not be hers but that of many hands. It offended her artist's sense, her belief in herself as a literary craftsman. She had worked in a great medium after taking years to master it and saw no need to be transposed into any other.

Critics were astute enough to deplore desecration of the novel, and sympathize with the actors. And they were able to say, as did the *New York Sun:* "Barbara Stanwyck, as usual, almost saves the day by giving one of her earnestly honest performances." "Almost" never made any actress happy. Nor was an "earnestly honest performance" one-tenth of what Stanwyck had at her command, if given half a chance. But she had three more of these wearisome program films to make before she would have a really good script.

What *The Secret Bride* (originally titled *Concealment*) offered Stanwyck in the way of a role was exactly nothing. She was completely wasted on this mystery story—which is one long bout with exposition and archaic phrasing, sorely in need of contractions. Picture anyone being convincing with lines such as Stanwyck's

> In the first place, I shall believe father when he denies all knowledge of the supposed bribe.

or Warren William's

> If it were known that Governor Vincent was my father-in-law, no one would credit me with any disinterested motive.

The story shows a secret marriage between Stanwyck and attorney general William which must be kept this way so he can work as a disinterested party in clearing her governor father of some accusations. As *Photoplay* put it, the actors "are lost in the wordy maze of this film's plot."

Director William Dieterle, who was as shortchanged by the script as Stanwyck, says:

> The work on the film *Concealment* was not very pleasant. The script was bad. I could not refuse it for contractual reasons. Why Miss Stanwyck did not reject the script, as Bette Davis would have done, I can only guess. She was not happy at Warners and wanted to get out of her contract as quickly as possible. Of all the films I directed, *Concealment* is the picture I don't like to think about any more.

Stanwyck completed her contract with *The Woman in Red*, an adaptation of Wallace Irwin's novel *North Shore*. Director Robert Florey (who later directed her on television—most notably in segments of *The Barbara Stanwyck Show*) says the film "was a contract assignment but the fact that Miss Stanwyck was in it made it much more than a routine job."

The Woman in Red is a society drama in which all the blue bloods are bored, snobbish and nasty and all the other characters good sports. Stanwyck plays a professional horsewoman who marries socialite Gene Raymond and has to contend with his snooty family and be suspected of adultery. She does have some good scenes in this one, however—including a chance to tell them all off.

Florey speaks of his position as a contract director at the time:

> A director under contract to a studio didn't have the power to choose a scenario. I would never have directed a picture if I had refused the ones assigned to me. I did take a suspension several times, in protest against a story that I disliked strongly. Sometimes I had to do the picture

The Secret Bride, *with Warren William*

The Woman in Red, *with Gene Raymond*

when I returned on salary. I suggested stories that I wanted to bring to the screen. I received a firm "No." It was disappointing when these were made years later by producer-directors or independent ones.

Another handicap of the contract director was the fact that he had no part in the final cutting and editing of the film. The producer and the studio boss would do as they pleased with editing, sometimes changing the order of the sequences, suppressing favorite scenes. And the director could object and try to influence them, but they had the power and the final word.

But, as Florey points out, "A director is not only a story teller. He is an illustrator. Part of his job is to create an interesting and imaginative atmosphere with artistic angles and composition." And Florey's ability with the visual is one of *The Woman in Red*'s assets.

Critics responded favorably to this and to Stanwyck's performance. But they noted that the story was cut to the same pattern as the others she had been faced with recently, and that her presence gave it more than it gave her back.

Florey adds:

Miss Stanwyck did not complain about the scenario. She understood the limitations of the profession. She was always very cooperative, pleasant, helpful and a favorite with all the directors. I only wish I had made more features with her. As far as I am concerned, she is the greatest.

The Woman in Red.
Photo by Scotty Welbourne

CHAPTER FIVE

A free-lancing Barbara Stanwyck was idle for about six months—then did producer Edward Small's *Red Salute*. Released through United Artists, the film was a minor one but gave her a chance to exercise her glibness with acid repartee.

She plays a college girl whose interest in a young radical has turned her to Communism. When her father sends her to Mexico to cool off, she becomes entangled with an American soldier, Robert Young, who is loyal to the States. In a cross-country trailer trip, they slug out their differences.

Although described as a romantic comedy, the film attacked student radicalism—which had been voicing itself—and drew angry picketers. Most critics blasted the film—either for attempting propaganda at all or for not doing a more competent job. Some were astute enough, though, to see merely a well-timed approach to getting a love story—in the manner of *It Happened One Night*—on its feet.

The ideas are clumsily handled, but the comedy is tight. Stanwyck and Young throw verbal darts with skill, and it's refreshing to see her playing in a lighter style for a change. However, except for the pleasure of batting its laugh lines around, *Red Salute* provided Stanwyck with little more than she had had at Warners.

After several inconsequential films, it was not a moment too soon that she landed in one that gave her an exciting role, a top director and a situation that could not have been more appropriate. *Annie Oakley* was the first Western for the girl who would one day be queen of them. Her personality was just right for their action, color and straightforwardness. And she was perfect casting for Annie.

Director George Stevens effected a stirring and humorous return to the days of Buffalo Bill's Wild West Show. Into this he splashed the dainty backwoods girl from Ohio—with spirit enough for ten and the ability to outshoot World's Champion Sharpshooter Preston Foster. Stanwyck gets a chance to prove this at their first meeting, but backs down and loses because Foster is just "too pretty." Her skill has been noted, however, and she is offered a job with the show. From here, the story concentrates on her involvement with Foster and her success as the "World's Greatest Woman Rifle Shot."

Stanwyck makes Annie a charming blend of conviction and kindness. Annie knows she is a crack shot. She has worked for this, and she is proud of it. Nobody can belittle her ability without ruffling her feathers. So, in their first meeting—when Foster is scornful of shooting "against a half-baked kid, and a girl at that"—she decides to give him a run for his money: "He'd look awful silly if I beat him in front of all these folks." She starts at the wrong end of the row of targets, picks off the smallest, and comments: "First pot shot I ever took." Annie has a devilish sense of humor.

When irritated further by the insinuation that she might be uncomfortable with moving targets, she makes it clear that "I never shot a quail while it was settin' down!" But when things reach the point where onlookers are suggesting the show's manager has signed the wrong shooter—and that Foster had better look for another job—her innate kindness takes over and she deliberately misses. She walks this fine line throughout the film.

Her fighting spirit and childlike naïveté are enchanting. When she has five birds thrown up, runs and jumps over a table, grabs her gun and hits them, she is a show-woman at her best. Yet she can—when chided for shaking the Czar's hand on their European tour instead of kissing it—react with a "Gosh, I suppose that was terrible." The impression left by both performances is reflected in the reply of the character who has teased her: "No, you were just yourself. That's why we all love you."

Critics knew a good thing when they saw it:

> The talented and attractive Barbara Stanwyck gives by far the best screen performance of her career.
>
> From the moment she appears . . . as the gawky little country girl of humble origin . . . to the time when she is acclaimed by the crowned heads of Europe for her unexcelled marksmanship, Miss Stanwyck plays the role with such commendable restraint and with such feeling for the character that she almost becomes Annie Oakley. [*New York World Telegram*]

> Barbara Stanwyck's presence, as well as an excellent script, pulls the picture definitely out of the "for children only" class. Her curious quality of sincerity, strikingly rare on the screen, gives the story unexpected tenderness and dignity. A western with Miss Stanwyck playing the shy, girlish young queen of the shooting range becomes a super-western indeed. [*New York Sun*]

> Barbara Stanwyck is splendid in the title role;

Red Salute

this is her most striking performance in a long time. [*The New York Times*]

Stanwyck had handled her role well. And she had done so with personal problems threatening the concentration an artist needs free from stress. In late 1935, she divorced Frank Fay.

Her triumph at RKO with *Annie Oakley* had caught the eye of Twentieth Century-Fox. The result was that she was signed by both studios. In a year and a half, this arrangement—plus loans—would have her working in four studios and lined up for a fifth.

Twentieth led off with *A Message to Garcia*. It was a contract assignment for director George Marshall and, as he describes it, "The whole picture was a struggle. A good beginning and a good ending. Nothing in between."

Critics were disturbed because it deviated sharply from the historical incident they presumed it represented. But Marshall points out that it was intended as "pure fiction, except for the basic idea" and was made from the title only.

The film is visually impressive. A stunning Cuban jungle was whipped up at Twentieth—complete with swamps, alligators, foggy mists and giant palms. And Marshall's work with cameraman Rudolph Maté produced a waxy and finely carved visual. But the script, as Marshall indicates, presented problems.

Stanwyck was badly miscast in this one (by Darryl F. Zanuck). A Cuban girl of Spanish descent is not a Stanwyck role. And, although Marshall explains her lack of a Spanish accent by stating that "she was supposed to have been in an Eastern school," there is no reference to this in the picture. *Variety* observed:

> She's no more a Cuban patriot's daughter than Carmen is a ballet dancer. She's a Cuban girlie who speaks her native language with an English accent and English with no accent at all.

And the *New York Evening Post*, hitting closer to the truth, said: "It bothers us that Barbara, cast as the Cuban senorita . . . should talk perfect Brooklyn." While the traces of Brooklyn in Stanwyck's speech have never been heavy ones, they should have made a producer think twice before putting her in *A Message to Garcia*.

Marshall did all he could to help her through the assignment. Double close-ups of her intensity, and of the attraction between her and John Boles—aided by

Spanish music and mosquito netting—prompted the *New York Herald Tribune* to state that, although she "is not particularly credible as the Cuban Joan of Arc . . . she is agreeable enough as the romantic interest." But Stanwyck was obviously uncomfortable in the role, and she could do little more than lose graciously to Boles and Wallace Beery, who were more believably cast. The *New York Post* sized up her plight fairly well:

> There's little for Miss Stanwyck to do—but she has been photographed attractively and she's a good enough trouper to keep in the background when the spotlight doesn't focus on her.

Marshall echoes this when he asserts:

> Barbara is a real professional. She not only knows her own part but everyone else's as well. That is why she has always been one of our better actresses. She knows what her character should be in relationship to the others. A director can give no greater praise, as she makes our work so easy.

And Stanwyck, speaking to an interviewer at the time (not about *Garcia*, but about her work in general) said:

> I like being busy. I like acting. Even if a picture turns out badly, I can remember the fun I had making it—and that's a good thing, when you enjoy the task that earns your living for you.

RKO's *The Bride Walks Out* provided plenty of fun. It is a romp which takes marriage apart, puts it back together with the same problems that destroyed it, and expects it to run. Storywise, it had to be kidding. And, of course, it was.

Director Leigh Jason, who began as a writer, had sharpened his wits—like most directors of the thirties—on silents. The screenplay of *The Bride* was done by two of Jason's favorite writers: Phil Epstein and P. J. Wolfson. But Jason—who was under contract to RKO—worked on it too. It shows Stanwyck and Gene Raymond trying marriage on the $35 a week he makes as an engineer. As a mannequin with "a certain kind of body you can hang clothes on" that would add $50 to their impoverished state, Stanwyck is cut down in the prime of her career and reduced to reading cookbooks, juggling furniture payments and settling for "Grade B milk" because Raymond is

Annie Oakley, *with Preston Foster*

Annie Oakley

Annie Oakley, *with Preston Foster*

stubborn about such things. It doesn't work. Nor will things be any better after the picture, when Stanwyck has returned to Raymond to prevent the self-sacrifice that will bring her his life insurance. They are still going to have to play house on $35 a week.

However, the laugh lines and the gags *do* work. Most of these go to two veteran sourpusses—Ned Sparks and Helen Broderick—who play an older couple chained to a lower-middle-class marriage and fighting all the way. Their skill and the originality of much of the dialogue inject life into a familiar routine.

> Stanwyck: Why did you two ever get married?
> Broderick: Ahhh, I don't know. It was raining, and we were in Pittsburgh . . .

The Bride Walks Out is a pleasant interlude for Stanwyck, and shows how much she has to offer for comedy—a facet of her ability that has been tapped far too seldom during her career. Stanwyck is best at high comedy, but manages a little of everything here, including a well-executed drunk scene. Her reactions to Billy Gilbert—as the repossessor from the Acme Furniture Company—are burlesqued to the point where she takes over a sneeze he has begun, and fumes at him for endowing her with his cold.

Of his gags, Jason says:

> I like to think that I added about twenty-five percent of the laughs on the set. It was rare to get a good idea from an actor. In the kind of "high" comedy I made, it was sometimes difficult to get the actor to just read the line, and not try to be funny.
>
> Billy Gilbert was a much broader comedian than I generally used, but I'd always add a lot when I used him. Sometimes the "reaction" was much funnier than the action, and Billy's "take 'ems" were really funny. Sometimes I had to make two or three takes because Barbara was laughing at Billy.

Aside from this, he adds "Retakes were mainly because of other actors, camera, etc." and that, in working with Stanwyck:

> Several script readings with the cast were all that was necessary. Barbara was always a delight. And a real craftsman. She was the only one I ever worked with who would dig to the bitter end for what you really wanted—and then give it to you.

The Bride Walks Out provided summer entertainment at Radio City Music Hall and was considered properly diverting by most.

His Brother's Wife was also good news at the box office—but for different reasons. In this one, it is the actors' lot to fall prey to a scenario aimed at twelve-year-olds. Or at least it seems this way. *The New York Times* got to the heart of the matter when it stated:

> Whatever else may be said of it, there is no disputing the formulary perfection of the Capitol's latest gift from Metro-Goldwyn-Mayer. Incredibly romantic, glossily produced, expertly directed and peopled by the sort of players most often encountered on the covers of the fan magazines, *His Brother's Wife*—even to its title —has been so astutely aimed at the box office that we can but stiffen resignedly and wait for the marker to cry bull's-eye. A triumph of machine-made art, it is a picture that will succeed no matter how we, in our ivory tower, rail against it for its romantic absurdity.

Stanwyck was once a lot less pretentious and more practical when she remarked that the picture set movies back twenty years.

An intricate and unlikely plot uses up a lot of the actors' energy and gives them little in return. Stanwyck is faced with that same girl from the wrong side of the tracks—but this one is merely a "stray cat" of indeterminate origin. Robert Taylor is loaded down with a combination of playboy and scientist. And Jean Hersholt has the thankless task of trying to bring the two together and concluding: "Love—it puzzles me more than science."

When science prompts Taylor to choose the tropics in preference to Stanwyck, she seeks revenge by marrying his brother in another of those *Mexicali Rose* mix-ups that doesn't seem like a very good idea. But this time she abandons revenge for nobility and wins Taylor by becoming a human guinea pig for his experiment.

The melodramatic race with death at the end of the film after Stanwyck has made use of a needle of spotted fever germs ("Rita! You deliberately injected that virus into your veins?") must have had the actors laughing—or crying—to the point of hysteria. With her life hanging in the balance, sweat on everyone's brow as they hurry to mix the serum that may—only may—save her, and Franz Waxman's score alternately tearing its hair and sobbing its heart

A Message to Garcia, *with John Boles*

The Bride Walks Out, *with Robert Young and Gene Raymond*

The Bride Walks Out, *with Helen Broderick and Robert Young*

out, Stanwyck becomes delirious and has to tackle lines like "Seven come eleven—roll 'em while they're hot!" What more is there to say?

Director W. S. Van Dyke's technical know-how put it all together effortlessly. But nothing could disguise the material. The actors do a decent job, the score is Waxman, and the production is slick. But the film just doesn't matter.

It mattered to the public though, and elicited the response sought. Whether or not an actress had much chance to act in a worthwhile vehicle probably concerned few besides herself.

At this time, however, Stanwyck was able to begin some work that would lead to many fine acting opportunities. *His Brother's Wife* was previewed on WABC, presenting her in one of her first radio appearances, and helping her become familiar with a medium in which she would spend a large part of her time for roughly twenty years. Her splendid voice quality as well as, of course, her talent and professionalism made her prime radio material—highly sought for the various shows that broadcast Hollywood to millions.

Her most frequent appearances were with the Lux Radio Theatre and the Screen Guild Players. She gave her first Lux performance on August 3, 1936—entering into what would be a long and happy association with the show and its producer-director-host Cecil B. DeMille. From 1936 to 1943 Stanwyck starred for DeMille in sixteen Lux shows—becoming the actress he cast most frequently. Many of the roles she played were re-creations of her film roles; but some gave her a chance at material different from that generally provided for her screen image. Her shows for DeMille were

Main Street
Stella Dallas
These Three
Dark Victory
Morning Glory
So Big
Wuthering Heights
Only Yesterday
Remember the Night
Smilin' Through
The Lady Eve
Penny Serenade
Ball of Fire
This Above All
The Gay Sisters
The Great Man's Lady

Often, of course, radio work was either not recorded or not saved, but a few of Stanwyck's performances exist to give an indication of what she did before mikes and audiences. In addition to screenplays, there were light sketches—particularly during the war years. (And it's hard to say which is funnier when she plays opposite master of comedy Jack Benny in some of these—her delivery of her lines or the cracking up she does over his!)

In the summer of 1936, John Ford filmed Sean O'Casey's *The Plough and the Stars* with Stanwyck, Preston Foster and a number of players from the Abbey Theatre. Against the 1916 Easter rebellion in Dublin, Stanwyck and Foster play a couple whose marriage is threatened by Foster's appointment as commandant of the Citizen Army, and by the subsequent danger to his life.

Stanwyck does not carry a heavy burden of dialogue, but she is constantly involved in the action and her presence is strong and expressive. There is, for instance, a scene where she lifts a blanket to see if a man brought by on a stretcher is Foster—and then uses her back and shoulders to indicate her feelings as she goes wearily up the steps to her house.

She is infinitely interesting in the opening sequence, which establishes her devotion to Foster and introduces the threat to their tranquillity. Her voice is mellow and her movements graceful enough to suggest dance. The sequence does, in fact, move to both an inner and outer rhythm—the latter provided by a street-singer.

The beauty of filming *The Plough and the Stars* lies in opening it out. And John Ford's masterful use of composition shines when survivors of the rebellion take to the rooftops. He brings Foster in through a skylight to unite him with Stanwyck, and sees that the rebels who follow do so quietly—both to avoid detection by the enemy and to key in with the couple's love scene. It is a fine synthesis of the practical and the dramatic and—like the rest of the film—contains a sense of something larger.

Both director and actress received some grief on this film. After Ford had completed it and gone to Honolulu, a new management—an executive producer—decided that there was nothing exciting about a married couple and that the film's stars should be lovers instead. An assistant director shot some scenes with this change—ruining Ford's film, O'Casey's story and Stanwyck's performance. Ford's version was shown in England and Ireland (where the other was

His Brother's Wife, *with Robert Taylor*

◀ His Brother's Wife, *with Robert Taylor*

The Plough and the Stars, *with Preston Foster*

The Plough and the Stars, *with Preston Foster*

Banjo On My Knee, *with Buddy Ebsen*

Banjo On My Knee, *with Joel McCrea*

Banjo On My Knee, *with Tony Martin*

refused) but prints with footage by the assistant director were released in the States.

Ford says Stanwyck gave him exactly what he wanted in her playing of Nora ("She is a superb actress") but that she was disgusted when the assistant director was brought in, and had little enthusiasm for what she did under this arrangement. The resulting compilation of footage—varying greatly in emotional intensity—was so erratic that some critics liked Stanwyck's work, some hated it, and all had different impressions of what she did. To study reviews of this film is to become hopelessly confused.

The London *Times* praised her performance for being "sensitive and restrained"; *The New York Times* found it "too well-bred to be true." The *New York Daily News* said her playing "places her in the class of the screen's great tragediennes"; *Variety* said the picture called for "an actress of considerable more gifts than Barbara Stanwyck here indicates she possesses." Probably the only valid review came from the *New York Sun* which said:

> Barbara Stanwyck, as the forsaken wife, must mourn bitterly from first scene to last, alternating reproaches with wails that men must fight and weeping is for the women. It is a character that does not lend itself to variety. Miss Stanwyck, unable to avoid a monotonous note, does give her Nora as much fire and warmth as the lines admit.

Banjo On My Knee (released before *Plough* but made after) shifted Stanwyck from RKO back to Twentieth for a bit of light entertainment. Director John Cromwell (for whom this is a trifle in his list of credits) does not consider the film any great contribution to motion pictures, but says it was fun to make. He enjoyed working with Stanwyck ("She is very easy to work with") whom he had admired in *The Noose.*

Banjo is aimed toward laughs. Shot quickly in late 1936, it made use of the studio tank for a portion of the Mississippi River containing "Island No. 21"—a sandbar to which a group of shanty boat people are moored. River boy Joel McCrea and land girl Barbara Stanwyck are married in the opening scene, but unable to consummate the marriage because McCrea takes off on his wedding night after a mix-up which leads to trouble with the police. This thwarts the wish of his "pappy" (Walter Brennan) who is determined

to have a "grandbaby." It takes almost nine reels of complication to get the couple together—moored in seclusion on a sandbar, and serenaded by a crafty and contented Brennan.

Stanwyck's character alternates between kind of a sweet thing and a spunky one. Cromwell says he wanted Stanwyck because "she was a natural for the role. She had just the right quality." He describes what she brought to acting as "full-blown"—that is, an ability with which she was born. All he ever had to tell her was the degree of emotion he wanted. He says her line readings reflect her instinctive sense, which is "so strong and so sure" and agrees that they are both right and unusual—"just different enough."

New for Stanwyck in this one was a chance to display her dancing ability, and she comes off well in a tap routine with Buddy Ebsen. She also sings—both alone and with Tony Martin. Her own voice was used for the songs (one of which was called "Where The Lazy River Goes By") and Stanwyck has quipped: "By the river—they couldn't have cared less!" (Actually, while Stanwyck's singing voice isn't on a par with her other talents, it's quite pleasing. Or, as *Variety* put it, her "deep and throaty . . . mike voice is good enough . . . to have her singing in plenty of pictures to come." There would be more songs in future pictures—some by Stanwyck, some dubbed. Those she would do herself she would do well.)

Stanwyck's first film at Paramount—*Internes Can't Take Money*—was also the first of the Dr. Kildare stories. Director Alfred Santell explains that "Paramount purchased the original story—then dropped the character. MGM was more 'series' minded . . . and they bought the character and additional rights." *Internes* should have been just another B film—but it became moody and interesting through Santell's eye for stirring visual effects which he combined with an awareness of the emotional impact they can create.

For this, he worked closely with art director Hans Dreier. Santell says: "Hans and I worked well together. He knew I knew what I wanted. If words could not convey it a quick thumbnail sketch would. Ours was a common language but Hans WAS the art director . . . and a damn good one."

Briefly, the film shows Stanwyck searching for her missing child. Joel McCrea—as Dr. Kildare—tends Stanwyck in the clinic where he works, falls in love with her, and (assisted by gangster Lloyd Nolan who owes him a favor) helps her locate the girl.

Internes Can't Take Money, *with Joel McCrea*

This Is My Affair, *with Robert Taylor*

Santell's approach—"a deliberate blending of silent and talking techniques held together by mood, intensity and sincerity"—produced a great deal of suspense. And it brought from Stanwyck a performance that has an aura of strangeness clinging to it. She controls her energy and pulls you toward her—instead of dissipating it through outbursts which release, and therefore relieve, her anguish. (Stanwyck would later display her most perfect use of this technique in *The Great Man's Lady*—with gorgeous results—when she holds a gun on Brian Donlevy, and when—believing her husband and children lost to her—she plays a woman who is "dead.")

Realizing what Stanwyck could give him, Santell arranged shots that would utilize it to the fullest. There is, for instance, a scene where she stands on the stairs of a decrepit rooming house and talks with another character standing above her. The setting is stark and Stanwyck wears a hat with a brim that dips over one eye. With a setup like this, and her annoyance at the character with whom she is dealing, Santell had only to shoot down on her looking up at the man from under that hat. The result could burn out the frame.

Santell says:

> Barbara is an artiste and needs little direction once she is told how you "see" the scene played. You merely block in the movements and run a rough rehearsal. From that you make corrections, rehearse again (or again!) until the scene is tight and plays well . . . then shoot it. If you're lucky you get it the first time!
> There were few retakes. . . . Barbara knew the whole script and had even memorized all the other parts. Occasionally, in rehearsal, she'd toss a floundering actor his next line!

Knowing the whole script is unusual for an actor; many of them don't even know their own lines. But it is not unusual for Stanwyck. In *Portrait: Barbara Stanwyck*, she explained how her way of working came about:

> I've always had to learn the entire script before I started. That goes for pictures or television. And that's the stage training. I must learn the whole thing—exactly as I would a stage play. [Then] I don't care where the director goes, because I know everything—and I'm adjustable for him.

Stanwyck went on to say that she is thus able to cope with unexpected problems ("an actor who gets sick, trouble with weather, trouble with the set") which might make it necessary to shoot something different from what has been scheduled. In addition, of course, familiarity with the entire script gives her a much better perspective as a performer.

Following *Internes*, Stanwyck returned to Twentieth for a melodrama decked out in turn-of-the-century décor: *This Is My Affair*. As a café entertainer, she is responsible for staying the execution of Robert Taylor when the mission entrusted to him by President McKinley—that of breaking up a gang of bank robbers—goes wrong. She is lovely to look at in period costumes and wigs, and she sings and dances with skill. Her first entrance—with a graceful song and alluring manner—is one of the highlights of the film. (Stanwyck did her own singing in this one too. For the record, her song in *Lady of Burlesque* would also be hers; those in *Ball of Fire*, *California* and *The Man With a Cloak* would be dubbed.)

The appeal, talent and discipline that were always evident in Barbara Stanwyck's performances would have assured her of continual welcome in Hollywood—both with those making pictures and with those watching them. But to remain a really top star, she needed one thing more: some good material. From the time of *Annie Oakley*—and for a while before that—she had had a number of scripts to which she gave much more than she received. Suddenly there was the possibility of a part with real substance—one that could give both her spirits and her career the lift they needed. When Samuel Goldwyn began casting *Stella Dallas*, Stanwyck wanted the role of Stella desperately.

She told Joel McCrea (with whom she was making *Banjo On My Knee* at the time) how much the part meant to her, and he spoke to Goldwyn. (As Stanwyck has put it: "Joel McCrea practically clubbed Sam Goldwyn into getting me into *Stella Dallas*.") McCrea explains:

> King Vidor, the director, wanted Stanwyck from the start, but Goldwyn wanted to test three or four other good actresses to be sure. Barbara didn't want to test, and I got Vidor to promise to hold out for her if she made the test. He agreed. Then I talked her into taking it. She was far and away the best, but she shouldn't have had to

test—any more than you would test Gable for a part. There is no better actress than Stanwyck if she is cast correctly. Goldwyn was a peculiar man, but he made fine pictures.

Concerning the experience, Stanwyck later told the *New York World Telegram:*

Goldwyn [had] flatly refused to consider me because he told me quite frankly that first, he didn't believe I was capable of doing it; second,

he thought I was too young; and third, I hadn't had enough experience around children.

[When] he finally agreed to give me a test, Anne Shirley and I did the birthday scene. We shot the scene for a whole day with King Vidor instead of in the customary few hours. When Goldwyn saw it he gave me the part.

And so—finally—Stanwyck was set for a role worthy of her talents. She would be Stella.

This Is My Affair

Part II
The Brass Ring

Stella Dallas

Barbara Stanwyck has played some widely varying expressions of human behavior. As Cecil B. DeMille once said: "She's a great technician—very versatile. She can play a great variety of roles." It is sometimes assumed that she hit her peak in *Double Indemnity*, but there is no "peak" in Stanwyck's career. She's hit lots of them—including one for a warm characterization in *Stella Dallas*, one for the opposite in *Double Indemnity*, one for cracking everybody up in *Ball of Fire* or *The Lady Eve* (take your choice) and one as Victoria Barkley in *The Big Valley*. As DeMille said: "She can play a great variety of roles."

Recently, Stanwyck was asked to select her favorite of all of her roles. And, again, there are many that remain favorites for her. She has also said: "I really don't think there can be a favorite. Every role is a challenge. If it's a success—it's a role you love." But—for purposes of answering the question—she agreed to talk about *one* of her favorites. And, for that one, she chose Stella Dallas.

When she began work on Stella in 1937, Stanwyck said: "I want to give the part I'm to portray a lot of thought. It will take a lot of thought." The Stella she created reflects the tremendous amount of care and understanding that went into it. To show something of the direction her thinking took—and why it produced a performance that has not lost its effect—the following, by Barbara Stanwyck, is printed in its entirety:

Picking one particular role as a favorite is a very difficult thing to do, since there were several that were personal favorites of mine. In this era when so many pictures are made for shock value, it may seem strange to some that my favorite role is one that was founded on sentiment, and which audiences remember because of the great heart which the central character in *Stella Dallas* showed. I have played many unsympathetic characters, like the ruthless Phyllis Dietrichson in *Double Indemnity*, and I know that such characters are sought after by many actresses who realize that roles in which they play evil women sometimes make a deep impression. Such parts have their own fascination for an actress.

However, for me there was even more enjoyment in playing Stella Dallas—it was a part which showed a woman moved primarily by unselfish motives.

The role was a challenging one for me (and I always enjoy a part that is a challenge) because it had once been beautifully played by the late Belle Bennett in the first version. In fact, it was a double challenge because the role had to be played on two levels, almost making Stella two separate women. On the surface, she had to appear loud and flamboyant—with a touch of vulgarity. Yet while showing her in all her commonness, she had to be portrayed in a way that audiences would realize that beneath the surface her instincts were fine, heartwarming and noble. Part of her tragedy was that while she recognized her own shortcomings, she was unable to live up to the standards she so painstakingly set for herself.

The story of her life was a study of mother love and of devoted sacrifice. Her ambitions for her daughter, Laurel, were so great and yet so utterly unselfish that she finally cut herself completely away from her child so that Laurel could attain the kind of life Stella wanted for her. She realized that she would be a discordant note in any attempt Laurel could make to achieve that kind of life.

Stella's tastes were cheap, her clothes loud, her manners crude. It was only as she grew older that she faced the realization that what she had thought were smiles of appreciation were actually smiles of tolerance, pity or contempt. To spare her daughter the humiliation of a mother with such surface commonness, Stella deliberately planned an affront which would leave Laurel free of any feeling of responsibility for her.

There is a point in portraying surface vulgarity where tragedy and comedy are very close; that thin dividing line had to be watched carefully. The characterization I gave had to be clear so that all the facets of Stella—a great woman in spite of jangling bracelets and bobbing plumes—were never confusing to the audience.

My Stella Dallas grew under the sensitive direction of King Vidor, and was aided by the warmth and brilliance John Boles and Anne Shirley brought to their roles. Anne played the exquisite Laurel very sensitively.

My favorite scene in the movie was the one where Stella Dallas stands by a rail outside a church as Laurel is being married to her well-born fiancé. I had to indicate to audiences, through the emotions shown by my face, that for Stella joy ultimately triumphed over the heartache she had felt. Despite her shabbiness and loneliness at that moment, there was a shining triumph in her eyes, as she saw the culmination of her dreams for her daughter.

While women identified with Stella Dallas and

suffered for her and with her, I like to feel that she was a woman who cheated failure. One who eagerly paid the full measure for what she wanted from life.

Some people may consider such a theme and such a character sentimental. But I think one must distinguish between sentimentality and honest sentiment. The theme of *Stella Dallas*—a mother's love and self-sacrifice—when properly handled in any medium is never maudlin, never dated. I still receive letters from fans seeing the film for the first time, either on television or at one of the various film festivals, and their comments make me doubly proud of the fact that I was fortunate enough to play this once-in-a-life-time role. [*Movie Digest*, January 1972]

The role is just that and, in 1936, it was a highly coveted one. In fact, the whole film was a plum for actors and gave rise to a lot of nervous testing. Samuel Goldwyn's special fondness for the picture—whose silent version he had made with great success—had given him definite ideas about what he wanted. In Stella's case, these had ranged from an older actress (he considered Ruth Chatterton who—apparently much lacking in perception—turned down the role "because Stella was such an unpleasant character") to an unknown (Anne Shirley tested with one of these—Bernadine Hayes). However, age and other preconceptions faded into the background when he saw Stanwyck's test, and she was cast by a satisfied Goldwyn. For the role of Laurel, he had wanted Bonita Granville (who proved too young to age in the later scenes). But, again, Anne Shirley—who would have her 18th birthday on the set—pleased with her test.

Director King Vidor recalls his own estimate of what Barbara Stanwyck would bring to the role of Stella Dallas:

> I do remember very well that I admired Miss Stanwyck's humanness and ability and the way she came over as a very down-to-earth person. And on the screen in anything she has ever done that has been her greatest asset to me, that she makes everything entirely believable—makes you think it is really happening when she does it. And this to me is the test for all acting and directing—if someone watching in the audience can entirely forget that he's looking at a movie.

To the choices already mentioned (Stanwyck,

Shirley and Boles) were added Alan Hale and Barbara O'Neil (the latter having won out over Mary Astor). And with this fine cast, Goldwyn—through the talents of his A-1 director, King Vidor—was equipped to turn out another memorable *Stella Dallas*.

Stanwyck had not seen the silent version of the film (and would not until after her own performance was released). But, as she states, its reputation presented "a challenge" to anyone who would try to equal or surpass it in a remake. She was determined to give her Stella everything that she could.

For the first time in her career, she did something that she does not like and has not done since: she bleached her hair. Although offered wigs (some of which she did use at certain points in the film) she insisted, most of the time, that she be able to work with her own hair. She explained that, to rely on wigs throughout the film would mean that

> I couldn't do anything with my hands, like running them through my hair. Furthermore, in her home Stella's hair was neglected, unkempt—and that just can't be done realistically except with one's own hair.

To further create the character's exterior, Stanwyck underwent a horrendous transformation at the hands of Goldwyn's head costume designer, Omar Kiam. Not only did she appear in trashy and outrageously overdone costumes, but she was surrounded by layers of lumpy padding. Even her legs did not escape. Nor, for that matter, did her cheeks—which were stuffed with cotton from time to time.

All was calculated to have its effect—on both audience and actress (to say nothing of those in the story with her)—and was useful to Stanwyck. She could completely submerge herself in such costumes and—more important—pull from them the essence of the woman who would wear them. She makes them work through her understanding of this.

But the real excitement is Stanwyck's presentation of the core of Stella. Crucial to showing this "great woman" is the expression of Stella's ability to accept and to grow. Without this, she could not have arrived at the maturity necessary for her unselfish action. She could not have seen things as she does or carried out the decision she makes. Stella's development—prompted by all she must face to achieve what she wants for her daughter—is what Stanwyck builds,

Stella Dallas, *with John Boles*

Stella Dallas

layer by layer, into the magnificence that reaches its culmination in the final scene. It is this that is so beautiful to watch.

Stella is sensitive to refinement—but incapable of acquiring it. Marriage with socially prominent Stephen Dallas (John Boles) gives her the chance. And her inability to succeed is splendidly shown at a country club dance where she has hoped to "get in with the right crowd." Dancing with race track tout Ed Munn (Alan Hale) she embarrasses Stephen with her enthusiastic bouncing and the tasteless gauze and glitter she is wearing.

It is right here that Stanwyck has to begin watching that line between comedy and tragedy. She keeps Stella's surface vulgarity from being offensive by showing what motivates her. Stella is a very natural creature. Impulse bubbles out of her before reason can suppress it. But she is not "an unpleasant character." She is engaging in her exuberance, her delight in living, her lack of airs. You enjoy Stella. You recognize that she is doing the wrong things but—as long as you can see what is fine in her, and how earnestly she wants to please—you like her and you do not laugh. Stanwyck controls the balance perfectly.

She uses a large number of physicalizations for the scene—and the role—because Stella throws her whole being into whatever she does. On the dance floor, she waves at some people at a table, slaps Ed's chest as she shrieks at his jokes, plays with the net of her gown, and shakes her curls and earrings as she reacts to his flattery and good humor. The zeal with which she gives herself—even if it does produce social unacceptability—helps maintain sympathy for her.

Stella's failure to fit in—and her subsequent separation from Stephen—doesn't bother her too much, because she replaces her ambition with something that matters more to her: her daughter, Laurel (Anne Shirley). She raises a happy and delightful Laurel—a combination of the surface refinement of her father and the inner fineness of her mother—or just about as perfect a child as she could have hoped for. And it is an agonizing moment for Stella when she realizes that she herself may mar this perfection. Her discovery is brilliantly played.

Laurel returns from a visit with her father, attracted to the social graces and the well-bred lady who is now the center of his attentions: Mrs. Morrison (Barbara O'Neil). Unaware of Stella's jealousy, she praises Mrs. Morrison—for all the things Stella is not. When Stella picks up the woman's picture to ask if those are "real pearls she's got slung around her neck" she accidentally smears it with cold cream. Laurel reacts violently and rushes to wipe it off.

Stella looks into the mirror at her cold-creamed face, her messy hair and sloppy condition—and sees how poorly she is equipped to satisfy Laurel's needs. She makes a pathetic effort to erase her feelings of inadequacy—to "improve" herself—by touching up her dyed hair. Realizing what has happened, Laurel returns and offers to help. As Laurel begins, Stella shrinks to a quiet, forlorn figure—contemplating her daughter and the situation. It is from this low a point that she must pull herself in order to reach the stature she has at the film's end.

She is close to it in the renunciation scene, where Stanwyck gives one of her most intricate and skillfully wrought pictures of the two levels on which Stella must be played.

When she attended the country club dance, Stella was innocent of her incompatibility with her surroundings. Now—seeking Mrs. Morrison in her gracious home—she is painfully aware of it. A determined but uneasy Stella awaits Mrs. Morrison's appearance. Needing encouragement, she gains it from the one object in the room to which she can relate—a picture of Laurel. Her need is so great that she touches the picture. At the same time, she sees how well Laurel fits in—and it helps her carry out the unpleasant task she has set for herself: that of giving Laurel to Stephen and Mrs. Morrison.

Stanwyck presents here a Stella who tries to curb her surface coarseness but cannot. In the middle of a speech whose volume and pitch have soared with excitement, Stella catches herself and lowers both. But other things get by her. In her eagerness to gain what she wants for Laurel, she pulls her chair up to the sofa on which Mrs. Morrison is sitting—then snatches away the pillow between them and plops herself down in its place. The beauty that radiates from Stella's words is especially moving because it must come through an exterior that is fighting it.

She is even closer to greatness in the "affront" scene, where she kills her relationship with Laurel. Bowing out nobly was one thing. But rejecting the girl and shattering her beliefs is another. Naturally, in both this and the renunciation scene, there is pain for Stella. Its elimination—or that triumph of joy over heartache which shows Stella in all her glory—will not come until she can reconcile her actions within herself and see that she has "cheated failure."

As she watches Laurel's wedding, Stella is searching for something. She is deeply involved. A handkerchief finds its way into her mouth, to give her support. Her major concern is to find out if Laurel is contented. When Laurel lifts her veil and kisses the groom, a pleased Stella tilts her head and lowers her eyes shyly. A tear falls and she accepts it willingly into her mouth. She turns—still holding the hankie between her teeth—as she questions her feelings. She finds that she is satisfied, removes the hankie and—with her head up—walks away fulfilled, picking up speed as she goes and breaking into a big grin.

Terribly important to all of this is Stanwyck's statement that "one must distinguish between sentimentality and honest sentiment." Her Stella works because Stanwyck handles the role with restraint and sincerity. You always see her thoughts. And emotional influence is revealed—not indulged—through careful selection of what will show it, and clear execution of this.

The whole film is shaped in this manner. King Vidor gives it its full value by letting it go only so far. He brings a scene to fruition and lets the audience—not the actors—react to it. His use of close-ups is sparing and brief.

Vidor stresses that the results his actors achieved were very much a product of teamwork: that is, of agreement on approach, followed by capability and invention on everyone's part. He remembers little about specific contributions because they were all working toward—and thinking about—the end result. He and Stanwyck were "in accord with the characterization" and it was "a question of sympathetic cooperation." He states:

> I think that the greatest results between actress and director come from a respect and a sympathetic understanding, and we certainly had that. There's no struggle going on if the director plays *his* part well and is capable and the actress plays *her* part well. And the more, I'd say, *psychic* understanding you have (I have cited, I think, in *A Tree Is a Tree* how I was able to direct Jack Gilbert even without *saying* much of anything) the better you can work. And when sympathy exists and respect exists between director and actress, it cuts out a lot of talk, and certainly no arguments are necessary, and they fulfill their

parts. And this is very important. If there is a mental conflict, then I—as the director—have to become like a psychiatrist and try to dig beneath the actor or actress's neuroses and reach him on some deeper level. But this did not happen with Barbara Stanwyck and myself simply because she was a pro. She was pleasant to work with; she was on the job at all times; and the whole crew felt this great professionalism and great rapport with her.

Of how he worked with Stanwyck, Vidor explains:

> I think it's a question of love. I think if love exists—admiration—love exists between director and actress, which I felt—I felt a deep feeling of love—it's like a family functioning. It's like a husband and wife functioning.
>
> A director also plays the part of the whole audience in film making. He reacts. He praises. He applauds—not with his hands—but with words and feeling, and you have a slightly different way for each person.

Of how Stanwyck worked with them all, Anne Shirley adds:

> The whole word is pro. Miss Stanwyck was hired and paid to perform a service. She presented herself for work before time. She was prepared to the very top of her ability. Dialogue learned perfectly. Hair, clothes, *energy* ready. There was no "I am not feeling well today" or "I have a personal problem" and then a request to be excused for the day, as happens with so many actresses. I believe she clearly felt she was in a business. By a business, I mean that it was not something in which you indulged yourself. You gave a day's work for a day's pay. Barbara Stanwyck did not think of it as a super art form, but rather as a business. And this is rare.

The type of work needed for *Stella Dallas* called for constant expenditure of emotion on the part of the actors, and equally constant exposure to this on the part of the crew. There were moments of hilarity in the script (such as the scene where Stanwyck dissolves in laughter after Alan Hale has spread itch powder among the passengers on a train). But the intense involvement created by the emotional moments called for some lighter ones *behind* the scenes to erase their effects. And Stanwyck—who has a knack for pulling people out of heavy scenes after

Stella Dallas

Stella Dallas, *with Anne Shirley*

Stella Dallas

Stella Dallas, *with Alan Hale*

Stella Dallas, *with Barbara O'Neil*

Stella Dallas, *with Anne Shirley*

they are over—was in fine form. Anne Shirley recalls that when they were rehearsing the scene in the train berth, an especially difficult one:

> It was terribly silent on the set. Barbara turned to me and said: "All these years I spend in movies and I have a scene in a bed with some-one, and who do I end up with? YOU! *Not* Clark Gable, *not* Gary Cooper . . ."

The set promptly broke up.

In addition to the requirements dictated by an emotional and high-aiming production, a day's work on the set of this film carried with it demands for endurance of another kind. A make-up and hairdress-ing strike had delayed the film's start. When it did go into production—with a skeleton crew in these de-partments—it was surrounded by trying circum-stances. The extent of the effect these could have is described by Barbara O'Neil, whose confrontation with a medium that was new to her was not helped any by the conditions then prevailing in it.

Barbara O'Neil was a theatre actress who had been spotted by a Goldwyn scout and brought to Holly-wood for the film. And the poise which she exhibits in her playing of Mrs. Morrison was extracted at a high cost to her nervous system. While she declares that her "life in the theatre and the acting profession" has been filled with "many rich and joyous experi-ences," memories of what she went through in *Stella Dallas* bring to mind for her what is "best described as 'total discomfort.'" She explains:

> There was a sane element at the center [of the situation] that gives perspective to the whole.
> I think Miss Barbara Stanwyck won't mind being called either a sane element—or a very attractive life raft in that miasmic tension-ridden atmosphere of strike plus Goldwyn.
> *Stella Dallas* was my first picture. There was a strike and a picket line to be crossed every morning which I hated.
> Being made up by a stranger during a strike in the early morning (instead of making myself up in the privacy of my dressing room backstage in the evening) was not a peaceful way to start the working day for me.
> I recall the head of the UA make-up depart-ment, a Mr. S- -. He kept the curtains drawn, peering out occasionally to see if the bomb would explode during my moments in his chair. He told me all through the operation just how dangerous it was for him to be doing my face at all.

By the time I landed on the set in the presence of Miss Stanwyck, Mr. Vidor and Rudy Maté [the cinematographer] I was an already shat-tered, New York-imported commodity.
> Rudy Maté would look at me sadly, but en-couragingly. He could see I hadn't slept very well. He was the dearest man out there, and his only mistake had been that when he made my original screen test he had made me look beauti-ful. His problem was to repeat that accomplish-ment each day! He was an artist—among the best in Hollywood—and he cared very much about his work.
> Mr. King Vidor was kind and respectful and very patient and, like a knowledgeable animal trainer, carefully managed to get a shot of me now and then that he could use.
> One day, when things were particularly rough and my ignorance of film technique was prob-ably costing time and money [Vidor: Goldwyn came on the stage, raised hell, and of course we knocked off work for the rest of the day] Bar-bara came over to my dressing room and, in a serious and friendly way, encouraged me to keep in there pitching and to try not to let Mr. Goldwyn bother me.
> She is a marvelous warm-hearted person. I knew it then while working with her, and—re-cently watching a rerun of *Stella Dallas*—I understood the depth and strength of her work. She is an inside actress—works from the inside out. And this privacy will make her pictures—but more particularly her performances—last with the new generations of audiences.
> Later, after I had parted company with Mr. G and was back on a stage with Walter Huston, I was invited to play Helen Morrison again—on the Lux Radio Theatre.
> Life is fascinating—because Miss Stanwyck had a bad moment before going on stage in front of a "live audience" and she let me encourage her. I told her to keep in there pitching and not to let that live audience bother her (as she had done for me).
> A couple of pictures later I was in the hospital having my tonsils out. She sent me a big glass bowl full of talisman roses. I think of her that way.

Critical reaction to *Stella Dallas*—and to the work of everyone connected with it—was excellent.

If only to view Barbara Stanwyck's dramatic triumph as *Stella Dallas*, this picture should be seen. Playing this emotional mother role with power, understanding and restraint, she gives her best performance yet. [*Film Daily*]

[Miss Stanwyck's] Stella is more restrained and credible than Belle Bennett's in the silent version. She gives an underlying strength to a weak, fatuous woman that makes the portrayal vividly sympathetic and lends needed motivation to the tale. It is her best acting in years. [*New York Herald Tribune*]

Miss Stanwyck's portrayal is as courageous as it is fine. Ignoring the flattery of make-up man and camera, she plays Stella as Mrs. Prouty drew her—coarse, cheap, common, given to sleazy dresses, to undulations in her walk, to (with the aid of pads and extra layers of this and that) fatty degeneration of the profile. And yet magnificent as a mother. [*The New York Times*]

Barbara Stanwyck gives the best performance of her cinema career. . . . her pathetic moments are handsomely pointed up by underplaying of a kind she has never delivered heretofore. The picture is her vehicle throughout and the star comes through in every scene. [*Brooklyn Daily Eagle*]

Stella Dallas is the sort of film that . . . could have been ruined by a less sensitive and understanding director than Mr. Vidor. . . . He never loses sight of the fact that the strength of [it] lies in its emotional appeal . . . [and] he puts over every poignant moment with devastating effect, but never in a cheap lachrymose manner.

Having always felt that Miss Stanwyck would prove herself one of the screen's finest actresses if given half a chance, this department is happy to report that in *Stella Dallas* [she] turns in a sensitive, beautifully shaded characterization and that there are moments of uncommon beauty in her playing.

No less superb is little Anne Shirley. . . . Excellent, too, are Alan Hale, Barbara O'Neil and John Boles, all of whom help to make *Stella Dallas* a film of warming satisfaction and deep, tender emotion. [*New York World Telegram*]

It is a notable personal triumph for one of the few really great directors of the screen. [*New York Herald Tribune*]

For her performance in *Stella Dallas*, Barbara Stanwyck received her first Academy Award nomination. While she did not win (Luise Rainer did for *The Good Earth*) she had finally been recognized—as she should have been from the start—(and Frank Capra points this out in his book) for *Ladies of Leisure*.

King Vidor last ran the film about a year ago and was "quite impressed with her performance and the other performances in it." Looking back, he states:

> I was pleased with the opportunity to work with Barbara Stanwyck and had great admiration for her as a most capable actress. It was a great pleasure to be her director, and I think she gave a superb performance.

Stella Dallas

Breakfast for Two

After the workout that *Stella Dallas* had given her, *Breakfast for Two* was just the thing to provide Stanwyck with exercise of another kind—the kind she terms "relaxation." She told the *New York Post* after completing *Breakfast:*

> I couldn't possibly have followed *Stella* with another emotional role. It had run the gamut. So I had to let down and give the boys a chance. I do very little in *Breakfast for Two*. It's practically Herbert Marshall's picture.
>
> I feel more comfortable in drama. It's more my field—but comedy has become relaxation. It's awfully easy—for me anyway—to do movie comedy. It's really like a vacation. I was playing—not working.

Breakfast for Two is one of those dizzy blends of gags and sophistication that prevailed in the late thirties, which director Alfred Santell states were known as "high comedy." In it, playboy Herbert Marshall—whose interest in wine, women and song is costing him the family fortune—battles with Stanwyck as a Texas heiress who decides to pull what's left of it out from under him and make him so mad that he straightens up, flies right, and takes the charming thorn in his side with him. Mounted in style against sparkling all-white sets, the film features smart dialogue—and grand high jinks on the part of Santell who, as he puts it, goes "back to the days of Mack Sennett and the Keystone Kops." Some of the gags, he explains, were in the script but most of them he developed as he went along.

Stanwyck and Marshall (and others such as that gentleman's gentleman *par excellence* Eric Blore) do full justice to Santell's inventions. Falls, slides and blows to more than the ego are executed with vigor and enthusiasm.

Probably the most outstanding gag given Stanwyck is the chance to kayo Marshall in a rowdy boxing match. After some wild swinging, the match builds to a climax when she is knocked against the wall, falls to the floor, and is bombarded by a supply of duckpins. This does it, and she charges. When the fight is over, Marshall and Blore—nursing black eyes—observe Stanwyck emerging from the gym and taking off her glove. A doorknob falls out of it.

Santell:

> A borrowed version from the old crooked prize fight game. It has been said that small horse-

shoes were secreted, at times, in fighters' gloves. I simply changed the horseshoe to a doorknob.

The film's most elaborate gag involves a series of well-timed interruptions in a wedding ceremony as Stanwyck tries to prevent another woman from marrying Marshall. The fun begins when the wedding—set against an expanse of windows—is stopped by a window washer with a heavy black beard who lowers himself on a scaffolding and begins to scrape on the glass. When he is shooed away, he hauls himself up and returns with four identical characters who scrape with him. The commotion—and another flooring of Marshall (this time with Stanwyck waiting discreetly outside the door as her uncle does the dirty work) leaves the knot *untied* and the groom fit to *be tied.*

Santell on the window washer gag:

> It had its origin years before when several friends and I actually did it at an opening of a vaudeville act of another friend who had graduated from the Gus Edwards Kids act, a fixture on the Orpheum circuit, into a "single" patter turn. We took the whole row center in the first tier nearest the footlights. We were all dressed alike and all wore beards which were exactly alike. When our actor friend made his entrance and saw us, he flipped and how!

Marshall has his chance to get even with Stanwyck in the final scene: a free-for-all of cake-throwing and pursuit over slippery floors in which he is the victor and the pair is united—for better or worse.

The film pleased in all departments. The *New York Herald Tribune* said:

> With excellent acting from a thoughtfully picked cast, cunning direction by Alfred Santell, and a steady flow of clever dialogue, this comedy is good entertainment.
>
> Barbara Stanwyck shows intelligent understanding of [her] role. . . . With commendable skill, she is both cocky and demure, assured and sorrowfully frustrated.

Santell states:

> Barbara is all things a performer should be. She is a real trouper. She arrives on the set ready and equipped to do her chores. And she does them! Always well. She has given much to the motion

114

Breakfast for Two, *with Herbert Marshall
and Eric Blore*

Breakfast for Two, *with Herbert Marshall*

picture industry—and more to those who were fortunate enough to work with her. One cannot be too complimentary about her.

Santell refers to Stanwyck's flawless promptness and preparation. Others have done so prior to this. In fact, the first to note that "Barbara Stanwyck always came on the set on time and always knew her lines" was Joseph Walker—who photographed her as early as *Ladies of Leisure*. Practically every director, cameraman and actor who speaks of working with Stanwyck—from the beginning to the present—mentions her dependability in these areas.

Stanwyck considers discipline a courtesy to the production and to those working with her, an essential to acting, and merely part of the job—which is what it should be. What makes her unique—and makes others recognize her for it—is the fact that so *few* actors function this way.

The period of "relaxation" that *Breakfast for Two* had afforded was soon followed by one of a different—and less welcome—kind. In the latter part of 1937, Stanwyck was suspended by RKO and Twentieth for turning down scripts she felt were unsuitable. During the suspension she found refuge and financial assistance in radio, where she appeared for the Lux Radio Theatre. Looking back on the experience a year later, she declared:

If you feel a thing strongly enough, you should have the courage of your convictions to carry it through. That's my philosophy, and it's gotten me into plenty of hot water. Somebody told me the other day that Bette Davis and I were the most suspended people in pictures, and wanted to know why we argued so. I don't know about Bette, but the reason I argue is because I know myself. There are things I know I can do, and other things I can't do.

A lot of times, a studio knows better than a star whether or not a picture will be a success. But I have to go on my instincts. Sometimes I've been wrong, but more often I've been right. Last year I was suspended for seven months because I wouldn't do two pictures at two different studios. They were rabid about these "great" pictures. But neither one has yet been made. That's vindication right there, I think.

I have to keep working to keep happy. They could work me every day and I'd love it. Those seven months away from the studio I didn't know what to do with myself. But if the same argument came up tomorrow, I'd probably go on another suspension. That's how I am.

To get back before cameras and complete her contracts, Stanwyck finally accepted *Always Goodbye* at Twentieth. It was a remake of the 1934 *Gallant Lady* that had starred Ann Harding and Clive Brook, and its theme was mother love and sacrifice. The resemblance to *Stella Dallas* stops right there. Actually, the films should not be compared but—coming so close together in her career—they were. Noble in intention, but inferior in script and direction, *Always Goodbye* wallows in sentimentality.

When the film is serious, Stanwyck's otherwise moving performance is weakened by close-ups that signal the story's big moments. Unlike Vidor's close-ups that grow slowly (as, for example, when he moves his camera unobtrusively toward Stella's reaction to what she overhears on the train) *Always Goodbye*'s are injected by abrupt cuts, and call attention to themselves.

Even more damaging is the saccharine approach used in the casting of the child (played by Johnnie Russell) whom Stanwyck, as an unwed mother, gives up and then wants back. Such excess clearly illustrates the difference between "sentimentality and honest sentiment"—and shows why *Stella Dallas* continues to move audiences and why *Always Goodbye* is dated.

Stanwyck's next picture—*The Mad Miss Manton* —remains one of the finer examples of "screwball comedy." It takes its attempts to solve murder very unseriously.

In this one, Stanwyck leads a pack of seven "public-spirited" debutantes through a series of daffy encounters with corpses and police—playing a character that is best described by the film's much-harassed police chief, Sam Levene: "She's probably the kinduva dame that'd come back ta haunt me. Otherwise I'd shoot ta kill!"

Leigh Jason's direction puts the picture together with rapid pace and a clear idea of what it is after. Roy Webb's score and Van Nest Polglase's art work are tasteful. And the film owes a lot to the work of Nicholas Musuraca, a most gifted cameraman, whose eerie shadows provide fitting atmosphere.

The Mad Miss Manton was shot in the summer of 1938. And Jason (who says "I've worked with perhaps eight or nine hundred actors and actresses. Barbara Stanwyck is the nicest.") had his hands full with the rest of the cast and some conditions similar to those in the script.

First, the picture was an exercise in group directing. There were seven lively girls surrounding Stanwyck. And most of them—except for Frances Mercer, who played the largest of the roles—had never been before a camera. This made things take longer. In fact, it was a challenge just to keep them straight (there was a temptation to put numbers on their backs, but Jason resisted) and give them bits of business that would keep them in the scene. The fact that some of the outside work was shot on the Warners ranch with fur coats and 100° temperatures did not help either.

Second, Henry Fonda, who starred opposite Stanwyck—as the reporter who questions her escapades, and ends up falling for her—had not fallen for the script. He says: "I was so mad on this picture. I resented it." His experience with a character who didn't appeal to him—and who had to spend his time being attacked by eight squealing females—makes him remember little except his frame of mind, which was none too healthy. Naturally, this did not stop a pro like Fonda from doing his usual fine job, but it did interfere with the fun he and Stanwyck would otherwise have had. Fonda says he wasn't receptive to anyone, including Stanwyck, and that later—when they hit it off during the making of *The Lady Eve* (because "as my daughter would put it, we had the same 'vibes' ")—Stanwyck reminded him of *Manton* in a friendly but direct manner: "You son of a bitch, you didn't pay any attention to me!" (Today this would not happen because Stanwyck remains for Fonda the favorite of all of his leading ladies. He says: "She is one of the dear people of the world—a perfect delight to work with. Great in her profession—not only in comedy but in her ability to tear you apart emotionally." He adds that there aren't enough superlatives in existence to describe her, and "I don't know a person who has been so loved by everyone as Stanwyck.")

For all its differences of ability and opinion, *Manton* is a successful ensemble film. However, its best moments are—naturally—those which bring the pros together. A parody of a death scene is milked to the fullest:

Fonda has been shot—with no ill effects—and is attacking his dinner with gusto in a hospital bed when Levene suggests they pretend he is dying, in order to pry information about the murder from Stanwyck.

Levene: I told her you were dyin'. She's out there in the corridor cryin' her head off for you. . . . In the condition she's in, she'd even tell ya her *age* if ya asked her.

Stanwyck bursts in weeping, and they go into action. A groaning Fonda requests his "favorite song"—"Home On the Range"—and policeman James Burke comes through in his finest Brooklynese. Against this, clichés get the works. Stanwyck breaks down and talks—in one of the funniest line-readings of the scene—and Burke and Levene rush out with their information.

But then she notices the tray of half-eaten food hidden under the bed, does a double take, catches on, and grabs a fork from it. Holding this behind her back, she baits Fonda:

Stanwyck: Are you still in pain, *sweet?*
Fonda: Oh, it's nothing, nothing—only when I move. But it's nothing.
Stanwyck: Peter, perhaps I did wrong in not telling Inspector Brent *everything.*
Fonda: You mean you held something back?
Stanwyck: *Ye-e-s,* Peter.
Fonda: Oh, sweet, you're so clever.
Stanwyck: Remember when I went into Ronnie Belden's apartment?
Fonda: Yes, dear.
Stanwyck: When I went into the bathroom? I *found* something.
Fonda: In the bathroom?
Stanwyck: Yes. Floating around in a foot of water in the *bath*tub.
Fonda: Louder, dear. I can hardly hear you.
Stanwyck: (with intent to kill) I'll come closer.
Fonda: Tell me, dear, what was it?
Stanwyck: The *Normandie,* you black-hearted faker, in *full sail!*

She gives him a spectacular jab with the fork and leaves.

You will not find more skillful timing or a better flair for comedy anywhere in the profession than that which characterizes the Stanwyck-Fonda combination. Watching this gifted duo clown, one can't help wishing that they had made more than three films together. (There are two actors who have been the perfect foils for Stanwyck's wit: Fonda and George Brent. Brent provides a bland opponent—Fonda a sharp one. She plays off both with ease.)

The New York Times observed that

Twentieth Century–Fox. General publicity—1938

Always Goodbye

Always Goodbye, *with Herbert Marshall*

Always Goodbye

Seven debs playing Philo Vance are almost as much fun as a barrel of monkeys—not quite, of course; but fun enough to encourage a visit to the Music Hall's current zoo.

The . . . script is dredged with bright lines and cheerfully absurd situations. The Ames-Manton romance, in the hands of Mr. Fonda and Barbara Stanwyck, is refreshingly natural, considering the unnatural background it moves against. And Leigh Jason's direction has kept suspense and comedy in exactly the right proportion.

Shortly after this, Stanwyck had the opportunity to play something a bit different (in the Lux airing of *Morning Glory*) and said:

I'd never done anything so light and frothy so I asked a certain producer to tune in. I wanted to prove to him that I could do something happy. I gave the lines everything I had. The audience in the theatre seemed to like it and I was feeling pretty good about the whole thing. Then, when it was all over, one of the technicians volunteered: "You've been off the air in Los Angeles for forty minutes. The local outlet broke down."

I squawked, "Well, how do you like that? A week's work shot to hell! This station's been here for fifteen years, and it has to break down just when I have a chance to prove I can do something besides woebegone mothers, with fourteen children at their skirts, heading over the hill to the poorhouse."

The *New York Post*, which *did* hear her efforts, said:

Barbara Stanwyck, to our surprise, polished off Eva in very nice style on last night's show. The voice was more expressive than we had remembered it, with just the right note of breathless awe to make the characterization click.

Stanwyck would not be doing any more woebegone roles (mothers or otherwise) for a while. She was now entering one of the most diversified and high-energy periods of film making in her career: one which would be filled with top roles, scripts and directors—and relatively few moments of woe.

Twentieth Century-Fox. General publicity—1938

The Mad Miss Manton

The Mad Miss Manton, *with Henry Fonda*

The Mad Miss Manton

CHAPTER EIGHT

I am sometimes asked who is my favorite actress, among those I have directed. I always dodge the question by explaining that I have to continue living in Hollywood. But if the tortures of the Inquisition were applied and an answer extracted from me, I would have to say that I have never worked with an actress who was more co-operative, less temperamental, and a better workman, to use my term of highest compliment, than Barbara Stanwyck. I have directed, and enjoyed working with, many fine actresses, some of whom are also good workmen; but when I count over those of whom my memories are unmarred by any unpleasant recollection of friction on the set or unwillingness to do whatever the role required or squalls of temperament or temper, Barbara's name is the first that comes to mind, as one on whom a director can always count to do her work with all her heart.

—The Autobiography of Cecil B. DeMille

These are the words of a man whose adherence to discipline was exceeded by no one's. The actress who could meet the standards of perfectionist Cecil B. DeMille—and please him above all others—would have to be exceptional. Four months on the complicated and sometimes trying *Union Pacific* (not to mention sixteen radio shows) proved to him that she was.

Union Pacific, begun in late 1938, is an epic treatment of the struggle to build the transcontinental railroad—given a million dollar budget and the DeMille concern for tradition and detail. Location shooting at Iron Springs, Utah (by a second unit under Arthur Rosson) provided the outdoor action sequences—tracklaying, wrecks, raids, pursuits—and fed studio process screens. Filming with the principals was conducted by DeMille at Paramount and on location at Canoga Park, which became "Promontory Point" for the driving of the Golden Spike.

Stanwyck plays Mollie Monahan: daughter of the Union Pacific's first engineer, and postmistress of "End of Track"—the town that moves westward with the railroad's progress. She enjoys the attentions of two suitors: Joel McCrea—a troubleshooter sent by Washington to control things, and Robert Preston—an irresponsible but good-hearted gambler. The uniting of east and west—and of Stanwyck and McCrea—is given its share of frustrations. As the *Brooklyn Daily Eagle* saw it:

*Columbia. General publicity—1939.
Photo by A. L. "Whitey" Schafer*

There are two bang-up train wrecks, a bloody Indian massacre, innumerable saloon brawls, a murderous mail-car robbery, perilous nocturnal horseback chases through wild Wyoming, and a mad dash by a battalion of U.S. regulars through fire and a barrage of Indian arrows to save two heroes and a heroine trapped by blood-thirsty redskins. That makes *Union Pacific* the largest conglomeration of thrills and cold-blooded murder since Pauline was in Peril.

As a matter of fact, "Pauline" *was* in peril in this one and—although most of her perils were handled by process work—when there was any action to be tackled, Stanwyck managed to get herself involved, as Joel McCrea puts it, "in everything. She is fearless and has more guts than most men." A high-energy Stanwyck scrambles over the top of a railroad car, spins on a brake wheel between two of them, operates a handcar with McCrea, runs after a wagon and jumps onto it, and battles her share of attacking Indians.

Her spirit and cheerful Irish tongue match the strength of her surroundings—making her a bright, colorful figure. All critics (except the three who rarely like her*) went for this one. Typical was *Film Daily* which had "nothing but the highest praise for Barbara Stanwyck, as the railroad postmistress in the midst of these brawling, fighting men" and the *New York Sun* which was taken with her "Mollie, with the Irish brogue, the coquettish manner, and the quick mind."

In keeping with the grand scale of *Union Pacific*, its premiere was a blockbuster too. After a five-day trip on a special Union Pacific train from Los Angeles—with stops and festivities at stations along the way—DeMille, Stanwyck (who had already begun work on *Golden Boy*), and a number of stars, featured players, and studio and railroad officials, arrived in Omaha, Nebraska, on April 28, 1939. They were faced with quite a display. As Lucius Beebe reported it in the *New York Herald Tribune*:

> . . . the atmosphere of frontier times [was

* There are three critics who have panned almost every performance Stanwyck has ever given: Winston Burdett, Archer Winsten and Howard Barnes. Burdett says she is not a great emotional actress; Winsten dislikes both her acting and her looks; and Barnes calls her wooden. You can pick up practically any review these men have written—whether on a good performance or a bad—and find the same evaluation.

Union Pacific, *with Robert Preston*

Union Pacific, *with Joel McCrea*

Union Pacific

spread] over a considerable portion of the Western countryside.

. . . most of the State of Nebraska, to the extent, at least, of some 400,000 persons, dug up grandfather's plug hat and Sharpe's rifle and tooled to town for the big doings.

False fronts were erected on the facades of buildings . . . More than 20,000 elaborate costumes [had been] imported from a Chicago mail-order house and sold at cost to the citizenry. Every known type of ancient vehicle was salvaged from the lofts of forgotten livery stables [and] every grown man in the community sported some variety of whiskers.

There were bands by the score; there were grand marshals, Sioux Indians, state and civic dignitaries, autograph fiends and beaver-hatted paraders by the hundreds. Three thousand school children sang "Crinoline Days" in the railroad station rotunda. Mr. DeMille made speeches. Mr. Jeffers [president of the Union Pacific] made speeches. Miss Stanwyck received approximately a hayrick full of bouquets. Urchins screamed and cheered. Bill Pine, Mr. DeMille's associate in the production of the film, was observed to be discharging an enormous horse pistol from the back seat of a lavender victoria. Maroons detonated in the heavens. . . .

Three theatres premiered the film simultaneously— one of them adding a midnight showing to accommodate crowds. And when it was all over, Beebe commented:

It was apparent to all observers that the festival transcended both in magnitude and enthusiasm anything in the nature of simple film publicity. It captured the public's imagination beyond anything that even Paramount's high-pressure exploitation staff could have dreamed up. Mr. DeMille, who is entirely accustomed to positively cosmic goings on, was a bit staggered by it all. He was also mightily pleased and so was Mr. Jeffers. Between them they had launched a film of the first magnitude, arranged the most amazing amount of interlocking publicity for Paramount and the U.P., and given Omaha and Nebraska the most magnificent games and circuses in the memory of the oldest inhabitant.

After this, a simple movie set might seem tame— but there was plenty to keep the filming of *Golden Boy* from falling into this category. Clifford Odets'

play (altered for the screen from an allegory of social struggle to that of a personal one) showed a man torn between his love for music—which would leave him materially poor but spiritually rich, and his attraction to fighting—which would do the opposite.

The search for an actor to play the title role had been lengthy. Columbia had tested some sixty-five actors—established and otherwise—and time was running out, when a young Paramount contract player caught their eye. Subsequent testing convinced them he was what they wanted—and the unknown William Holden was set to begin his film career.

A crash program followed to shape him to the role's requirements. It was a rough experience and had its effect on a new and nervous actor. Holden says:

I don't think there's anyone who's done more for me in my career than Barbara Stanwyck. Maybe ten percent of the actors you're fortunate enough to work with are real pros. They will do everything to cover and protect you. A lot of this has to do with integrity.

When they were about two weeks into production, Holden explains, "serious consideration was given to replacing me." It started with the replacement of the original cameraman (Nicholas Musuraca took over) and a kind of replacement "fever" spread—resulting in a "nervous, unhappy situation." When doubts were expressed about keeping Holden, Stanwyck "went to bat for me and had a meeting with Harry Cohn. She said, 'Look, you haven't given him a chance . . .' "—and she saw to it that Cohn was convinced.

Then, after a hard day's work, she began spending a half hour or so running lines with Holden for the next day. Robert Taylor, who would be waiting for her (Stanwyck and Taylor were married shortly before the film's completion—on May 14, 1939) also helped. Holden would go from there to a violin lesson, dinner, the Hollywood Athletic Club for a boxing lesson—and what sleep he could get before the next day's early call.

It was a grim schedule and Stanwyck, knowing this, tried to relieve the tension for him. When he was having trouble—and "in every actor's approach to his work" there are times when "you realize you haven't done well"—Stanwyck "would say encouraging things about something that *had* gone well." And

Paramount. General publicity—1938

130

Golden Boy, *with Joseph Calleia,*
Adolphe Menjou, Edward S. Brophy

Golden Boy, *with Lee J. Cobb*
and William Holden

Golden Boy, *with William Holden* ▷

when tempers were on edge because of his lack of experience, Stanwyck always "managed to straighten things out." What it all came down to was that "she wouldn't allow anyone to fall short of what was expected of him."

Holden recalls that—in the midst of this—director Rouben Mamoulian "pulled a trick on us" that backfired one day. Mamoulian's way of working involved a loose first rehearsal, a second one to tighten, and a third which he would call a take. "But rather than waste the film, which was precious in those days, he would do the final rehearsal without it." To get them "to give more," Mamoulian had a habit of sometimes telling his actors the camera was rolling when it wasn't. Holden had been subjected to this "pressure," but the day that Mamoulian tried it on Stanwyck, he "lost a damn good performance" and precipitated a touchy situation.

Stanwyck had given what would have been a great take, and no film had been exposed. She was highly irritated and told him: "you ask me as a professional to perform for you," that she expected him to function just as professionally, and "Don't tell me it is rolling when it isn't!"

Such deception was unnecessary. As Holden puts it, Stanwyck "is always good. She's so consistent. She rarely deviates from the artistic level she has set for herself." And "she would never expose herself to a poor take. She would have had whatever was awkward ironed out before." Her "artistic judgement" is excellent.

In their scenes together—as is well known—the intensity of Stanwyck and Holden proved a joyous combination. Stanwyck's Lorna Moon is a woman of the world who's "been kicked around." But beneath her façade she has a reverence for life which, paired with that of the idealistic Golden Boy, makes her fire itself. Their scenes go sky high.

Holden's performance triggered his long and successful career—and he has since sent flowers to Barbara Stanwyck each year on the anniversary of the picture's beginning.

Remember the Night, Stanwyck's next film, was one of those rare blends of script, cast and director that can do no wrong. It is so finely balanced and understated, so warm and real, that it will always be a joy to watch. Director Mitchell Leisen shaped Preston Sturges' script into a moving personal statement which *The New York Times* called "the real curtain-raiser for 1940." The *Times* went on to say:

Perhaps this is a bit too early in the season to be talking of the best pictures of 1940; it is not too early to say that Paramount's nomination is worth considering.

Remember the Night is a title which critics never figured out. (Leisen: "That was the title Sturges gave it. I don't know why.") But the film speaks a language common to all.

Assistant D.A. Fred MacMurray has his Christmas visit with his family in Indiana threatened by the need to prosecute a last-minute case. He manages to get the case—that of a shoplifting Stanwyck—postponed, takes pity on the fact that she will have to spend Christmas in jail, and bails her out. Finding that she is from Indiana too, he offers to drop her off to see her mother on his drive home.

The mother—who is responsible for Stanwyck's inability to go straight—rejects her, and he takes her home with him. There, Stanwyck is exposed to a way of life that changes her outlook. She and MacMurray fall in love and when—back in New York—he attempts to free her by losing the case, she pleads guilty to save him from jeopardizing his career. The film ends with her acceptance of a jail sentence for her mistake and their decision to marry when she is released.

The production has class from the moment Leisen opens it with a shot of Stanwyck's black-gloved hand admiring a jeweled bracelet—until he closes it with a shadowy view of Stanwyck and MacMurray clinging to each other in the prison corridor. Leisen's elegant use of the visual (developed during his years as costume and set designer, art director and assistant director for Cecil B. DeMille) is accompanied by strong concern for the substance of his characters. He creates the right moment always.

The Christmas which shows Stanwyck some real people is typical of what the film achieves. Beulah Bondi, Elizabeth Patterson and Sterling Holloway represent more than life on a farm, or a quaint contrast to the city life Stanwyck has known. When she plays the piano as they listen to Holloway sing "The End of a Perfect Day," the camera focuses on contentment that could be found anywhere that people appreciate each other.

Stanwyck's performance is one of her finest. Lee Leander is a mixture of wit, intelligence and sensitivity—which Stanwyck puts across with the same. Not the least of Lee's many sides is her mischievous one. To do justice to the humor with which Sturges explains Lee's lack of ethics, Stanwyck makes her a pixie. Sturges gives her pranks to play, but it is Stanwyck who supplies the line readings and facial expression. Sometimes Lee even seems to surprise herself with her ingenuity! She gets great delight from setting a wastebasket on fire so she and Mac-Murray can escape the consequences of small-town justice by running away in the confusion. When he learns she set the fire and accuses her of arson, she replies gaily, "Well, it's better than going to jail, isn't it? I told you my mind worked differently!"

One of Stanwyck's best scenes—because it shows how deftly she can underplay comedy to make it both natural and funny—involves her and MacMurray in a classic routine with a cow. Having parked their car for the night in a farmer's field, they are awakened in the morning by a cow's head poked through the window, nuzzling Stanwyck's neck. Subsequent efforts to milk the beast find Stanwyck pushing its rear toward MacMurray—who is contending with this, the cow's swishing tail, and a thermos which leaves little room for error. Stanwyck pushes too far. MacMurray and the thermos end up on the ground. And she peeks underneath the animal (upside down) and scolds: "Oh, you spilled the breakfast!"

Leisen loved working with Stanwyck. He says: "I have great admiration for Stany. She is a tremendous professional, a woman of unlimited ability and, with Carole Lombard, is the easiest woman I ever worked with." He appreciated her sense of humor, her consideration for the crew—and the fact that one-take Stanwyck never failed to come through the first time.

Director and crew found Stanwyck a help in many ways on this production. *Remember the Night*'s 42-day schedule was reduced to 34 (saving over $50,000)—partly because some of Sturges' overlong script was not shot, and partly due to Stanwyck's lack of concern for time-consuming glamour treatment.

Prior to this, Leisen had made *Midnight* with Claudette Colbert. While Colbert was lovely to work with, she was very fussy about how she was photographed. Sets sometimes had to be rebuilt in order to present her at her best angle. This, and other requirements of his star, made *Midnight*—budgeted at 44 days—take 47 days to shoot. Leisen expected he would do *Remember the Night* a little faster but—because its script was longer—he planned on a schedule similar to that of *Midnight*.

He soon found, however, that Stanwyck liked to work as rapidly as possible. She would let them shoot her from any angle that could be set up quickly. This, and the fact that she was perfect on the first take, imparted a speed to the proceedings that became contagious. Everyone picked it up and, in the end, *Remember the Night*'s average number of pages shot per day came out to 4½—or the fastest Leisen ever shot anything in his whole career.

Stanwyck's endurance of physical discomfort also amazed Leisen. The scene with the cow was shot at the Paramount ranch in the heat of summer, with the crew wearing swimsuits. Stanwyck was bundled up in heavy winter clothing which she would not remove between setups because time would be lost while she put it back on. This reduced three days of shooting to two. Nor—when they were filming the barn dance sequence—would she take off the tightly-laced corset used for her old-fashioned dress. Despite urging from Leisen that she relax during the hours between scenes, she preferred to remain ready in case he should need her.

In addition to finding her a help, the crew found her fun. One day cameraman Ted Tetzlaff was giving them a hard time with the perfection he wanted in his lighting: "A little more to the left, down a little, more to the right . . ." Their anguish was neatly voiced for them by Stanwyck (who had gone up to the gallery to chat) when she hurled down a "For Christ's sake, Ted, make up your mind!"

Leisen (with whom Stanwyck did only one other film: *No Man of Her Own*) wanted to work with her more. He had planned to star her in *The Night of January 16th* (right after *Remember the Night*) but complications resulting from a rewrite demanded by Don Ameche—who would have played opposite her—killed this. Stanwyck, with no other film offers that pleased her at the time, made a number of radio appearances instead—preferring to wait until a really good screenplay came her way. (In one of these—the Lux Radio Theatre's *Wuthering Heights*—she is a fittingly headstrong and romantic Cathy. Her touch of accent is becoming, and her gentle death scene moving.)

The really good script came—and with it came the satisfaction of working with Frank Capra again. *Meet John Doe* was Capra's first independent picture. From a story treatment by Robert Presnell called *The Life and Death of John Doe*, Capra and writer Robert Riskin (having formed Frank Capra Productions, Inc.) had put together a scenario of epic proportions and been given carte blanche to film it at Warners.

Paramount. General publicity—1939

Remember the Night

Remember the Night, *with Beulah Bondi*

Remember the Night, *with Beulah Bondi*
and Fred MacMurray

All of Capra's "first-choice dream cast—[Gary Cooper], Barbara Stanwyck, Edward Arnold, Walter Brennan, James Gleason, and Spring Byington . . . accepted their roles before reading the script—which is about the highest compliment a director can be paid."(NT) In Stanwyck's case, the conversation went something like this:

Capra: Will you do it without seeing the script? Will you take a chance?
Stanwyck: Is it an honest role?
Capra: I give you my word.
Stanwyck: I'll do it.

When Stanwyck *did* see the script, she was delighted—and it was with enthusiasm that she began filming. Soon after she said:

Everybody is so terribly interested in his work, it's a pleasure to be there each day. And, of course, Capra is in a class by himself. There's no one really quite like him and when people ask, "What's so different about him?"—you just answer, "He's Capra, that's all." You make other pictures to live, but you live to make a Capra picture.

Meet John Doe is one of Frank Capra's greatest films. It tackles a heavy theme: the threat of fascism to the Christian-democratic ideal—and comes up with a sturdy glorification of principles and a monument to the "little people" Capra loves. It is also the ultimate in cinematic showmanship. Five hundred umbrellas over a rally—that moves from silent prayer to seeing its hopes dissolve in the rain—has to be the most powerful crowd scene Capra has ever directed.

For Stanwyck, the film offers fitting material. The character she plays is a veritable dynamo, and Stanwyck sails through the picture—alternately sharp and tender. As the sob sister whose circulation-boosting stunt turns John Doe into a national hero, she must carry a large share of responsibility for keeping things moving at fever pitch. This she does.

No one can move faster than Stanwyck. Spurred by Capra's technique of "kicking up the pace," her quick mind and agile delivery of ideas set a new record for bowling people over when she confronts her editor with the possibilities in the "fireworks" she has injected into her "lavender and old lace" column. He gets more than he can handle. Stanwyck comes up with one of the smoothest, most sophisticated attacks she has ever given a scene. She hardly stops for breath. Yet she is not merely hammering out speeches. She is providing them with every conceivable nuance and building the scene steadily to its climax.

She maintains this hard-hitting approach throughout. And, when she helps save what is left of Doe at the film's end—in the scene, chosen from five versions shot in an icehouse at twenty below, which Stanwyck later said put her in "the hospital to be defrosted"—she is the hottest thing there. The intensity of her playing—and of Frank Capra's glorious staging—lift the scene to a level that will accept a passage from Beethoven's Ninth without batting an eyelash.

Meet John Doe was chosen by *Film Daily* as one of the ten best pictures of the year, and it was a top-grossing one. For Barbara Stanwyck, it was a prelude to what would be a run of exceptional portrayals. Of the four performances she turned out next, three would join the list of her greatest.

Paramount. General publicity—1939

Meet John Doe, *with Gary Cooper*

Meet John Doe, *with Gary Cooper*

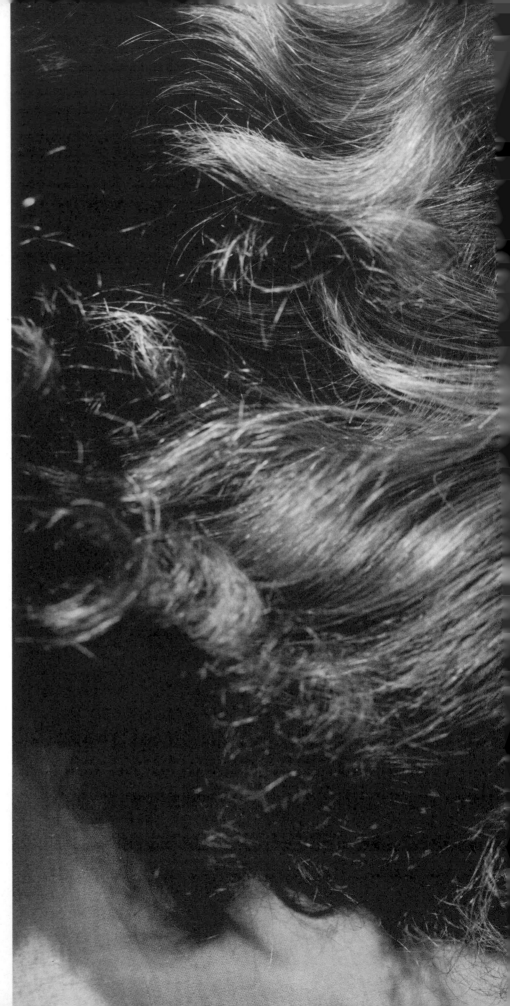

142

CHAPTER NINE

We call Sturges the "Mad Genius." You never know what he'll do next. Wore his hat all day the other day "so we'd recognize him." Came on the set the day we were working in my bedroom wearing a horrible-looking bathrobe!

It was while she was filming *The Lady Eve* that Stanwyck voiced the above. She added that she felt Sturges had "a wealth of talent" and would be "one of our 'biggest' some day." When the picture was completed, she told *The New York Times* she had never had more fun in any role than as the girl card-sharp in this Preston Sturges comedy. She continued:

He'd ask us how we liked the lines. If we didn't we'd say so, and he'd say the script-writer was fifty kinds of an imbecile—and change them. But, you see, he wrote the thing himself.

Henry Fonda looks on *The Lady Eve* as one of perhaps five films he is really proud to have made, and recalls what a ball they had putting it together. In fact, "Sometimes, during filming, Sturges would be laughing hysterically at his own lines. He was a total egomaniac." Fonda explains that he means this in a complimentary way. In Sturges, he says, it was "almost an endearing quality because he was naïve about it."

Preston Sturges had had phenomenal success with his first two director-writer efforts (*The Great McGinty* and *Christmas in July*) and was as delighted as a child with a new toy. Fonda remembers that at lunch in the commissary Sturges "practically demanded that you sit at his table." He had a long table—with himself at the head of it—and Stanwyck, Fonda, cameraman Victor Milner, and the principal actors lining it. One day, a Sturges "henchman entered with a stack of photos of a marquee" from a theatre showing a Sturges film. Sturges "had had the marquee photographed from every conceivable angle" and proceeded to pass the results along the table, wanting everyone to enjoy them.

With *The Lady Eve*, Sturges not only maintained his rating; he turned out one of the screen's classic comedies—considered by many to be his finest work.

If it is brilliant Sturges, it is also brilliant Stanwyck. While she had played comedy before, Stanwyck had never met up with such a sparkling and carefree role. Her best light moments had occurred in *Remember the Night* (another Preston Sturges script). And she had done them justice. But the heavy

volume of her earlier "woebegone" roles had caused a couple of critics to label her "lugubrious" and expect her to stay that way. Both did double takes on *The Lady Eve*.

This was a new and different Stanwyck—and an enchanting one. *The New York Times* found her "a composite of beauty, grace, romantic charm and a thoroughly feminine touch of viciousness." The *New York Herald Tribune* said the film was "played to breezy perfection by Barbara Stanwyck and Henry Fonda, who are not usually associated with sly clowning," and felt that Sturges had "disclosed hidden talents in both stars"—including, in Stanwyck, an ability to be "alluring as well as artful." And the *New York Morning Telegraph* put it right on the line: "Miss Barbara Stanwyck, who plays the title role, becomes one of the hottest things of the moment in the way of portraying high comedy and sex at one and the same time."

Cardsharp Charles Coburn sets the tone for it all when he says to his equally adept daughter, Stanwyck: "Let us be crooked, but never common." In the elegant fleecing of millionaire snake-enthusiast Fonda that follows, Stanwyck plays two shrewd and disarming characters—and has a field day.

The forte of the first character, Jean, is seduction. On board the pleasure cruise she and her father are "working," she meets Fonda by tripping him up in the dining room (throwing him into the first of five falls which he remembers all too well to this day) and traps him into escorting her to her cabin to replace the shoes he has ruined. This sets up what *The New York Times* called "one of the most satiric lust-scenes ever filmed."

Its context is simple: her presence and perfume are overpowering—and he's been up the Amazon for a year where "they don't use perfume." He is invited to pick out a pair of evening slippers (she goes to a trunk of them and leans on it suggestively: "See anything you like?") and put them on for her ("You'll have to kneel down"). A gown slit to her knees by Edith Head does the rest. And a reeling Fonda is brushed neatly aside when he attempts to make a pass at the elusive Stanwyck. He is, however, allowed to follow her back to a little card-playing with her father, where it becomes "every man for himself."

The second character, Eve, uses something even trickier: wit. Despite her dishonorable intentions, Jean falls for Fonda and—when he learns of her racket and jilts her—Stanwyck has the opportunity

The Lady Eve

to pose as the "Lady Eve Sidwich" who descends on his estate in "Bridgefield," Connecticut to undo him again.

She appears before an audience of expectant "your ladyships" as modest, soft-spoken gentility ("Just call me Eve"). Then, spurred by a coterie of admiring males, she takes stage with a stream of smart stories —dazzling with her charm, her accent, and her busy ostrich fan. It is a bravura performance—filled with bold strokes and subtle rhythms—which captures Fonda and continues to delight film audiences.

Contributing to what was played up as a "new screen image" for Stanwyck, was an interesting transformation which had taken hold of her behind the scenes. Edith Head had first designed for Barbara Stanwyck on *Remember the Night*—a picture during which Stanwyck had floored people by donning hats with no mirror and no concern for how they looked on her. She had explained her behavior by saying: "I like to have my mind free to give a performance; it's my performance I'm concerned with—not how I look."

But, on the set of *The Lady Eve*, things went a little differently. As Edith Head described them in her book *The Dress Doctor*:

> Some actresses fit in three minutes, some take three days. The subjective actress thinks of clothes only as they apply to her; the objective actress thinks of them only as they affect others, as a tool for the job. There are those who stand before the mirror absorbing each minute adjustment. Barbara Stanwyck is the one who stood with her back to the mirror! As for fashion, she couldn't have cared less. . . .
>
> . . . *The Lady Eve* was strictly a *dress* picture, and I was about to inoculate her with flattering furs, evening sheaths and diamonds!
>
> Barbara walked about while director Preston Sturges explained her dual role as two sophisticated ladies: a titled Englishwoman, a lady gambler. Any diagnostic eye could tell there'd be no difficulty in Stanwyck's carrying high fashion. She's small, but she has excellent carriage, a good figure, an innate poise. She listened to our diagnosis and said nothing. Barbara would make a first-rate hand at poker.
>
> Her first fitting involved an evening gown for the love scene with Henry Fonda. It was of clinging black crepe, a sheath with the slimmest of slim looks (she *hated* tight skirts), the lowest of necklines, a very high, very tight cummerbund

(she *hates* anything tight around her midriff), and a short jacket covered with black glitter.

> When she finally turned around toward the mirror and *saw* herself side view first—"More people look at you sideways or walking away, how many people see you straight on?"—she was stunned. And she fell in love with high fashion! I worked on all Stanwyck's pictures for years. . . . [Head has costumed Stanwyck in 23 of them.]
>
> It was the beginning of a long and happy relationship. I enjoyed it, because Barbara, with her clean-cut, arresting beauty, wears clothes well; but she has a sense of humor that keeps her from ever taking fashion too seriously. She's extraordinarily honest: "This looks pretty repulsive on me, don't you agree?" . . . Brutally frank: "It may be winter-white jersey, Edith; it looks like long underwear to me." . . . There is no equivocation or beating around the bush; she doesn't say "Oh, yes" to you and then tell the director, "I wouldn't be caught dead in *that!*" . . .
>
> The only argument we ever had concerned wardrobe tests. The average female showing clothes just automatically *models*, puts one hand on her hip and walks thus . . . She'll turn her best angle to the director and the cameraman. Barbara puts on a beguiling costume and just stands before the camera, turns around, walks. I'd gesture wildly from behind the camera.
>
> "Hand on the hip, Barbara. Come on, girl . . ."
>
> Barbara'd have none of it. "I'm not a model, why should I act like one?" she'd say. Once a costume was in action, an actual scene being shot, the clothes became part of her characterization.

Skillful handling of costumes has always been part of a Stanwyck performance. And, in 1957 and 1964, it would be recognized through presentation to her of the Motion Picture Costumers' Award (fittingly titled "Eve") for "Artistry" and "Unfailing Cooperation."

The Lady Eve was chosen by the National Board of Review as one of 1941's ten best pictures. It is probable that it would also have provided Stanwyck with an Academy Award nomination if *Ball of Fire* had not done so in the same year.

The concept behind her next film, *The Great Man's Lady*, promised something very special. Stanwyck's role was a beauty—and a challenge which resulted in one of her finest pieces of work.

The Lady Eve, *with Charles Coburn,*
William Demarest, Henry Fonda

The Lady Eve, *with Henry Fonda*

The Lady Eve, *with Henry Fonda*

The Great Man's Lady (which began as *Pioneer Woman*) shows how idealist Joel McCrea builds the city of his dreams in the West and becomes a public hero—inspired by the devotion, courage and self-sacrifice of his wife (Stanwyck). It opens in the present with a 109-year-old Stanwyck embarking on "100 years of memories—some good, some bad" for a girl who is writing a biography of McCrea, and tells its story through flashbacks that begin in 1848 when Stanwyck is 16.

Preparation for a role that would age the 33-year-old Stanwyck to 109 was extensive. Charles Gemora (who worked for the picture's make-up artist, Wally Westmore) created brilliant make-ups for the ages she would portray. Edith Head did graceful things with costumes for a period that is a designer's delight. And two weeks of tests followed. In *The Dress Doctor*, Head recalled these and said of Stanwyck:

> . . . she's absolutely loyal. If she feels something is right, no one can change her mind. She'll stand up against director, producer and writer, come hell or high pressure.
>
> [At one point in] *Great Man's Lady* she played the owner of a gambling hall, one of the richest women in the early West. I copied a dress worn by a noted woman of the period: black velvet embroidered with diamond birds. Stanwyck loved it; so did I. When we ran the test, several executives suggested that, wonderful as it was, it would look even better without the birds.
>
> "If the birds go, the dress goes," Stanwyck said firmly. "I like 'em; so does Edith."
>
> Rather than spend the money to make an entirely new dress . . .

Along with the externals being planned for her, Stanwyck was working on a set of her own—one that would be prompted by her understanding and use of internals. Her research took her and director William Wellman to an Eastern Star home, where she absorbed some of the real thing. Stanwyck's talent being the deciding factor, she was able to put together a careful, knowledgeable job of aging. It advances by degrees from the willful girl who elopes with McCrea to the selfless woman who saves his career. And, when she appears at the age of 109, it is with a change in physical rhythm (the details of which she makes hers, as she does costume and make-up) that does not wipe out her character. She remains a woman of spirit and intelligence.

The script of *The Great Man's Lady* was a strenuous one—giving Stanwyck plenty of exercise of the kind she likes: sliding down the bannister of her "stuffy" Philadelphia house, galloping off on horseback to elope with McCrea, being married on the prairie in a driving rainstorm, shooting and slitting rabbits, throwing crockery, and crawling onto a bank of mud from the studio tank where she has lost her babies and almost drowned in a flood. In addition, the physical workout had nothing on the emotional one which produced some of the most intense scenes she has ever played.

The character of Hannah is many-sided, and Stanwyck makes her register at all times.

As the romantic young girl in ruffled nightgown and cloak, she flirts boldly with McCrea, challenging him to swing her onto his horse and race off with her in the moonlight.

As the resourceful pioneer bride, she puts on a grand show for the man who attempts to interfere with her husband's goal. Using a nasal twang and a pretense at dullness that make a most amusing scene, she primes the man for the moment when she hurls a knife in his direction and follows it with insults and dishes that send him fleeing an uncivilized "prairie woman."

As the determined defender of her husband's interests, she confronts Brian Donlevy—a gambler who has taken advantage of him—with a revolver and a gaze guaranteed to get back everything McCrea has lost.

And as the woman stripped of husband and children—a woman who is "dead"—she places McCrea's needs before her own, giving him the strength to pursue his ideals by relinquishing her chance to be reunited with him.

Barbara Stanwyck's portrayal of Hannah is a tour de force. It is one woman's life—and one actress's versatility—combined. Hannah—as the film's title indicates—is always a lady. But she is a flesh and blood one—capable of learning the skills that will help her husband, enduring the hardships that are a part of their life, adhering to what she believes in, and giving up whatever she must in order to provide him with what he needs. Stanwyck plays this with depth and conviction—creating a wealth of beautiful moments. The scene in which she learns that her drowned babies were buried by Donlevy is one of the most brilliant she has ever played, as is the one in which she returns briefly to McCrea before giving him up for good. But then, there are so many excep-

The Great Man's Lady, *with Joel McCrea*

The Great Man's Lady, *with Joel McCrea
and Frank M. Thomas*

The Great Man's Lady, *with Brian Donlevy*

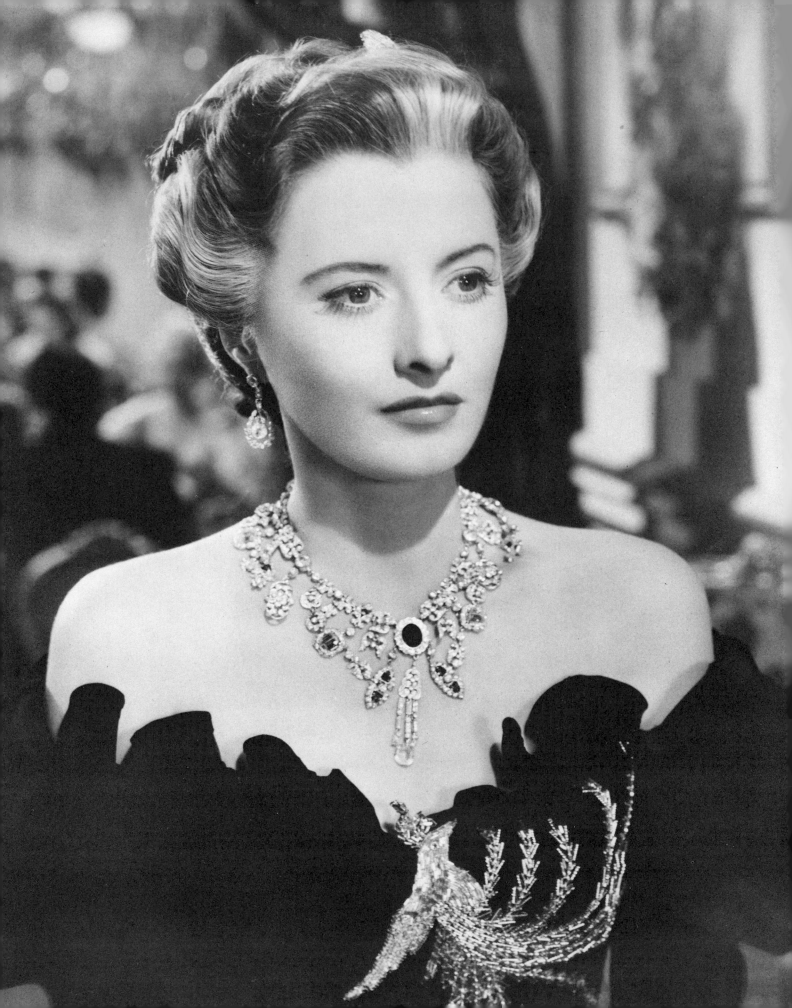

tional scenes for her in this picture that it's hard to single them out. Joel McCrea puts it best when he says: "Stanwyck should have gotten an award for this film—if ever anyone deserved it."

In an attempt to capitalize on *The Lady Eve*, Stanwyck and Fonda were brought together again in *You Belong to Me*. The picture gave *Eve* no competition but—on its own terms—was enjoyable enough. Anything that stars Stanwyck and Fonda is worth watching. And there was the added plus of Joseph Walker's lenses—marking his sixth and final feature film with Stanwyck. (Walker and Victor Milner tie for having photographed Stanwyck in the greatest number of films.)

In what *The New York Times* called "a bit of well-turned fun," the film explores a wealthy, idle playboy's insane jealousy over the men patients of his doctor wife. This takes the pair through a series of stock situations—from Fonda's explosive entrance into Stanwyck's office while she is examining a patient, to his refracturing of the sacrum of another to make sure it stays that way.

As always, Stanwyck and Fonda are in fine form. The material they have to work with isn't the greatest, but they help it out considerably. Director Wesley Ruggles said of his stars:

> Because of them, I've been on a vacation. This is the most delightful job I've had in years. They seem to be able to read a director's mind. They know exactly what he expects of them without being told. Sometimes, too—when I have a scene about as perfect as a director can expect it to be—Barbara and Hank will throw in a bit of new business during a rehearsal, just for a gag, and I'll find it improves the scene even further.

And *Variety* added:

> The performances of Miss Stanwyck and Fonda merit fulsome praise. Their strokes are keen and deft regardless of whether they're playing farce, romance, or the film's more serious moments.

Ball of Fire, like *The Lady Eve*, had everything going for it: an excellent director, script and cast. Billy Wilder (who would begin filming his own scripts right after this and who "spent a good [deal of] time on the set observing" *Ball of Fire*'s director, Howard Hawks) says:

The story was an original called *From A to Z*, written in German by me in Paris sometime before I ever came to Hollywood. The late Thomas Monroe helped me Americanize it. We then sold it to Mr. Goldwyn when he was looking for a vehicle for Gary Cooper. The casting of Miss Stanwyck came later.

The screenplay by Wilder and Charles Brackett bears a resemblance to *Snow White*—as some writers have put it—"in reverse." Wilder says he did not think of it that way but "maybe it was in our subconscious." At any rate, it is a kind of fairy tale.

Seven whimsical professors, led by a pedantic one (Gary Cooper), are compiling an encyclopedia in a hallowed brownstone. Their sanctuary is invaded by strip-tease dancer Sugarpuss O'Shea (Stanwyck)—a gangster's moll who hides from the police by helping Cooper with his research on slang. Sugarpuss has magical powers. The professors have been marching in step for nine years—from their constitutional in the park to their work on the project. But it is with glee that they toss this aside to follow "a pair of ankles" through four days of conga lines and similar hooky-playing devices. As for the Prince of the tale: Cooper was a child prodigy with no time for the more primitive pleasures of life. The tempting Sugarpuss blows the "dust that has piled up on his heart smack into his eyes"—and he is in love.

Woven through this is a serious statement which director Howard Hawks puts across expertly and pleasantly: a respect for two ways of functioning— and the ideal produced by their fusion. Sugarpuss starts out taking the "kids" for a ride—but ends up as devoted to them as they are to her. Thus, "eight squirrelly cherubs" have their instincts sharpened by Sugarpuss's vitality, and some of their gentle manner and moral soundness rubs off on her.

Stanwyck plays "the kind of woman that makes whole civilizations topple" with the poise and glamour she displayed in *The Lady Eve*. But Sugarpuss is an entirely different kind of *femme fatale*— probably best described by the reviewer in the *Newark Evening News* who called her "Little Miss Smartypants." She's fresh. And totally lacking in inhibition. And—as Stanwyck delivers this—totally beguiling.

An energetic fingernail, lacquered to kill, taps on the curtain before she enters in a burst of spangles to

The Great Man's Lady

The Crew's Great Lady. April 1941

You Belong to Me, *with Henry Fonda*

Paramount. General publicity—1941

Ball of Fire, *with Gary Cooper*

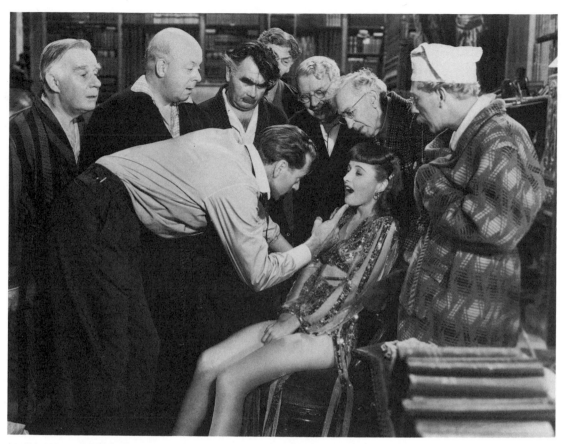

Ball of Fire, *with Gary Cooper, Henry Travers, Aubrey Mather,*
Oscar Homolka, Leonid Kinsky, S. Z. Sakall, Tully Marshall, Richard Haydn

Ball of Fire, *with Gary Cooper*

sell her nightclub number. Equal surety of purpose accompanies her greeting to Cooper when she shows up on his doorstep to exchange her knowledge of slang for a hideout. She knows what she's doing too when she sheds her mink and blinds Cooper with her brief and sparkling costume—Gregg Toland's lights turning her into a Tinker Bell. And when she gives Cooper a cold, wet and very nude foot to feel—and then undulates up the stairs telling him to look at her "as another apple . . . just another apple"—it is clear that Cooper is in for the works.

She makes the most of suggestive lines and business. In answer to Cooper's apology for the fact that he hasn't got his tie on, her response of "Oh, you know, once I watched my big brother shave" ought to have made the Hays office at least uneasy. Similarly, she turns a wicked pencil sharpener for the benefit of Cooper's housekeeper who has lost out to Sugarpuss's ability to get her man—and her way.

There is another reason for this character's appeal: Sugarpuss is fun. She is a cheerful thing to have around. The color she brings to the musty quarters of the Totten Foundation is enough to gladden any susceptible bachelor's heart. And her seven "push-overs" are not without symptoms of revolt before her appearance. One has succumbed to a craving for strawberry jam; another has raised a shade to let the sun in; and, since a third is just beginning his article on sex, she probably has not arrived a moment too soon. The joy she gives them—whether they are blushing before her stuck zipper, dressing up to please her or capering through an energetic conga—makes her quite a treat.

And, when "mink coat" learns that there is something in the world besides the opposite of this ("bungalow apron"), her reaction to the situation she has created—as she wrestles with her conscience and desires—is just as gratifying. The Sugarpuss that raises a glass in genuine appreciation to what she has seen produces a moment—filled with loss of innocence—that Hawks leads gently into the film's most touching sequence.

From the peddling of slang to the meeting of dramatic crises, the role required versatility. Sugarpuss has many dimensions. Barbara Stanwyck made them into a character quite her own—winning audiences and an Academy Award nomination.

CHAPTER TEN

"Moody" and "different" were terms applied to Stanwyck's next film appearance, and they were appropriate. *The Gay Sisters* brought the bitter, argumentative people of Stephen Longstreet's novel to the screen with no apologies.

Three generations of aristocratic tradition stand behind the refusal of Stanwyck and her two sisters to sell their Fifth Avenue mansion to make room for "progress"—the building of Barclay Square. Stanwyck is also held back by her hatred of the man behind the project, George Brent—an engineer whom she tricked into marrying her so she could claim a badly needed legacy. She had intended to pay him off and leave on the wedding night, but he refused to let her go until morning—thus providing her with a child she has hidden from the world for six years, and a ferocious disposition.

In some ways the situation is a *Cherry Orchard*. One of the characters says of Brent: "Perhaps he sees the world we once loved is ending"—and Brent *does* want to hurry this along to his advantage. But, in its strongest statement, it is a psychological study of Stanwyck's character: Fiona Gaylord.

Fiona is Stanwyck's first projection of a type of woman that would appear frequently on the screen from now on: a dark, discontented one—the product of a changing world. In 1942, her iron will and complex nature were still a bit startling. (Of course Fiona, and even the bloodthirsty Martha Ivers, seem like pastel personalities in a world which now eats aberration for breakfast.) But Stanwyck saw—as she would with all her dark characters—that Fiona's actions were prompted by understandable motivation.

Fiona learned self-reliance as a child, when her father's death left her head of the house. She also learned that the self-reliant person does not show vulnerability—and even her housekeeper is convinced that "she's got no heart, only a stomach." There are indications she would like things to be different, but she fights them: "Love is something you cut out of yourself, or it moves in and cuts you apart." She gives in to it eventually, but not until she has exhausted every other way out of her problems.

The Gay Sisters is admirably honest and Stanwyck's work perceptive. With humor as pungent as her character, she provides caustic narration for a flashback which shows her trapping Brent into marriage by playing the role of "girlish modesty." A real gem, the sequence moves from "bucolic love-making" amid apple blossoms ("I'll never forget the *stink* of

those apple blossoms") to an old-fashioned wedding in which she suddenly has "an attack of the vapors, sways weakly and totters toward the stairs" where she "drapes herself over the bannister like Monday's wash" and "swoons" in Brent's arms ("Katharine Cornell couldn't have done it better"). She meets her downfall when—having sent Brent to the village drugstore for some "sal volatile" so she can make her getaway—she is headed out with her suitcase as he returns. The background music (a Max Steiner score which has been enjoying itself thoroughly) helpfully throws in "My mama done tole me."

Director Irving Rapper speaks vividly of the experience of working with Stanwyck. He found her "*terribly* cooperative and the easiest lady to work with" and says he is in a position to know, having worked with "a few tough girls." She is "so simple— so unassuming—so disciplined."

He mentions that the picture's inexperienced players slowed things down at times, but one of these—Nancy Coleman—states that, for her:

> The making of this film was one of the smoothest and most rewarding of my motion picture experiences, and I think a great deal of this had to do with Miss Stanwyck. She seemed to accept me as a much more experienced actress than I actually was and, by this acceptance, gave me great confidence.

Concerning another newcomer, Rapper had some qualms which his leading lady treated in an equally professional—and typically Stanwyck—manner: "Irving, don't worry about him. The producers will forget all about me and he'll be a great star." After the previews—as predicted—the producers were saying they wanted to see more of this actor. His name, identical with that of another, had to be changed. And to capitalize on the impression he had made in *The Gay Sisters*, he was named after the character he played: Gig Young.

Stanwyck's next film was the imaginative *Flesh and Fantasy* (shot in 1942 and released a year later). Three separate stories and casts (linked by prologue, epilogue and connecting commentary) concern themselves with fate versus free will—implying that faith in yourself is insurance against fear. In the third story, Stanwyck is a fugitive from justice with whom circus aerialist Charles Boyer becomes involved, after a dream in which he sees himself falling, during his

Warners. General publicity—1942.
Photo by Scotty Welbourne

The Gay Sisters

The Gay Sisters, *with George Brent*

The Gay Sisters, *with Nancy Coleman*

Flesh and Fantasy, *with Charles Boyer*

act, as she screams in the audience. Stanwyck's role is an interesting one which she handles well.

The film is very much a mood piece and gave cinematographer Paul Ivano atmosphere galore for his camera. Ivano's recollections:

The Julien Duvivier film was started by Stanley Cortez. I had just finished *Shanghai Gesture* with Josef von Sternberg. After two weeks of shooting, Duvivier and Stanley had a fight and I was called to Universal to meet Duvivier. He looked at my eyes and said "Okay, it's your film—you have light eyes. I do not like directors of photography with dark eyes . . ."

The film was a Charles Boyer–Julien Duvivier production. I was born in France—so Julien spoke French with me and Boyer. Barbara did not like this since she does not speak French—but I could not help the situation because Duvivier addressed me in that language.

However, Miss Stanwyck and I became friends. I had a crane shot in the circus tent that went from a long shot to the close-up of Barbara's ear [to point up an earring Boyer sees in his dream]. As I was on a big crane I realized how dangerous that was, so I started with the ear and pulled back, cranking the film backwards. Barbara realized I did that for her safety and we became friends.

Ivano has since photographed some of Stanwyck's television work and says:

Every time I light and set a close-up, Barbara says to her stand-in, "Please get me coffee. I want to talk to Paul." She knows my close-ups are better if I line up and light her. I do not like stand-ins because it is better with the real actress.

With Barbara there is never any trouble. Everybody adores her and so do I.

There was considerably more "flesh" than "fantasy" in Stanwyck's next film—and certainly nothing psychologically complex about her character. The last of her chances to work with "Wild Bill" Wellman, the unique *Lady of Burlesque* also gave her a chance to let her hair down. And, as the *Brooklyn Daily Eagle* phrased it: "Barbara Stanwyck is a lively girl and knows her way around roles like this." Playing Dixie Daisy, star performer of a group of burlesque "artistes," she is involved in four shows a day *on* stage and a murder mystery *back*stage.

Gypsy Rose Lee's novel, *The G-String Murders*, came to the screen with a different title because producer Hunt Stromberg—working on his first independent picture—had had a survey made in a number of cities and found that very few people knew what a G-string was. Most of them thought it had something to do with music.

The Hays office kept its eye on things, but let the film get away with more than might be expected. Strip-teasing was out, and bumps were either toned down or registered in the reaction of another performer watching—but scanty costumes were allowed as long as everybody kept them on.

In addition to solving murders, Stanwyck puts over a couple of neat song and dance routines. One of these is an accomplished rendition of wisecracks, off-camera stripping and a song called "Take It Off The E-String, Play It On The G-String." The other keeps her busy with cartwheels, splits—and a pair of spike heels that makes her agility all the more impressive. She is equally proficient with a series of gags in some comedy skits.

Film Daily said: "Miss Stanwyck plays a burlesque star to the breath." And *The New York Times* found her wriggling "through a couple of song and dance numbers" one of "the bright spots of the picture" and proof "that she hasn't forgotten her early chorus-training on Broadway."

Barbara Stanwyck had now starred in 43 films, and shown versatility with many styles. There remained one kind of role—an integral part of the spectrum of an actress—that she had never done, and the time was right for it. It was still early enough for audiences to be shaken up by a thoroughly evil woman.

Stanwyck was well aware of the potential in the role of *Double Indemnity*'s Phyllis Dietrichson (Director Billy Wilder says: "She jumped on it instantly") but she did have one fear. She stated in *Portrait: Barbara Stanwyck*:

When Billy Wilder sent me the script of *Double Indemnity* and I read it . . . I had never played an out-and-out killer. I had played medium heavies, but not an out-and-out killer. And [because it was an unsympathetic character] I was a little frightened of it and, when [I went] back to his office, I said: "I love the script and I love you, *but* I am a little afraid after all these years of playing heroines to go into an out-and-out cold-blooded killer." And Mr. Wilder—and rightly so—looked at me and he said, "Well, are you a mouse or an actress?" And I said, "Well, I *hope* I'm an actress." He said, "Then do the part." And I did and I'm very grateful to him.

Barbara Stanwyck was Wilder's first choice for her role, but he says:

> I had great difficulty finding a leading *man*. In those days none of the big ones dared to play a murderer. When I told the story to George Raft he told me he would play it if the lead turned out to be an FBI man at the end, trying to pin down Miss Stanwyck as the murderess.

(Faced with Raft's refusal, Wilder was sure he had a good picture.) Fred MacMurray had some fears about accepting the part too, and one can only be grateful for all that worked to bring together the final combination of Stanwyck, MacMurray and Edward G. Robinson to become—under Wilder's superb direction—one of the most memorable trios in film history.

The screenplay—fashioned by Wilder and Raymond Chandler (from a James M. Cain short story in his book titled *Three of a Kind*)—went into production in September of 1943 with a harshly made-up, brassily blonde Stanwyck. The blonde wig was Wilder's idea. He used it "to complement her anklet. I wanted to make her look as sleazy as possible." Cinematographer John Seitz recalls that "when Buddy DeSylva, then production head of Paramount, saw the first shots he remarked, 'We hired Barbara Stanwyck and here we get George Washington.' All in good humor, of course." Wilder adds, "The wig was not much good, I must admit."

Double Indemnity, as is well known, traces an almost perfect crime from its inception to the point where it "comes apart at the seams." Stanwyck's calculating Phyllis Dietrichson persuades insurance salesman Walter Neff (MacMurray) to fix her husband up with an accident policy and murder him so they can collect $100,000 on its double indemnity clause. The fact that the story is told through flashbacks by a confessing Walter (wounded by the unfaithful Phyllis just before he polished *her* off) substitutes—for the need to discover "whodunit"—an involvement that pulls for the murderers' success, and tortures when this is threatened. Despite assumptions to the contrary, Billy Wilder states: "We had no problems whatsoever with the Hays office."

Director and cast gave their best (which is nothing short of perfect) and Wilder—who has "the highest regard for Miss Stanwyck both as an actress and a person"—says: "She is as good an actress as I have ever worked with. Very meticulous about her work. We rehearsed the way I usually do. Hard. There were no retakes." He also stresses that

> Everybody helped [to make the picture what it is]. There was my collaborator on the screenplay, Mr. Raymond Chandler, the cameraman, Mr. John Seitz, the Art Directors, Mr. Hans Dreier and Mr. Hal Pereira, and, ultimately, Mr. Miklos Rozsa, who wrote the music score.

Stanwyck's performance is a beauty and—for some—it is the one they remember most vividly. As she said when discussing Stella Dallas, "roles in which [actresses] play evil women sometimes make a deep impression." There is no comparing Stella and Phyllis—except to say that they are opposites. Stella is a very open creature—Phyllis a mysterious one. Each draws because of the artistry Stanwyck brings to her.

Barbara Stanwyck's Phyllis Dietrichson is an undiluted study in greed, cunning and ruthlessness. From her determined heels clicking down the stairs at their first meeting, to her shooting of Walter at their last, she is cool complete control. No pity. No excuses. No nerves. Phyllis is "rotten to the heart."

There is a way of putting this across with dignity and class. Stanwyck knows how. Her Phyllis is attractive—with the appeal of the smooth, the powerful, the fatal. She is a curve of assurance—with a steel spring coiled inside.

In her first meeting with Walter she plans her moves for effect. She uses her anklet, her perfume, her sensuality. As she and Walter test each other, it is clear that this will be a fight to the finish—with all the fascination such a contest holds.

She is still planning when she shows up at his apartment, with her hands in the pockets of her coat, and a "You forgot your hat this afternoon." There is no hat. There is a dame in a tight white sweater who brushes against him until he grabs her and signs his death warrant.

Phyllis, in fact, never makes random movements. What she does, she does for a reason. And she makes very *few* movements—so when she *does* make one, it counts. Stanwyck brings to this one of her greatest assets: her ability to cut out superfluous movement and direct her energy where she wants it.

Lady of Burlesque

Double Indemnity, *with Fred MacMurray*

Double Indemnity

Double Indemnity, with Fred MacMurray

Double Indemnity

She also gets plenty of mileage from props—subtle and right on target: a lipstick, a piece of lemon thrown into a glass of iced tea, the lowering of a pair of sunglasses, a massive emerald cut ring on her finger. She punctuates her ideas with just the right movement at just the right time.

The above is not new for Stanwyck. Her coordination and handling of props have always been outstanding. But *Double Indemnity* illustrates exceptionally well the ability she has at her command, and the precision with which she can employ it. (So does *The Strange Love of Martha Ivers*. Watch how she wraps a bandage around Kirk Douglas' hand in this one; if it were a noose, he'd be dead.)

So impervious to the feelings of others is Phyllis that she is able to use them as conveniences. And, since she experiences no involvement, she remains free to operate without a sense of guilt. The killing of her husband finds her aglow with satisfaction. A Walter who tries to pull out of their deal is verbally poisoned. And when he shows up later with murderous intentions toward her, he is faced with the same. What makes her so attractive is the *way* in which she operates. Walter hits on it when he says: "Murder can sometimes smell like honeysuckle."

Six Academy Award nominations were given to *Double Indemnity*: Best Picture, Actress, Cinematography (Black and White), Music (Scoring of a Dramatic or Comedy Picture), Sound Recording (to Loren Ryder) and Writing (Best Written Screenplay).

John Seitz says, "The film was shot in 'newsreel style.' We attempted to keep it extremely realistic." One of Seitz' touches of realism was "the effect of waning sunlight" in the cheerless living room of the Dietrichson house, which he achieved through the use of "some silver dust mixed with smoke." Enhanced by his low-key lighting, it wraps the characters in atmosphere that is both realistic and an accompaniment for their deeds.

Billy Wilder—while he has not seen the picture in years ("I never look at my old stuff")—regards it as one of his favorites: "because it has the fewest mistakes; because it was taut and moved in the staccato manner of Cain's style." The *New York Herald Tribune* stated:

Billy Wilder has adapted the . . . story with uncompromising artistry. His staging makes the offering one of the most vital and arresting films of the year. With perfectly co-ordinated acting by Fred MacMurray, Barbara Stanwyck, Edward G. Robinson and the lesser players, it hits clean and hard right between the eyes.

Wilder has made a sensational contribution to film-making in *Double Indemnity*.

Of Barbara Stanwyck's portrayal, the *New York World-Telegram* had "nothing but whoops and bravos for the vicious conniving spirit she has woven into the girl." The *Tribune* found her "vibrantly malignant and attractive as the homicidal wife." And the *Brooklyn Eagle* said she "has never given a more striking performance. [She] proceeds to give us all a lesson in feminine beguilement that ought to go down as a classic in film history."

It did. And Phyllis opened up a whole new direction for Barbara Stanwyck. The fact that audiences not only accepted her as a heavy, but liked her, meant that she had added the final dimension to what she could play. Comedy or drama, heroine or villainess— she would have her choice from now on.

Part III
Three-Ring Circus

March 1, 1945

Dear Barbara Stanwyck,

This afternoon, in a Nissen hut "somewhere in England," My Reputation had its first showing.

We were the audience. We came from the planes and the hangars. We wore flying clothes and dirty coveralls. We sat on benches mounted atop empty bomb crates. We watched, we listened, we enjoyed. We are the officers and enlisted men of the 467th Liberator (B-24) Bomb Group, Eighth Air Force.

We thank you, Barbara, for this "Premiere," and we ask you to pass our thanks along to your friends and associates in the Motion Picture Industry for the movies we enjoy so much . . . at the "Trans-Lux" (as we call our hut theatre)—a big link with home which helps to keep our spirits in top fighting form.

Stanwyck received the above while she was working on *The Two Mrs. Carrolls.* It was inscribed on a sheet of parchment bigger than she was, and carried the signatures of all who had "watched, listened and enjoyed."

My Reputation was begun shortly after *Double Indemnity,* and its overseas release was one of the many efforts to bring home to those in the service. "Home"—in this one—takes a jaunt to Lake Tahoe for skiing and hot rum, gathers around the piano for "Silent Night," and dances through a tangle of streamers on New Year's Eve. It revels in such stuff as security is made of and—against this—concentrates on Jessica Drummond: an upper-middle-class widow of 33, "hermetically sealed" most of her life, and expected by her sons and a domineering mother to stay that way. A nervous breakdown looks likely until she meets George Brent—a wolfish bachelor who, as director Curtis Bernhardt puts it: "tries to convince her that sex is not sin, and that the defense of so called 'reputation' in that field is a lot of nonsense."

Stanwyck's portrayal is one of her best—mature, real, deep. The gentle nature of this character wins the audience instantly, and wit and intelligence keep them interested. Jessica may look easy to do, but she's not. She has to be timid without washing out, have hysterics without being showy, and be funny without appearing to try. Stanwyck meets the challenge so subtly that her Jessica "hatches" in a most artful—and, seemingly, artless—manner.

Emotionally, Jessica scores whether she is reading a letter from her dead husband with all the control she can summon—or sitting quietly on a sofa wrapped in a satin comforter and her loneliness. She is under great pressure and Stanwyck shows why.

On the lighter side, Stanwyck is just as effective with what Bernhardt calls her "tremendous sense of comedy—of timing." This sparkles as she and Brent sit on a sofa and make small talk—while he tries to seduce her, and she pretends not to notice. When he touches the pearls she is wearing around her neck, she practically jumps out of her skin—but it is done within the framework of the character's inhibitions and she remains a believable person, even though Stanwyck is playing for laughs. It's very delicate work.

Bernhardt's "foremost memory" from making the film is

> . . . a good feeling of smooth production work, not interrupted by the usual tantrums, difficulties, etc., brought about by some prominent members of the cast, mostly feminine. . . . Barbara . . . was greatly instrumental that work on this film went ahead cheerfully and smoothly. [She was] never adverse to . . . helping with a practical joke on the set whenever spirits began sagging. She is a most pleasant figure in the paling memory of those days.

My Reputation, following its overseas premiere, was released in the States (in 1946) and became a top-grossing film.

Another heavy money-maker (filmed intermittently in 1943 and 1944) was the all-star *Hollywood Canteen*—made for, and with, servicemen—and released in December of 1944. Stanwyck appeared—as herself—in what writer-director Delmer Daves refers to as

> . . . one of the dozens of starring players' voluntary "bits" that made up the mosaic of that film, the profits from which are still being distributed to servicemen's funds, thanks to the canny investments of those profits by Jules Stein —still as much as a quarter-million a year!

Following the filming of *My Reputation,* Stanwyck made her first of three films with director Peter Godfrey: *Christmas in Connecticut.* Also timely and destined for high grosses, it invited returned war hero Dennis Morgan to spend Christmas on the farm of a Stanwyck whose column in "Smart Housekeeping"

. . . as in Connecticut

My Reputation, *with Warner Anderson,*
Bobby Cooper, Scotty Beckett,
Eve Arden, John Ridgely

My Reputation, *with George Brent*

◁My Reputation

bills her as a gourmet cook and "ideal" wife and mother. Only trouble is, the column is a fabrication—and she has to find a husband, farm and baby fast in order to fool her unsuspecting publisher. Reginald Gardiner, with hopes of making it real, plays the husband. (He has one of those "I'm sure I can make you care for me in time" attitudes, but at least she has an original answer: "Could you wait that long?") Gardiner's farm, a neighbor's baby, and café owner S. Z. Sakall—posing as her uncle and doing the cooking—complete the ruse. And a farcical Christmas is had by all.

The film is clever, fast-paced and filled with opportunities for improvisation. Its cast of pros (the above plus Sidney Greenstreet and Una O'Connor) makes it lively and entertaining.

For some tricky coordination of props and action, watch Barbara Stanwyck in this one—especially when she gets her hands on a large figurine. Her rapid-fire line readings, with some unexpected twists, are fun too. In fact, there is a wealth of inventive detail in her performance.

Christmas in Connecticut also has a less frantic side and, when it relaxes, it does so profitably. Stanwyck and Morgan are very happily teamed. The charm they project (in their first meeting as they gaze at each other across a rocking chair, in his song to her while she trims the tree, and in their involvement in a Virginia reel and a sleigh ride) gives the film some of its best moments.

Quite a different mood prevails in *The Two Mrs. Carrolls*—shot in 1945 and released in 1947. Stanwyck plays the soft-spoken and agreeable wife of a psychopathic Humphrey Bogart who spends his time marrying, painting his wives as "The Angel of Death" and getting rid of them with poisoned milk.

The film is large on atmosphere—as are all three of Peter Godfrey's with Stanwyck. To Franz Waxman's superb score, Godfrey adds an intoxicating mixture of church bells and stormy weather. Stanwyck's realization of Bogart's intent, as the bells sound and wind batters casement windows; his shady phone call from a rain-soaked booth; the shock of confirmation when she sees herself as The Angel of Death through shadows from a rain-drenched skylight; his hasty drive through wind and rain—all of this leads effectively to the attempted murder when Bogart crashes through the window in a sweep of rain and blowing draperies. And in the confrontation, Stanwyck and Bogart pull off a skillful climax to what they have built.

Although drama is her forte, for a good ten years now Barbara Stanwyck had been playing comedy as well. Often she alternated the two so that she was able to unwind in something light after she had completed a serious picture. But 1946 would see her last performance in a comedy—until television brought this wonderful side of her talent back in a few segments of *The Barbara Stanwyck Show* and *The Big Valley*. This was not because Stanwyck wanted to abandon humor. Quite the contrary. She just couldn't find a worthwhile script. She told Hedda Hopper in 1953: "I've always got my eye out for a good comedy. Remember *Ball of Fire* and *The Lady Eve*? But they don't seem to write that kind of comedy any more—just a series of gags."

Sadly, too, the last humorous film she did was marred by silly lines and clumsy direction. Stanwyck and Bob Cummings are to be commended for the excellence they brought to *The Bride Wore Boots*, because it was much less considerate of them.

This comedy—about a wife who loves horses and a husband who doesn't—finds its stars bickering constantly and expertly. They bring off their vicious little exchanges and their romantic make-ups between bouts with all the believability and style such a script requires.

But, in the midst of this, as *The London Observer* put it:

> . . . director Irving Pichel tries, with all sorts of extraneous tricks and incidents, to make it seem far funnier than it is, with the result that the real humours of the outline are lost in a mass of silly, superfluous and occasionally unpleasant device.

The worst of these was described by the *New York Sun:*

> The script writer, or maybe it was the director . . . had a curious little trick. . . . When in doubt about any situation he simply had the principal characters laugh. Sometimes it would be Barbara Stanwyck, and sometimes Robert Cummings. Sometimes it was both, in unison or in opposition. This saved a lot of writing. The Paramount's film, instead of a punch line to finish a sequence, has a laugh—by one of the actors.

In addition, it has words like pretty-witty and gunsy-wunsies, and lines such as Stanwyck's "Antiquarian—it sounds like somebody against fish. Is

The Two Mrs. Carrolls

Hollywood Canteen, *with Robert Hutton and Jane Wyman*

Christmas in Connecticut, *with S. Z. Sakall*

Christmas in Connecticut, *with Dennis Morgan*

The Two Mrs. Carrolls

The Two Mrs. Carrolls

The Two Mrs. Carrolls, *with Ann Carter*
and Humphrey Bogart

The Bride Wore Boots, *with Patric Knowles and Bob Cummings*

The Bride Wore Boots, *with Bob Cummings*

there a name for them—people against fish?" Stanwyck is smart. She throws that first "fish" away and gets off the whole subject in a hurry. This is how she and Cummings make the picture work—by remaining a jump ahead of both script and direction. As *Film Daily* saw it: "The cast is the saving of the film, the performers exacting all the laughter possible from each situation. . . ."

During the making of *The Bride Wore Boots*, Stanwyck played a fine scene *off*-camera (better than any she was given in the film) and Bob Cummings writes an expert account of it. Cummings refers to Stanwyck in his story as "Missy." And it should be made clear that "Missy" is the name given to Stanwyck by her maid and friend, Harriett Coray—who explained in *Portrait: Barbara Stanwyck:*

> When I first started working for Miss Stanwyck, I never seemed to be able to get her full name out when I wanted to ask her something—like "Miss Stanwyck, this" or "Miss Stanwyck, that"—and she'd cut me off. So it finally wound up that I could just get "Missy" out. And after a few weeks of that, she got so she liked the name and just sort of adopted it.

Since Harriett Coray is always on a Stanwyck set, "Missy" has been picked up by casts and crews and become a term of affection used by them for Barbara Stanwyck.

As Cummings tells his story:

> The three months of filming were memorable as I learned what an extraordinary woman Barbara Stanwyck is. She is one of the most honest, forthright, compelling people I've ever known.
>
> On a hot July afternoon at the Midwick Country Club near Los Angeles, we were in the midst of filming the thrilling steeplechase scenes. Director Irving Pichel had ordered the race—run down the entire length of the country club—to be shot over and over again. I say it was "thrilling" because we were using a dozen real race horses—running at full gallop—being photographed from a camera car carrying long shot, medium shot and close-up cameras, which were all focused on the central character in the scene: a "gentleman jockey" who was supposed to be on the verge of falling off and scared to death all the way. I can vouch for the fact that he was scared to death, because the "gentleman" was ME.
>
> We had made a total of thirteen takes, all of which seemed excellent as for the action. And several had some truly hair-raising moments, as I actually slipped down under the horse's neck at full gallop a few times, and then desperately worked my way up on his back again. These pieces of action were not in the script. I was "ad-libbing" whatever came to mind—and some of it I wished hadn't come to my mind.
>
> After each race, the man from the Society for the Prevention of Cruelty to Animals would take over and see to it that the horses were cooled down properly and given a rest, and that twelve fresh mounts were saddled up. Markings, such as white blazes on the horses' noses, were painted on for "matching" purposes with non-injurious S.P.C.A. approved water color, so it would always look as though I was riding the same horse.
>
> After the thirteenth take, we all sort of walked around holding our breath—praying director Pichel would hand down an OK verdict so we could print the take and be through with this series of defying equestrian gymnastics. Everybody knows that movies are all "trick photography." Well, the trick with this photography was staying alive! Slowly Mr. Pichel picked up his megaphone, and everything stopped, and we heard him say: "ONCE MORE, it's not good enough yet!" All of us jockeys bit our lips, resigned to one more do or die effort. Make-up men started wiping sweat off everybody and repairing the greasepaint on my dripping face. Out of the corner of my eye, as the artist dabbed at me, I noticed a tiny figure coming across the wide expanse of grass. It was "THE BRIDE" of the film and she was wearing "BOOTS!"
>
> The song hadn't been written yet, but THOSE BOOTS WERE MADE FOR WALKING! and she was WALKING the calm, cool, self-contained assurance that only Barbara Stanwyck can WALK! On and on she came—and for some mysterious reason almost everyone, including the horses, stopped what they were doing and stood transfixed. Eventually "Missy" reached our side of the field, walked up to Irving Pichel, stopped a few feet from him—and with that strange enigmatic Stanwyck smile on her mouth, but *not* in her *eyes*, said quietly, "MR. PICHEL, IF BOB CUMMINGS RIDES THAT RACE ONCE MORE, YOU WILL NEVER DIRECT ME IN ANOTHER SCENE!" She waited just the right moment for it to sink in—then with enormous poise turned and walked the two thousand or so feet back to her palatial air-conditioned trailer dressing room.

The sun was sinking low in the west. All eyes and ears were focused on director Irving Pichel. He now was biting *his* lip. "PRINT TAKES ONE, FOUR AND THIRTEEN!" he said. "THAT'S IT FOR TO-DAY!"

He turned and walked toward his limousine as a hundred technicians and actors watched and stopped biting their lips.

Anyone who saw *The Bride Wore Boots* in 1946—or even last week on the late late show—realizes that Missy was right. The steeplechase was spine-tingling and hilarious. There was no need to risk the lives of men and horses again.

BARBARA STANWYCK?
GREAT ACTRESS!
GREAT STAR!
GREAT PERSON!
LOVABLE SOUL!
"MISSY"

The Bride Wore Boots

The Strange Love of Martha Ivers.
Photo by A. L. "Whitey" Schafer

Barbara Stanwyck and Kirk Douglas are playing to the hilt two of the meanest and most seriously interesting characters that addicts of homicidal melodrama are likely to meet with on the screen for a long time to come. . . .

Miss Stanwyck is twice the hard-boiled, lustful vixen that she played in Double Indemnity. *. . .*

The New York Times' assessment of what Stanwyck brought to *The Strange Love of Martha Ivers* was correct. Having broken the ice as a villainess with Phyllis Dietrichson, she no longer had fears about being a nasty dame on the screen.

Martha Ivers has everything going for it: a superior script, hard-hitting direction, a score by Miklos Rozsa and exciting camera work. The script was written by director Lewis Milestone in collaboration with Robert Rossen, and Milestone explains: "I didn't take screen credit for it, but then I seldom did."

In the film's opening scenes, Martha Ivers—as a child—murders her aunt. Some eighteen years later, Stanwyck's Martha has married Kirk Douglas—who witnessed the crime—to keep him from talking. They have had an innocent man hanged in her place; and Martha, who inherited her aunt's wealth, has pushed Douglas into public office where he is going to be "whatever his wife wants him to be." He has turned to drink and she to lovers. When Van Heflin—to whom she was attracted as a child—returns to Iverstown, she tries to get him to kill Douglas. This fails and she and Douglas commit suicide—in an impressively staged scene that Milestone will speak of shortly.

Film Daily called the picture "blue-ribbon" and said: "If the season discloses a drama related with greater intensity or one more intriguingly developed, it will be nothing less than a miracle." Important to this is the way the film probes its characters. Their deeds, motives and guts are laid bare inch by inch.

Like *Double Indemnity*, *Martha Ivers* shows a crime—prompted by hate and greed—that would be perfect if people did not "come apart at the seams." But the character of Martha is more complicated than that of Phyllis. She does not come apart in a normal way; she is sick—her sense of values distorted by her childhood experience. When the young Martha killed her aunt (in a justifiable moment of rage) she found that "that night I slept heavily. Peacefully." What should have seemed wrong to her did not, because the

"right" she had known from her aunt was tied up with cruel treatment. Murder freed her as a child; she continues to turn to it as an adult.

Then there is the matter of her background. The aunt had been "trying to wash the dirt and grime" of some bad breeding off Martha. But neither a change of name nor the polish she eventually acquires can completely change Martha Smith into Martha Ivers. She retains her affinity for the earthy and violent. It is inevitable that, when given the chance, she will tie up with "Sam the superman—the dirty little boy from the other side of the tracks" in an effort to get rid of her spineless husband.

Such a role has Stanwyck suggesting both a black widow spider and what Douglas calls "a little girl in a cage, waiting for someone to let her out." Stanwyck wrings every particle from the conflict. As the venomous Martha, she wears power well—and she has a way of encircling her victims with grasping hands and a seductive manner as she goads them to do what she wants. As the trapped Martha, she is mercurial—shifting moods and tactics rapidly.

One of the reasons *Martha Ivers* is such a good film is because Lewis Milestone was inventive and his actors responsive. Milestone talks of their work together and of the reactions of an always alert Stanwyck who

. . . was very knowledgeable about all phases of film production. She would come on a new set and carefully examine the placement of camera, lights, etc. Then she would call the cameraman over and introduce him to the mysteries of her own favorite key light. She astonished everybody with her knowledge of lighting and her technical know-how in general.

We rehearsed for more than two weeks, and during that time each member of the cast had an opportunity to perfect his or her own part, and to work with the other actors to achieve a cohesive dramatization of the story.

During the rehearsals, we were faced with the problem of how to establish the fact that Van Heflin had become a professional gambler. Build a casino? Expensive! And lengthy! Then I recalled a piece of business I had noticed at many of the casinos in Las Vegas. [Some of] the dealers, superlatively skillful with their hands . . . could take a coin, a dollar or half-dollar, insert it in the space between two knuckles, and deftly manipulate it to twist it end over end,

The Strange Love of Martha Ivers,
with Van Heflin

The Strange Love of Martha Ivers,
with Kirk Douglas

The Strange Love of Martha Ivers,
with Kirk Douglas

The Strange Love of Martha Ivers,
with Van Heflin

over and over, to and fro across their knuckles. I decided that this would be the perfect piece of business to help Van establish a believable character as a professional gambler.

When I suggested this to [him] I told him it wouldn't be effective unless he practiced it a long time so he would be able to do it mechanically. He would have to become so dexterous that he could concentrate on his dialogue without paying any attention to the business with the coin. Van practiced for hours, and everybody was amazed at the skill he acquired. He could deliver pages of dialogue while his hand performed the coin trick automatically.

Barbara watched this during rehearsal. "Van, that's a wonderful piece of business, but if you do that during my important lines, I have a bit of business that will draw attention away from yours." She pulled her skirt up way above her knees. "Any time you start twirling that coin, I'll be fixing my garter. So be sure you don't do that when I have important lines to speak."

(The observant will notice that the traveling coin appears in only one of Stanwyck's scenes—one in which Heflin is *supposed* to be antagonizing her. It makes three bold journeys across his hand—and then gets the hell out of there!) Milestone continues:

Our main problem on *Martha Ivers* was the ending. While fishing around for one, I thought of an actual incident in the life of the famous, or infamous, Owney Madden, the King of Hell's Kitchen. It happened when he was a very young man. Another young Hell's Kitchen hood decided he could make himself a great reputation if he could rub out Owney Madden.

One evening, as Owney came into his favorite saloon, the young hood confronted him with a gun. Madden stared at him for a full minute while everybody held his breath. "You punk, you haven't got guts enough to pull that trigger. So I'll do it for you." With that, Madden thrust his thumb through the trigger guard and pressed the trigger—and shot himself. But he had tipped the barrel of the gun aside just enough so the bullet didn't hit him in a fatal spot. This daring act of bravado saved his life.

I asked Barbara if she could see herself doing a scene like that. She had known Owney Madden when she was a young chorus girl, and she was very enthusiastic about having such an ending. So we developed the scene, with Kirk Douglas trying to kill her, and she was delighted with it.

Milestone was equally delighted with Stanwyck. He calls her "from A to Z, the greatest lady of the screen" and says:

You ask what I got out of my association with Barbara Stanwyck on *Martha Ivers*, in addition to a fine film. My answer is simply: Barbara's friendship.

Stanwyck went next into what was announced as "the first of Paramount's postwar outdoor epics": *California*. In this one she is an adventuress with an unhappy past, the ability to clean everybody at cards, and a love-hate relationship with Ray Milland that causes a lot of trouble. Underneath her protective callousness is a softness that responds to decent treatment when this is accorded her.

The transformation from downtrodden and vindictive to appreciated and gentle was a familiar one for Stanwyck—and certainly not unusual for actresses in Westerns. She would play such parts often—with a distinction that makes them count. The setup allows her to elicit sympathy, yet match the tone of her surroundings.

In *California* she is more of an ornament than the vital force she would be in future Westerns. But this is because the film is concerned with so much else, and because her character—as written—soon becomes more decorative than active. She spends most of her time beautifully gowned (in Edith Head's copies of museum pieces)—either entertaining at "The Golden Lily" or otherwise adding elegance to her surroundings. (Stanwyck did record her own songs for *California* but "those in power" decided to dub them.) However, she also plays a mean poker game, saves Milland by shooting the man who would have killed him, and exhibits nerve and intelligence throughout. If she does not have as much physical action as she would in later Westerns, she does have as much composure.

This was Stanwyck's first color film, and it was photographed by master of Technicolor Ray Rennahan—who had done her early screen test in the two-color process. Rennahan states:

With Barbara Stanwyck, Ray Milland, Barry Fitzgerald—and John Farrow directing—(all very fine people and real professionals) there was little chance of any problem [on *California*].

One small one happened quite often. When Barry Fitzgerald got excited at times, he talked

California

very fast, and the faster he talked, the thicker his Irish brogue came on. The sound man finally would cut the scene and call out, "I can hear everything fine but cannot understand a word."

To most of us who have worked with [Stanwyck] she is the all time best actress—very considerate to her co-workers. The American Society of Cinematographers is comprised of the top directors of photography in the world and, at a recent meeting, one of our members was moaning about his star giving him a bad time and trying to be difficult. A half dozen voices called to him: "Have her take a lesson from Barbara Stanwyck!"

In the early days, Mary Pickford was known as "America's Sweetheart"—and by the same token, Barbara Stanwyck was and still is The Sweetheart of the Motion Picture Industry.

There is no denying the difference between the finely wrought picture of a sick mind in a script like *Martha Ivers* and that which is shown in one like *Cry Wolf*. However, *Cry Wolf*—although described as a murder mystery with psychology—is not all that concerned with psychology; it's just having a good time as a thriller.

A secret marriage brings Stanwyck to the residence of Errol Flynn—the scientist uncle of her recently deceased husband—to collect a large inheritance. The suspicious Flynn tries to prove she is not the widow she claims. She, in turn, investigates the possibility of his being a murderer with a yen for the money himself. The film's resolution (the "dead" man turns up, hidden on the estate because he is insane, and meets with accidental death) softens the pair toward each other and unites them.

Actionwise, *Cry Wolf* gives Stanwyck a fine workout. Another Peter Godfrey–Franz Waxman creation, it is filled with strangeness: sinister servants, a locked laboratory, screams in the night. Stanwyck's attempts to find out what is going on put her in some tight spots. Or, as the *New York Herald Tribune* phrased it, "This idea of creating suspense by sending a dame alone into danger is as good a trick now as it was in the nineteenth century. . . ."

Cry Wolf makes full use of it. To gain entrance to the mysterious laboratory, Stanwyck resorts first to hoisting herself up in a dumbwaiter. (A neat bit of tension is created when she bumps into a water cooler; Flynn investigates only a short distance from where she hides, wondering if he will see the moving water.) A later attempt finds her scrambling over rooftops to drop through a skylight—this time into a direct confrontation with the waiting Flynn.

Further hazards surround her in an overgrown game preserve, where she is thrown when a rabbit frightens her horse. Making her way through a wood alive with crickets and startled birds, she becomes aware of footsteps besides her own—and meets up with the husband that is supposed to be dead.

A final encounter with her demented husband sends her crashing through French doors to escape. (And a final struggle between Flynn and the husband sends the latter over a balustrade to his death.) All great fun for an actress who prefers "doing" to "talking."

A very different world surrounds her in *The Other Love*—a gentle picture from a story by Erich Maria Remarque. Stanwyck portrays a renowned concert pianist, afflicted with consumption, who enters an idyllic sanitarium in the Swiss Alps where she falls in love with her doctor, David Niven. When she learns she is dying, she flees restraint for a last fling in Monte Carlo with playboy-sportsman Richard Conte. But love for Niven and her failing strength bring her back to the mountains where—married to him—she spends her final days in security and acceptance.

The role of Karen Duncan is a wonderful one for Stanwyck and she makes it sing. Witness what happens when she sweeps into a room filled with flowers, stops abruptly, then moves enchanted from one bouquet to another. This is a classic Stanwyck entrance. It is a classic entrance, period. But when Stanwyck learned how to make it (early in her career) she added presence of her own. While that is to be found in every entrance she has made since, this one in *The Other Love*—with Miklos Rozsa's music, her white gown in motion, and flowers everywhere—seems to be the epitome of it.

Such vitality produces both a romantic spirit (essential to the film's style) and a fighting one (essential to the portrayal of an artist). As the artist, she is deeply involved in her work. There is a scene in which she struggles with a desire to play the piano as she listens to one of her recordings. Her thoughts are easy to read as she succumbs, finds she is out of practice, wonders if she will play again, and smashes the disc in frustration. A good bet for a showy display with a lesser actress, the scene—with Stanwyck—is real. On the romantic side, her warmth and

Cry Wolf, *with Geraldine Brooks*

Cry Wolf

charm, balanced by Niven's, give the film a bitter-sweet quality. And a breathy voice (no more than a whisper at the film's end) is equally touching.

Director Andre de Toth was aware of the pitfalls in the script for overplaying, and of the kind of acting needed to maintain believability. He states:

> We [Enterprise Studios] prepared the screenplay with Harry Brown and Ladislas Fodor. From the inception only Barbara Stanwyck was considered to play the part of Karen Duncan—which needed the rare combination of sincerity, sensitivity and reality which she possesses. Of course it was most gratifying that she not only accepted the script but was extremely fond of it. All of us connected with this picture have fine memories.

One of these for de Toth is the type of work he was able to attempt. He explains that

> The picture was shot in late 1946—early 1947. At that time the motion picture industry was still shackled to Hollywood. We who were seeking reality not only in portraying characters but also in presenting true geographical locations had a great deal of difficulty and many obstacles to overcome. William Fox's dogma, "a rock is a rock, a tree is a tree, shoot it in Griffith Park," had not yet been broken. It was a great triumph that we could venture away with this picture. Some of it was shot on Mount Wilson, a hot 35 minutes' ride from Enterprise Studios. It was an exciting challenge to make the audience feel they were in the Alps.

The picture is a constant blending of location and studio footage—and its atmosphere is one of its joys. Of how he worked with his actors, de Toth says:

> I don't believe in "chopped up rehearsals." I rehearse the sequence as a whole. [Stanwyck] was delighted with this method and I was even more delighted to work with her, a sensitive professional, both searching for the best we could deliver under the circumstances.
> . . . it was a happy occasion for all concerned. We had a motto, easy does it, and it worked. Sometimes with a detour.

Along with Rozsa's classically inspired score, the film has several scenes where Stanwyck's piano playing is synchronized with a sound track recorded by Ania Dorfman. You never doubt Stanwyck's author-ity as a pianist, and there is a good reason for this. De Toth explains:

> Miss Stanwyck was coached for playing the piano by Ania Dorfman. True to her desire for perfection, Stanwyck practiced two to three hours daily for about a month. At the end she herself could play the relevant pieces.
> My office was across from her bungalow on the lot; in spite of my affection for her and admiration for her tenacity, three hours a day practice of the same piece was just too much for me, and I presented her with a silent keyboard. I found out later from her husband, Bob Taylor, he too appreciated the silent keyboard!

Stanwyck's love of physical action (she calls herself a "frustrated stuntwoman") would lead her to take on increasingly spectacular challenges. And, even in a safe little picture like *The Other Love*, she managed to find herself some danger—but not for her usual reasons. As de Toth tells it:

> We had a scene where Barbara is driving along a road from the sanatarium. The horses gallop briskly when a racing car unexpectedly crosses the intersection—the scene where she meets Richard Conte, the racing driver.
> During rehearsals the stunt double was slightly injured. My staff did not want to worry me and I was not told. Before the take Stanwyck came to me saying it was a very difficult stunt, and how much was the stunt girl getting for it. At her insistence I inquired from the production manager and was told the figure. All this happened during the last few days of shooting and Barbara had never asked for anything special till that day. She thought that the girl should have four times as much, as the stunt was dangerous. Naturally I agreed, and gave orders accordingly.
> We set up for the take and barrelling along comes the carriage, to my horror driven by Stanwyck. The take is in the picture and of course the stunt girl received her quadruple reward. What else can one say about Stanwyck?

De Toth does say something else though:

> Stanwyck for me is the softest diamond in the world. The difference between a star and a player is when you have a scene with a star you can let it run just 20 frames longer before you

cut. With Barbara you can let it run 24 frames longer.

At about this time—along with just about everyone else on the Paramount roster—Stanwyck put in a brief appearance, as herself, in *Variety Girl*. The film was a tribute to the philanthropic work of Variety Clubs for underprivileged children, and she opened it by explaining how this work had begun. (From there, the film moved to a lot of cutting up on the part of its other stars, and made lots of money.)

A practical Stanwyck cut her hair for her next film—*B. F.'s Daughter*—shaping her image to fit changing times and fashions, the latter designed by Irene. But there was one concession that she would not make. Her one-time seventeen-inch hair style had been boasting stray glints of white since the early '40s. By 1947 Stanwyck had two superb streaks of this—one on each side of her forehead—which retouchers generally eliminated on photographs. She refused to dye them. (Destined for prematurely white hair, she would soon grow more of it so rapidly that alterers would throw up their hands in despair—and let her alone. The reason she would not dye it: she had no desire to lie about her age, and "I simply couldn't face sitting there six hours every two or three weeks." Her natural hair has since, of course, been recognized for the asset it is.)

B. F.'s Daughter is a mature script that comes smoothly to life in the hands of its performers. (Critics argued that the film side-stepped in coming to grips with its conflicting ideologies; but critics usually get hot under the collar when a film touches on social issues—no matter how it deals with them. The screen version of John P. Marquand's novel decided to abandon soapboxes and resolve itself in terms of human relationships. This is a choice to which it was entitled.)

Stanwyck and Van Heflin play—respectively—an heiress who wants to buy her husband greatness, and an economist who wants to achieve it on his own. An understanding script lets them make a new try at a wrecked marriage. Stanwyck and Heflin are an excellent screen team—extremely natural together. They make acting look deceptively easy. This was apparent in *Martha Ivers*; it would be so in *East Side, West Side*.

B. F.'s Daughter was completed in a record 37 days, and cinematographer Joseph Ruttenberg says this was "because of Barbara's cooperation." He cites an example of her beyond-the-call-of-duty performance:

It is customary for the star of a production to have her own stand-in: someone who, as much as possible, has the same facial features and height. This is to save the star from standing in the hot lights while the cameraman adjusts them. But Barbara, knowing it will be easier for him to do a better job if he is lighting her, likes to do her own standing in.

One day I was arranging my lights on her for a scene. When I finished, I neglected to tell her and walked away. About five minutes later, when I returned to the set, Barbara was still standing there waiting to be dismissed. Now this is what I mean by cooperation.

Ruttenberg was impressed by Stanwyck's talent and professionalism—and by her sense of humor. She may not have been destined for much fun in front of the cameras for a while, but she would continue to find—or create—it behind them. As it happened, the *B. F.'s Daughter* set was a gold mine of opportunity. As Ruttenberg tells it:

Robert Leonard, who directed *B. F.'s Daughter*, was a most outstanding director and a wonderful person. His philosophy was that a little fun on the set keeps the crew happy, and that makes for doing a better job, etc. So "Pop," as Mr. Leonard was called by everyone, was always thinking up gags to play on someone. This time he picked on Van Heflin.

There was a scene in the picture where Van was to pick Barbara up and carry her over the threshold into their home. It was rehearsed over and over—many times—and, by the time they got it right, lunch was called. The morning had dragged along without much being accomplished. So Pop decided that after lunch he would do something to perk everyone up and get a few laughs—and maybe also get some work done.

Barbara and Mr. Leonard used to have their lunch on the stage and, while they ate, they dreamed up something on Van. When everyone returned, the assistant director got them ready for one more rehearsal and to make a take. Van and Barbara went through the scene, and when Van got to the part where he had to carry Barbara over the threshold, he couldn't lift her off the floor. The following had happened.

The Other Love

The Other Love, *with Richard Conte*

The Other Love, *with Mary Field*
and David Niven

The Other Love, *with Richard Conte*

The Other Love

Before people had returned from lunch, Pop had placed Barbara on the spot where Van was supposed to pick her up. He had had one of the crew wrap a bunch of iron chains around her body and then she had put on her mink coat that she wore in the scene. She must have weighed two hundred pounds! [Heflin's line before he attempts the impossible is: "I'm not very good at lifting things, but here goes . . ."] It was a very funny situation, watching Van try to pick her up. Of course, Van didn't think so. He liked playing tricks on others, but he couldn't take it himself.

Everyone *had* to take it on this set, because you never knew where it would strike next. Stanwyck pulled a gag of her own on Richard Hart—by having a prop man nail a folding bed to the wall. Hart was slightly humiliated by his lack of strength when he couldn't pull the bed down during a rehearsal.

And, of course, Stanwyck was fair game herself. Leonard gets credit for wrapping things up with this one: On the day Stanwyck had a bet on a horse, he wired a loudspeaker to the set and had the race called by a professional announcer. Her horse came in the winner by five lengths on the phony announcement— and sixth in the real race. When she learned of the trick, she said: "I'm not sure, but I think I've been topped for good!"

B. F.'s Daughter, *with Van Heflin*

B. F.'s Daughter, *with Charles Coburn*

B. F.'s Daughter

Director Anatole Litvak states that "many years before" *Sorry, Wrong Number*, he had "admired Barbara as an actress and had only hoped that one day we might work together." He continues:

> But in spite of [this], not knowing her personally, and just from talk around town, I was a bit afraid of our working together because of her strong personality.
>
> However, from the time I met her during a lunch we had together in a small restaurant across from the Paramount Studios, any doubts I might have had about her vanished. I'm not one who pays compliments easily, but I can tell you that in all my years as a director I've seldom known an actress not only so extraordinarily talented but so unselfishly professional.
>
> . . . the part she played in this film was not an easy one. We didn't have a very long schedule and Barbara had to work practically every day from morning to night. There was never a word of complaint—only encouragement and enthusiasm, which certainly influenced and helped not only me in my work but everyone connected with the film.

Sorry, Wrong Number (with Stanwyck as the bedridden neurotic marked for murder who tries to summon help on the telephone) is one of the screen's classic suspense films. Lucille Fletcher's 22-minute radio drama (rebroadcast, according to a 1948 *Cue*, "seven times since 1943 in fifteen languages") was so successful that Hal Wallis had had the author expand it into a full-length screenplay. The original was a tour de force for Agnes Moorehead. Heard today, it has lost a lot. But the screen version—which opens out with flashbacks—is expertly enhanced by Litvak's direction, Sol Polito's camera, and a Franz Waxman score—and captures the full excitement of Leona Stevenson's battle for survival.

To fit this larger-than-life treatment, Stanwyck gives a performance on the grand scale—described by *Life* magazine as "the most extended emotional jag in recent movie history." Leona is arrogant, querulous and demanding. And Stanwyck takes her from irritation to terror in strong, sure strokes. Such work requires a great expenditure of emotion, if one is going (as Stanwyck does) to live a role. And the way the phone scenes were filmed was important to what she was able to achieve.

Asked by Ralph Nelson (in *Portrait: Barbara Stanwyck*) if it was difficult for her to build up her terror

throughout the picture, Stanwyck said that it was, and continued:

> But I was very very lucky. Anatole Litvak was the director, and a very fine director and a marvelous person to work for. I had twelve days of the terror in bed. And he very kindly—which as you know, being a director yourself, is difficult for a director to do—asked me did I want to do those twelve days all at once or spread them in between continuity. And when I thought it over, I thought it would be better if I could do the twelve days at once so that I myself might have continuity. And he very graciously fixed his schedule as such. And I did twelve days—consistently.

Continuity was helpful—to both actress and director—but it did have one drawback. The existence of a rumor—concocted by the side of Hollywood that likes to make something out of everything, and speculated that it was the making of this film that hurried Stanwyck's white hair along—led to a statement on her part of the demands her work *did* carry with it. In a 1965 promotion tour for *The Night Walker*, Stanwyck was interviewed in Boston by Bill Hahn for his WNAC radio show. Hahn—who had done his research—asked her about the rumor regarding her hair, and she replied:

> I don't know whether it was the part. Of course, I worried every night that I went home, because all the scenes in bed were filmed consistently— which means that at six o'clock at night if I have hit a high emotional peak, then I must come back the next morning and *start* up there. Well, this worries the life out of a performer, because how do you go home and eat and shower and sleep and then at nine o'clock in the morning start way up there? It's rather difficult. So I worried quite a lot about it. Now I don't know whether that was part and parcel of [the change in hair color] but it did start on that.

Hahn, with a gentle sense of humor, speculated: "I was just wondering what other trick making another suspense and horror film would do." And Stanwyck, quick to pick up his tone, bounced it back to him:

> Well, I think it's gone as far as it can go! It's *white* now. So I don't think it would have any influence. If that was part of it. I don't know. Or

whether nature just started to let it turn grey. I don't know . . .

A more amusing—but just as constant—hindrance to what Stanwyck was trying to sustain emotionally was described by Edith Head in *The Dress Doctor:*

> To indicate her wealth and elegance, we arranged with a Beverly Hills jeweler to lend her a fortune in gems. In addition to full insurance coverage, he insisted upon an armed guard to accompany her at all times. As small Barbara walked off the set—even when her destination was the powder room—she was shadowed instantly by a large man with two guns. A very impressive gentleman, as Barbara said, "At least they picked a good-looking one."

None of the above interfered with what Stanwyck gave. If anything, she worked harder—because she knew there were obstacles to be overcome. Litvak says:

> There was a scene in the last part of the picture just before she was to be murdered by hired killers. I remember, being an incorrigible perfectionist, asking her to do the scene over and over again. At a certain moment I decided to stop to give Barbara a little time to recover as it was a highly emotional and difficult scene. As everyone in the crew simply adored her (because of the incredible kindness and respect she had for everyone working on the film) it seemed to me that there was a kind of a small revolt growing, because they all felt she had already given a brilliant performance and that there was no need to do it again. They all felt this way but she didn't. She trusted her director completely and wanted to do it again and again, for the best of the picture.
>
> Later I found out that when I left the stage to get a drink she was told by the crew that it was ridiculous of me to ask her to do this scene again—that what she did was good enough. But instead of agreeing with them as many artists in similar situations would do, she gave them hell, saying that it was not for them to judge but for the director—that good was not enough.

The result of all this is indelible for anyone who has seen it. A spoiled woman, used to having her way. A hypochondriac, to make sure she gets it. Insecurity in the midst of luxury. Boredom, ill-temper, hysterics and nerves. A hot summer night—and a restless Leona focusing on medicine, magazines, lace and brocade; on curtains drifting in heavy air; on the lights of an indifferent city; on a staircase leading to the unknown. And in the final scene: the killer's shadow on the stairs, eyes that are black with fear, a train that drowns her screams, and hands that clutch and go limp.

Stanwyck received her fourth Academy Award nomination for *Sorry, Wrong Number* and critics pulled out all stops. *Time* magazine said:

> It gives Barbara Stanwyck her fattest role since *Double Indemnity,* and she makes the most of the pampered, petulant, terrified leading character.

The *New York Herald Tribune* stated:

> With Anatole Litvak's brilliant direction, and taut performances by Barbara Stanwyck, Burt Lancaster and the others, the show is calculated to scare the wits out of a spectator. . . . No compromises have been made in keeping the offering an astringent study of neuroticism and evil. . . . Both of the principals succeed in holding *Sorry, Wrong Number* to its mood of savage and unrelenting horror.

And *Cue* magazine added:

> For sheer, unadulterated terror there have been few films in recent years to match the quivering fright of *Sorry, Wrong Number*—and few performances to equal the hysteria-ridden picture of a woman doomed, as portrayed by Barbara Stanwyck.
>
> Miss Stanwyck gives one of the finest performances of her career—a carefully calculated, skillfully integrated picture of developing psychological terror that provides a filmic highlight of the year.

Jumping ahead for a moment (to January of 1950) will provide another look at Stanwyck's Leona Stevenson. The Lux Radio Theatre—then under the direction of William Keighley—presented her and Burt Lancaster in an S. H. Barnett adaptation of *Sorry, Wrong Number.* It was a fine blending of the script's original impact and what it had gained from screen treatment.

Sorry, Wrong Number

Sorry, Wrong Number, *with Ed Begley*

Sorry, Wrong Number, *with Burt Lancaster*

Here—with complete continuity and only an hour in which to live through Leona's torturous evening—Stanwyck is superb. She starts high, moves fast, hits hard, and—by the time she has finished—is pretty well drained. Anyone who wants to know how much this actress gives to her work will find out here. Following the performance, she has very little voice left and—as she pants her way through questions from Keighley (to the delight of an understanding audience) she laughingly comments, "I sound like Andy Devine."

In October of 1948, Stanwyck added a new radio show to those in which she had been appearing: The Prudential Family Hour of Stars. A CBS presentation, it offered a line-up of actors who were billed as members of "Hollywood's most glittering royal family." They were to be featured on a rotation basis and—in addition to Stanwyck—included Humphrey Bogart, Bette Davis, Gregory Peck, Ginger Rogers and Robert Taylor. Later, Ray Milland replaced Bogart. (Stanwyck would continue to perform for the Lux Radio Theatre, Screen Guild Players, Hollywood Star Playhouse, Tums Hollywood Theatre and others throughout the mid-fifties.)

For her next film, Stanwyck took on another emotionally disturbed character—this one certain to be rough going, since she appears in almost every scene (generally, much agitated). The director of *The Lady Gambles*, Michael Gordon, says:

> I seem to remember that [Stanwyck] had some hesitation about accepting the role when it was first offered to her. I think she had some sense of the emotional demands it would make and, although she was intrigued, a degree of persuasion was required to induce her to undertake it.

A kind of *Lost Weekend* of the gaming tables, the film certainly does ask her to suffer. But Stanwyck's role is a fine one to display her versatility—and it needed a natural actress to make it work. It profits greatly from the quality she brings to it.

The Lady Gambles shows a "clean, warm, intelligent human being" who is overtaken by a thirst for gambling that lands her in the gutter. In a happy marriage with Robert Preston, she is carefree and fun; but when wheels, tables and tracks get hold of her, she falls apart. Stanwyck runs the gamut—from warmth and humor to hysterics and despair. And it is the use

of her child-woman balance that makes this one special.

Gordon, who guided his actress with great perception, says:

> Barbara's is a talent that, in my opinion, has never been sufficiently recognized and appreciated—except by those of us who've been fortunate enough to work with her. Looking back over forty years of professional life I can think of no actors who gave themselves to their work more fully than she did. Her responses to the extremely demanding role she played for me were more intuitive than intellectual, but because of her honesty and generosity in her use of herself, her intuitions were almost invariably truthful and exciting.
>
> One illustrative incident that I recall occurred during the shooting of the pawnshop scene. Houseley Stevenson, who played the pawnbroker, was getting along in years and had difficulty in remembering his lines. Because the scene was so emotionally draining on Barbara—there were no fake tears in her performance—after several takes I reconciled myself to settling for a less than satisfactory performance on the old man's part rather than ask her to keep repeating the scene. But Barbara insisted on my staying with it until she knew I felt we'd gotten it right. The wear and tear on her nervous system that day was considerable—but that's the way Barbara worked.
>
> Her respect for her work and her co-workers—combined with her extraordinary warmth, energy, and good humor—elicited a reciprocal respect and love that not only enveloped her, but bathed the entire company in a glow that I still remember vividly a quarter of a century later.

In early 1949, Stanwyck began what would be practically nonstop filming of five pictures in one year. The first of these was *The File on Thelma Jordan*, an exercise in murder and suspense directed by Robert Siodmak. Fine performances, dramatic staging and George Barnes' shadowy low-key lighting are the picture's strong points—along with a script by Ketti Frings that has unusually intelligent dialogue.

In trouble again, Stanwyck plays a woman accused of murder whom Assistant D.A. Wendell Corey falls for and has acquitted—by becoming her prosecutor

Sorry, Wrong Number

The Lady Gambles

The Lady Gambles, *with Robert Preston*

The Lady Gambles

The File on Thelma Jordan

The File on Thelma Jordan,
with Stanley Ridges

The File on Thelma Jordan

and losing the case. The surprise is that she *is* guilty and has been two-timing him.

Siodmak says:

> Barbara always had the character completely worked out. Before we started shooting, she would be sitting in her chair, her eyes closed and her concentration on the scene she was to play. The make-up and wardrobe people would be working to get her ready. But she never looked in the mirror. Completely absorbed in her work, she would go without a word in front of the camera.
>
> One day, before a very difficult scene, I tried to give her some last minute advice. That was the only time she showed any temper. She brushed me impatiently aside. I didn't mind, for I was sure she knew what she wanted to do.

Stanwyck plays two people: a dame with a shady past and one who reforms when she develops an attachment for Corey. Most of the time, like Corey, you believe she's on the level. But Stanwyck livens this up with a few glimpses of what lies behind it—mainly through the use of some smouldering intensity, combined with what Siodmak calls "her feline catlike grace." It is shown in her relationship with her lawyer (a slippery Stanley Ridges) and in an exciting walk which she takes from the jail to the courthouse for the verdict. Victor Young's score is a triumph here as it follows her, nonstop, on her lawyer's arm—through corridors, into an elevator, out the door, through lines of photographers and up flights of stairs. Director, actress and camera work to a rhythm which builds to fever pitch as crowds surge in and take over.

A velvet-voiced Stanwyck opens her next film, setting a mood for director Mitchell Leisen who moves his camera into the house where she and John Lund are waiting to be arrested for murder. *No Man of Her Own* is one of those 1950 features that was not released to television until 1972. It is fine Leisen and Stanwyck (enriched by the ensemble work Leisen characteristically gets from a cast) and it is well worth watching.

Although *No Man*'s screenplay is credited to Sally Benson and Catherine Turney, Leisen says:

> I adapted the script myself from *I Married a Dead Man* by William Irish. Catherine Turney

wrote the introductory scenes; all the rest was mine. We threw Sally Benson's version out entirely.

Paramount had not originally been interested in filming this novel but Leisen—who was—had given it to Stanwyck to read. She liked it so much that she told the studio she wouldn't do anything for them *but* that.

Done as a flashback, the story begins with a pregnant Stanwyck being kicked out by her lover, Lyle Bettger. She is subsequently involved in a train wreck from which she emerges mistaken for the wife of a man who died in it. Needing a home and a name for her child, she decides to continue the deception. Life with the family of the dead man—and an attachment which she forms for his brother, John Lund—changes her. But the return of a blackmailing Bettger brings them all a lot of trouble before the latter is killed (by another woman he deserted) and she and Lund can live in peace.

This, actually, gives little indication of what the picture contains. Nor will description do much for it. A Stanwyck down to her last 17¢ making an urgent call from a phone booth; dragging eight months of pregnancy up the stairs of a cheap rooming house to plead hysterically outside Bettger's door; being brushed off with an envelope pushed out from under it that contains a one-way train ticket and $5; and being shrieked at by another tenant for the noise she is making—such images are not enough to convey what comes across on the screen.

Leisen blows up the essence of his characters—both in his visual treatment and in the acting room he allows. The pace of the above sequence, the way it is shot, the completeness with which Stanwyck plunges into it—all of this makes the material moving and urgent. Stanwyck is at her best, and she remains so throughout the film.

There are many startling uses of the dramatic, but the most outstanding is the train wreck. And it's even more startling when you know how it was staged. Leisen explains:

> The set of the rest room [in which Stanwyck and Phyllis Thaxter are trapped when the train crashes] was built inside a gigantic steel wheel, about twenty feet in diameter. The camera was stationary and was suspended from the catwalk. When the train crashed, we just turned the wheel, and all the spills they took were genuine.

No Man of Her Own, *with Lyle Bettger*

No Man of Her Own, *with Lyle Bettger*
and John Lund

224

East Side, West Side, *with Van Heflin*

East Side, West Side, *with James Mason*

East Side, West Side

East Side, West Side

Stany would never have a double if she could help it. There was a scene in which Lyle Bettger slapped her around, and that was real too.

The "slapping around" was rough for both Stanwyck and Bettger. She had a hard time persuading him, during rehearsals, that he should really hit her. When she finally succeeded, Leisen ended up with as brutal a take as a director could want. (But don't look for it in the film; it isn't there.)

No Man of Her Own was brought in one day ahead of schedule and—as with *Remember the Night*—Leisen, the crew, and the other actors were impressed with Stanwyck's help. Lyle Bettger says:

No Man of Her Own was my first film. I was brought to California by Paramount (after a New York test) to play the heavy opposite Miss Stanwyck. For reasons that I still don't know, the studio entertained second thoughts about me and it was decided to test me again. Mitchell Leisen prevailed upon Stanwyck to make the test with me, and she very graciously agreed.

This was a break for me, as ordinarily a young starlet would have been assigned the job. No inexperienced contract player could possibly have given me the support and prestige that Miss Stanwyck provided. It helped me to deliver a better performance; and this erased any doubts the studio might have had as to my suitability for the film. It clearly demonstrated her high degree of professionalism, as there were, and are, few stars of her stature who would have bothered to help a newcomer in this way.

The morning of the test, Leisen introduced us on the set, and I was struck by Barbara's friendly forthright greeting. It boosted my confidence, and after a couple of run-through rehearsals, Mitch said, "Would you like to try one?" Before I could answer, Barbara said no, she'd like to go through it once again. So, with camera and sound ready, we went through one more rehearsal. It went smoothly, and I was satisfied that I was doing as well as I ever could. Then I noticed that everyone was sort of staring at me, including Barbara and Mitch, who were both smiling. It scared me, and I asked quickly, "What's the matter?" Barbara laughed and said, "Now that didn't hurt too much, did it?" I was bewildered and stammered, "Huh? Whatta ya mean?" Mitch said, "Lyle, that was your first

take. We rolled one without telling you. Barbara and I thought it might remove a little pressure from that first take if you thought it was just a rehearsal."

Throughout the ten weeks of actual shooting, my admiration and respect for Barbara Stanwyck grew each day. And by the time we were finished, she had spoiled me for wanting to work with anyone else. She is a lady with guts, consideration, kindness, and great good humor and integrity—a real pro. There are not many like her left.

After completing *No Man*, Stanwyck—who had liked to alternate the kind of roles she played—indicated that a Hollywood which had gone humorless was getting her down: "My God, isn't there a good comedy around? I'm tired of suffering in films. And I've killed so many co-stars lately, I'm getting a power complex!"

But there was more suffering to come. In M-G-M's *East Side, West Side*, she is mistreated by an unfaithful husband—James Mason. A comfortable Van Heflin helps her through this and offers her the devotion Mason has not.

Stanwyck's work is subtle and fine. The character she plays is gentle and, as she says, "quiet." Outwardly. But inside—because of her situation—she is torn up. Conflict must be expressed carefully, and it comes through best in a scene where she reveals her distress to Nancy Davis. Playing on two levels, she must try to convince Davis—and herself—that everything is all right, while showing—at the same time—that it isn't. Stanwyck draws on a great many skills to do this, but her trump card is a technique that she employs often in her "suffering" pictures. She has a way of holding tears or strong emotion back—and then letting her voice break on the last word of a line. It gets an audience every time. The technique is a standard one, but difficult to do; unless it is supported by real emotion, it will not convince.

Barbara Stanwyck's performances were taking on a maturity that would become increasingly beautiful to watch. Even though she was still very young, she had gained beyond her years from what she calls the source of her training: "experience, life." And her voice was deepening to match this. The deeper both her outlook and her voice became, the more satisfying she would be.

CHAPTER FOURTEEN

In addition to unbelievably noble heroes, despicable villains and innocent schoolteachers, the old West also contained real flesh and blood people. These latter are the subject of Paramount's taut and stirring drama, The Furies.

Ambition, revenge, jealousy and passion—emotions usually displayed in less rugged surroundings—are the concern of this superior film.

—*The* New York Mirror, *1950*

As the above indicates, *The Furies* was given honesty and adult treatment in its filming. Direction by Anthony Mann, a score by Franz Waxman, and camera work by Victor Milner (whose diffusion and silhouettes won him an Academy Award nomination) complement a no-nonsense cast, headed by Stanwyck and Walter Huston. As a self-made cattle baron and his equally iron-willed daughter, these two are perfectly matched: in principles, capability and drive.

Stanwyck has said: "The kind of script I like best is one in which the man's part is equally good. Then you have to work twice as hard. You try to top each other and that's fun." This is just what she and Huston do in *The Furies*. And a strong, high-energy Stanwyck is most welcome after all the long-suffering females she'd been playing, no matter how well she had done them.

When Stanwyck plays opposite an actor whose vitality is as great as hers, it is magnificent to watch. She, herself, might say that she couldn't top Huston. But she certainly holds her own. When faced with his powerful voice and movements, she stands perfectly still—smouldering with contained energy. And when goaded by him to let loose, she rises to the occasion with equal fire. The challenge they throw to each other is apparent in all their scenes—as is the delight they get from meeting and seeing that challenge met.

Stanwyck is excellent in this film. The spirit which had shown itself in her first Western, *Annie Oakley*, is now mature and completely at home in its surroundings. She has courage, her riding is fast and purposeful, and it is apparent that the medium of the Western—which she loves so well—is one to which she can make a unique contribution.

Much of *The Furies* was filmed on location near Tucson, Arizona, where cast and crew came to know each other well. Stanwyck developed a great admiration for Huston—as he did for her—both on and off camera. And his fatal heart attack shortly after the film's completion was as hard on those who had known him as it was on the motion picture industry. She was asked to dedicate a scholarship in his name at the University of Arizona when the film was premiered in Tucson. Her speech was a moving one—and in the quiet that followed it, she unveiled the portrait of Huston that had been used in the film. Hal Wallis had presented it to Huston's son; and John Huston, in turn, had presented it to the university. Later, at the film's premiere, she paid tribute to Huston again with the words:

> Ladies and gentlemen. You are about to see the Hal Wallis production of *The Furies* in which, unfortunately for our industry, Walter Huston plays his final role. It is Walter's picture. Mr. Wendell Corey, Mr. Gilbert Roland, Miss Judith Anderson and myself are in the supporting cast. For me, this is the greatest honor I have ever had.

Walter Huston's last line in *The Furies* is "There'll never be another like me." And the *New York Herald Tribune*—commenting on this—stated:

> According to his stature as an actor he was right; and those who knew him as a man would say he was right, too.

The combination of Barbara Stanwyck and Clark Gable is another that can do no wrong. And in *To Please a Lady* they prove it. This romance between a newspaper columnist and a racing driver has some rough dialogue. But the intensity of the stars cuts right through it. They can take lines like Gable's "It's time somebody roughed you up a bit. I can handle you, baby. You're just another dame to me" and Stanwyck's "You're nobody until somebody loves you" and make them brand new.

What keeps it lively is not only the ease with which they handle the situation, but the way in which they stand outside and kid it at the same time—always gently, and never without involvement in what the script asks of them. They're obviously enjoying themselves—as were Stanwyck and Huston—because they're so evenly matched, and because the script gives them fun things to do. A Stanwyck following Gable around the racetrack as he checks its condition is told to go get in some other guy's hair—and teases him with "But I like being in yours!" And you know how things are going to go from there. Of course she

The Furies, *with Judith Anderson*

The Furies, *with Walter Huston*

The Furies, *with Walter Huston* ▷

breaks a heel—and of course he has to carry her—and would anyone want it otherwise?

Make no mistake, however. Around all the humor, this pair delivers some very sultry scenes. Or, as *Film Daily* put it, the production provides "a highly suitable display of the talents of Clark Gable and Barbara Stanwyck. The script . . . is an astute job slanted for the players and they make every moment of it count."

In late 1950, Barbara Stanwyck and Robert Taylor announced that they would divorce, and issued the statement:

> In the past few years, because of professional requirements, we have been separated just too often and too long. Our sincere and continual efforts to maintain our marriage have failed. We are deeply disappointed that we could not solve our problems. We really tried. There will be a California divorce. Neither of us has any other romantic interest whatsoever.

Stanwyck's next film, *The Man With a Cloak*, was a mystery in which she played a scheming housekeeper trying to do Louis Calhern in for his money. In black wig and period gowns, she is both regal and forbidding—and she had no qualms about making the character what it should be. Director Fletcher Markle recalls:

> We were nearing the end of the picture when a question arose concerning a change in a scene. The change, if made, would have put Miss Stanwyck's screen character in a better light with audiences, making her less of a villainess. However, she turned it down as a weak compromise. Her intelligent point was that if she were going to be hated it might as well be all the way.

Markle says: "I have never had the privilege of collaborating with such a totally professional actress in the star category. 'Missy' is a lady of quality" who "through the long hours of many a rough day" was "the essence of good cheer with an unselfish concern for the welfare of her colleagues."

Good cheer took some doing on this film, since there were problems for almost everyone connected with it. Joe DeSantis, who played the butler that schemes with Stanwyck, states:

> This was my second major picture and it was loaded with top stars. I was fifth in the pecking order and believe there is very little left in the barnyard. Also I was new in Hollywood, having been flown in from New York by Fletcher Markle, who had used me a great deal in radio.
>
> There seemed to be a great deal of interpersonal tension on the set. First off we spent almost ten days rehearsing the entire picture in sequence, and there seemed to be much personal unhappiness.
>
> Little Leslie [Caron], I remember, was always red-eyed, and [Joseph] Cotten was a little short-tempered and testy. I recall one morning he was late, and young Pola (who was dying of leukemia and knew it) decided to make me up to save some time. When Joe found me in the chair he snapped at Pola, "I'll be in my dressing room when you're ready for me!"
>
> Miss Stanwyck, through the first days, was properly remote and aloof as befitting a great star. I seem to recall one incident during rehearsal when I interposed a mild objection to some procedure and she turned to me for the first time and addressed me as "Sonny."
>
> We had many scenes together, but we were not on the same social level. I got along famously with Louis Calhern who was a good friend. One day, to while away the tedium of waiting, I suggested that he pose for me for a small bust in his character of King Lear which he had done on Broadway. He agreed, and I whacked a good likeness in an hour or so. That afternoon Miss Stanwyck happened to see me working on it through the open door of my dressing room. She stopped and watched me for a minute and murmured, "That's beautiful, Joe." I thanked her and invited her in and we talked. In the course of half an hour she gave me, as the Italians say, "confidenza" and she revealed to me many personal things which had contributed to her deep unhappiness in this period of her life. Then at a point she had to prepare for another scene and a new costume and she held out her hand and left. What we spoke about, of course, is privileged, and I do not betray confidences.
>
> That is the extent of my contact with Missy—although years later I did work her show. But that was TV and pace was hectic and fast. What do I think of her? She's a pro. One of the few left and she don't take no guff from nobody. She knows her lines and she hits her marks and her work is her work and she's good.
>
> Of course I remember her also as the first and, I may add, only star I ever got to kiss "in de movies"—and that's like walking on the moon.

Cinematographer George Folsey (who would also photograph Stanwyck in *Executive Suite* and *These Wilder Years*) says: "Barbara was a joy to work with and a great privilege to know. I love her, as do all who have worked with her. She was very keenly aware of my problems and ever willing to help solve them." He explains:

A cameraman is mainly concerned with the appearance of the star he is photographing. Each day I found a flaw in Barbara's make-up which I had to have repaired on the set. She would stand there while I told the make-up man what was wrong and had him fix it. She was always patient and pleasant about it. I could never seem to iron this difficulty out with the man who put Barbara's make-up on in the department (not the man on the set). He saw a problem and fixed it one way. I saw it another way. My point is that Barbara's attitude and patience helped keep everything on an even keel.

The Man With a Cloak was the first film to employ the 12-tone scale in its scoring, and David Raksin's music is fittingly sinister. But it made a mistake when it gave Stanwyck a song for which her voice was not even considered. (Markle cannot recall who made this decision or why.) Although she does a fine job of lip-syncing, the song is a total loss because the voice quality of the woman dubbing it bears no resemblance to Stanwyck's. However, this is a small point in a long film which, otherwise, makes intelligent use of its star.

A really excellent role came her way next—in *Clash By Night*—and it was one that she wanted very much to do. She was also eager to work with the picture's director, Fritz Lang, whose touch on any film guarantees excitement.

In an Alfred Hayes rewrite of the Clifford Odets play, Stanwyck is a bitter restless woman who returns to her home town and marries a simple fisherman, Paul Douglas, for security. Her eventual dissatisfaction leads her to adultery with a cynical movie projectionist, Robert Ryan. And the result is violence and a wrecked home until she decides to go back to Douglas and their child.

Clash By Night shot exteriors with its cast in Monterey, California, in October of 1951. Shortly before this, Lang and cameraman Nicholas Musuraca had spent several days there filming documentary footage to enhance the story. Much of it did serve this purpose but, in addition, it so impressed the picture's producer that three hundred feet was selected for an introduction: a powerful and significant look at the locale which would affect the lives of the players. Crashing waves and a matching Roy Webb score begin under the opening credits, setting the tone for the battle of raw emotions that will follow.

Back in Hollywood, Lang explains that—before starting to shoot—he spent a week rehearsing with his actors, much as one would for a stage play. This was possible because the main scenes involved only three people.

While things went smoothly with the rest of the cast, Lang (and everybody else) had a difficult time with Marilyn Monroe—playing one of her first important roles. In 1965, Stanwyck recalled for the *Toronto Telegram*:

She was awkward. She couldn't get out of her own way. She wasn't disciplined, and she was often late, and she drove Bob Ryan, Paul Douglas and myself out of our minds . . . but she didn't do it viciously, and there was a sort of magic about her which we all recognized at once. Her phobias, or whatever they were, came later; she seemed just a carefree kid, and she owned the world.

Lang mentions that, during the scene where Stanwyck had to hang clothes on a line while talking to Monroe, the latter blew her lines maybe eight or ten times—making it very hard for Stanwyck to get anywhere, but he says: "Not once did she have a bad word for Marilyn. She understood her perfectly." He continues:

I have never worked—here or in Europe—with any artist who was more cooperative than Barbara.

From the beginning, Barbara had insisted that she not have to work after 6 p.m. This was in her contract. In my opinion the request is perfectly legitimate, because one shouldn't make any close-ups of an actress after a whole strenuous day of shooting.

One day we were lining up a scene and, in spite of the hard work of the crew and the brilliant cameraman, Nicholas Musuraca, it was quite obvious that we wouldn't be able to start shooting before six.

At about a quarter to six the producer, Harriet Parsons—who worked under the executive producer Jerry Wald—came to the set; and when she learned that we probably would not be able

To Please a Lady

To Please a Lady, *with Clark Gable*

The Man With a Cloak, with Leslie Caron and Joe DeSantis

The Man With a Cloak, with Joseph Cotten and Joe DeSantis

to shoot the scene before 6 p.m., she said she would ask Barbara to stay longer. I warned her not to do it because it was not a question of five or ten minutes that Barbara would have to stay, but maybe half or three quarters of an hour. But, in spite of my warning, Miss Parsons insisted. She went to Barbara's dressing room from where she emerged after ten minutes, seemingly very upset, and left the studio without saying a word to anyone.

Some minutes later Barbara asked me to come to her dressing room where she told me that if it would help us to keep on schedule, she would be willing to shoot the next morning at 8:30—half an hour earlier than the usual 9 o'clock start of the shooting day.

Such an understanding of the intricacies of shooting and such willingness to help was typical of Barbara. As I said, I have never worked with anybody like her.

Another example to show why I as a director like her so very much: One day before shooting in the morning, she complained to me about a scene and said it was very badly written and she could never play it. I knew the scene, which I thought was very well written, and said, "Barbara, may I speak very frankly and openly with you?" She said "Naturally," and I continued: "I think the scene reminds you of a rather recent event in your private life, and that is why you think it is badly written and you cannot play it." Barbara looked at me for a second and then said slowly, "You son of a bitch"—went out and played the two-and-one-half-pages-long scene so wonderfully that we had to shoot it only once.

Clash By Night is charged with volatility. The house in which Stanwyck and Douglas live stifles her with domesticity. Ryan's projection booth becomes a jungle where the two men battle—and slam an interfering Stanwyck against a hot projector before they come to their senses. Symbols and dramatic camera angles present an explosive Ryan bursting through the corners of frames to satisfy his desires, a bungling Douglas as incapable of controlling a ringing alarm clock as he has been of satisfying his wife, a trapped Stanwyck pacing like an animal in the cramped kitchen where she is caught between the two men.

This is one of Stanwyck's best performances—so good, in fact, that it won her the *Motion Picture Exhibitor*'s "Laurel" award. Probably the hardest job she has in the film is making the character's turning point acceptable. The script has her saying: "People change. You find out what's important and what isn't. What you really want." Stanwyck leaves you with no doubt that the character *has* changed when Douglas takes her back. As she starts to enter a room where he has told her she will find her sleeping child, she moves softly, with the attitude of a person who's been given a great gift: the chance to start over.

Another fine role was Stanwyck's in the clever *Jeopardy*—a 69-minute exercise in suspense built on accident and circumstance. A family of three—Stanwyck, Barry Sullivan and their small son, Lee Aaker—are vacationing on the Mexican coast when their fishing trip turns into a nightmare. Sullivan is pinned to the ground by a timber from a rotting jetty and Stanwyck has just four hours in which to get help before the tide comes in. To save him, she is forced to give herself to escaped convict Ralph Meeker.

Director John Sturges says:

Making a picture with Missy is such a stimulating and productive experience, it's hard to think how it could be better.

I recall one aspect of her approach to her work that struck me as meaningful. I commented one day on how purposely and yet gracefully she moved, the marvelous sense of contained power in the way she walked, stood, sat down, or whatever.

She told me years ago in New York she had the standard heel hitting clack-clack jolting walk of a chorus girl, which she was then. She went to the zoo, and for days and weeks studied the tigers, and made herself move as they did. That straight-on attack to become what she wanted to be seems to me a strong indicator of the kind of make-up she has as a person.

The purpose, the grace and the straight-on attack have always been a part of Stanwyck, but she has improved her use of them over the years. Compare—as was mentioned previously—*Annie Oakley* and *The Furies*. Compare *The Furies* with *The Big Valley*. She only gets better. This is because Stanwyck knows herself and works carefully—nothing she does is accidental. As Cecil B. DeMille said, "She's a great technician." Stanwyck knows how to use her poised neat body and the intensity at her command—and she knows, too, how *not* to use them.

Clash By Night, *with Paul Douglas*

Clash By Night, *with Robert Ryan*

Clash By Night, *with Paul Douglas*

Jeopardy, *with Ralph Meeker
and Barry Sullivan*

Jeopardy, *with Barry Sullivan*

Jeopardy offers Stanwyck physical action which she brings off in style: bouncing along a dusty road in an uncomfortable car, smashing windows, battling Meeker, and struggling with ropes, timbers and a vicious sea as they race to save the drowning Sullivan. But the sense of *contained* power shows best in her psychological action. When she realizes that only through seduction will she get Meeker to help her, she changes completely. She looks and talks and handles her body differently from that instant. The way she smokes cigarettes, leans against the wall of a crumbling shack or back over the side of the car—challenging him to take her—is as overwhelming as it must be in order to trap him into doing what she wants.

While all this is going on, Barry Sullivan is suffering up to his armpits in water and futile attempts to capture the attention of a passing boat. However, despite this, he says:

> Of the films I did with Miss Stanwyck only *Jeopardy* sticks in my mind as having any merit, but all three occasions [the others were *The Maverick Queen* and *Forty Guns*] cling to my memory as fun experiences. This may seem a minor thing in discussing a fabulous artist, but dammit, in my book it looms very formidably. We start out in this business thinking of it as a glorious adventure and "fun," and all too often it seems like drudgery. You know you're not doing your best work when something is drudgery. When you work with this lady you know damn well it *is* fun, and thus the glorious adventure you always dreamed about, and you, come up a couple of octaves.
>
> All great artists have this one thing in common. Tracy had it, Bette Davis has it, George C. Scott has it, young Robert Foxworth has it. They give their very best shot regardless of the calibre of the material. And Barbara most certainly has it in large quantity.
>
> We don't always get Arthur Miller or Lillian Hellman to perform. It is common knowledge that most of the material today borders on the mediocre. It would be easy, and *perhaps* forgivable, if one were to "walk through it"—using only part of whatever God has given. You'll never find Barbara doing that. I think maybe she might have worked harder when the writing was thin. She just damned well pulled it up to her level and everybody else in the cast could do no less.

> I guess I am labeling her "inspirational," and she would laugh uproariously at that word. The ability to laugh, though, is perhaps what makes her so damn great. The set was always loose. No phony tensions to distract from the job at hand. Young actors and actresses, perhaps on a first job and understandably nervous, would lose the nervousness and begin to enjoy. I've seen her do the same thing with some of our senior performers who might be uptight (it happens at both ends of the spectrum, God help us). Her infinite patience, her joshing way, her generosity in blaming herself to reduce pressures when a scene would blow—all these things are marks of professionalism maybe, but I rather feel they are the marks of one great human being.
>
> This carried over to the technical people, too. She knew their problems—always their mechanical ones, and almost always their personal ones. If a director goofed because he had a hangover, she was better than Bromo; if a prop man forgot something because his baby was sick, she was better than a pediatrician; if a make-up man started applying the wrong color because he had had a fight with his girl friend, she was better than Max Factor. None of this was phony bleeding heart concern. It was genuine.
>
> If all this gush sounds like I'm in love with the lady I plead guilty. My fondest hope is that I will walk on a set one day soon and find her waiting (as she will tell you, I am always late dammit). I know I will have one helluva good time.

Of her role in *All I Desire* Stanwyck told the *New York Morning Telegraph*: "It's the type of part I've had many times—a bad woman trying to make up for past mistakes." As the wife of a school principal in 1910, she returns to him and their three children after deserting them ten years earlier because of gossip caused in their small town by her romance with another man. Stanwyck continued: "When I return I'm about as welcome as a typhoid carrier. It's the old Biblical story of adultery."

Wicked women had become something of a specialty with Stanwyck by then—a condition that was fine with her because "I like gutsy roles. Namby-pambies have no interest for me. I'd rather not act at all than do a Pollyanna. I've got to play human beings. . . . I think I understand the motives of the bad women I play. My only problem is finding a way to play my 40th fallen female in a different way from my 39th."

All I Desire pits a romantic Stanwyck against a lot of petty middle-class people. And maybe if director Douglas Sirk could have fashioned the novel *Stopover* into the film he envisioned, it would have made a worthwhile statement. But the picture is hindered by a happy ending (which Sirk did not want but producer Ross Hunter did) and a saturation of weepy music. Under the circumstances, *Variety* said:

> The Ross Hunter production and Douglas Sirk's direction pull all stops to make the picture a 79-minute excursion into sentimentality. With help of Miss Stanwyck's performance, the soap-operish tear-jerking is palatable.

and *The New York Times* added:

> Since Miss Stanwyck is an accomplished veteran she gives a better performance than could reasonably be expected under the enervating circumstances.

Her next film was the beautiful *Titanic:* fine enough in its script to win writers Charles Brackett, Walter Reisch and Richard Breen an Academy Award; fine enough on Stanwyck's part to win her another "Laurel" from the *Motion Picture Exhibitor;* and fine in every department—directing, acting, editing, sound.

Titanic is predominantly a script about human beings. The brief glimpse of each character it shows is the essence of that character: a lifetime of understanding—or misunderstanding—telescoped into a few scenes. The realization which the audience has from the beginning that the ship will sink and separate these people from their lives or from each other throws everything into high relief. Director Jean Negulesco wisely understates. He lets the tragedy speak for itself—pacing it brilliantly and building it steadily.

An outstanding contribution to this is the fact that *Titanic's* sound track has no background music except for what stems from realistic sources: the ship's band, a church service, a group of people singing around a piano. The tremendous amount of quiet that exists before the ship's collision suspends actions in time and imparts a sense of waiting and urgency.

Even during the disaster, sounds are styled to contribute to a dramatic purpose.

One can hardly say enough for what Stanwyck does with her role. The great humanity that is Julia, her grace and dignity, and the courage with which she tries to improve things for her children yet accepts when she cannot—these are all deeply real. Stanwyck has a great role and sensitive direction—and does complete justice to both.

Perhaps one of the best ways to look at what she achieves is to know what she put into it, and her description to Hedda Hopper of what she lived through in the filming of the final scene speaks for itself:

> The night we were making the scene of the dying ship in the outdoor tank at Twentieth, it was bitter cold. I was 47 feet up in the air in a lifeboat swinging on the davits. The water below was agitated into a heaving rolling mass and it was thick with other lifeboats full of women and children. I looked down and thought: If one of these ropes snaps now, it's good-by for you. Then I looked up at the faces lined along the rail—those left behind to die with the ship. I thought of the men and women who had been through this thing in our time. We were re-creating an actual tragedy and I burst into tears. I shook with great racking sobs and couldn't stop.

Robert Wagner was very young when *Titanic* was made. He recalls the poem that Stanwyck read to him in the film: A. E. Housman's "When I Was One and Twenty" and says:

> The content of that poem sort of sums up where I was at that point in my life. Barbara was very helpful. She's a sensitive lady beneath that kind of sharp front. She changed my whole approach to my work—made me want to learn the business completely. She really started me thinking. It means a great deal when someone takes that kind of time with a newcomer.

Wagner adds that, when they made *Titanic*, "It was like a big family then at the studio." He speaks of the party at the end of filming and of sketches which Negulesco did of everyone. Wagner still has his, as well as "fond memories of great times together," of "great enjoyment and love" and of Stanwyck who is "a great memory."

All I Desire, *with Maureen O'Sullivan,*
Richard Carlson, Marcia Henderson, Richard Long

All I Desire, *with Billy Gray*

Titanic, *with Clifton Webb*

Titanic, *with Clifton Webb* ▷

CHAPTER FIFTEEN

While finishing *Titanic*, Stanwyck was busy taking shots (the preventive kind) for a trip to Mexico where she would film *Blowing Wild*. It's too bad she couldn't have been inoculated against the script too. In a story of wildcatting and banditry, this one shows her married to Anthony Quinn and wanting former lover Gary Cooper. She is a tramp with a lot of stormy things to do—an earthy, violent and determined one. She hates her husband; she hates being where she is; and she will hate Cooper when he rejects her. Nor does she find it difficult to push Quinn to his death in the mechanism of a pumping oil well. The *New York Herald Tribune* said:

> *Blowing Wild* is labeled cheap from the very beginning, when it has some difficulty making up its mind whether it is imitating *High Noon* or *Treasure of Sierra Madre*. It soon lapses into its very own brand of corny sensation in a story about strong men fighting bandits in the Mexican oil fields, with Barbara Stanwyck climbing all over Gary Cooper in a dime-novel version of grand passion.

Another critic noted that "Barbara Stanwyck is hampered by a trite love theme and too many scenes in which she must emote." And *The New York Times* called the film "an initially lost cause" with "painfully familiar dialogue, such as Barbara Stanwyck's 'Why do you always fight against me?' and Mr. Cooper's 'Because you're no good.' " The *Times* added: "There's no getting around the little matter that Philip Yordan's script is a loose miscellany of random actions. And so, as a consequence, is the film."

Stanwyck's next picture was bearable only when she and Fred MacMurray were in it. *The Moonlighter* had a scenario by Niven Busch that is hard to account for after *Duel in the Sun* and *The Furies*. *The New York Times* called the movie "a shapeless, dull and low-budget affair" and added:

> Barbara Stanwyck and Fred MacMurray are still actors of estimable magnitude. So it comes as a mild shock to find them tempting prestige in the Globe's new and dinky little Western called *The Moonlighter*, made, for no discernible reason, in 3-D. Exactly why the protagonists of *Double Indemnity* should have elected to participate in such cow-town petty larceny is a mystery.
>   Warners' Natural Vision process, viewed through polarized glasses, merely pulls a few

cliffs, trees and modest panoramas into clearer focus, which is more than director Roy Rowland accomplishes with the visible or underlying text. Mr. MacMurray seems jittery throughout, Miss Stanwyck as cool as a cucumber. Whether toiling honestly or inspirationally for their 3-D debut they have picked themselves a sow's ear.

There is no arguing with the above. But there are two moments of glory for Stanwyck in *The Moonlighter*—moments that foreshadow many she would create later.

The first comes in a gun battle with Ward Bond that finds her dodging bullets behind rocks and brush, and winning by trickery. It's amusing, in retrospect, to look at the *New York Herald Tribune's* reaction to this:

> You may fidget a bit as Barbara Stanwyck, stylishly thin and looking mighty small beside a horse, fights it out with rifles with Ward Bond and wins. This, as anyone who has ever seen a Western knows, is practically impossible. Bond may lose a screen battle here and there but never to a wisp of a woman with rifles at fifty yards.

Stanwyck's other moment is a stunt of no small magnitude from which she emerged with nothing but bruises—and you wonder why. Roy Rowland says:

> She was capable of doing her own stunt work and completely unafraid. She always wanted to do her stunts, but we could not risk the possibility of an accident. Barbara understood this, but she still pleaded to do [them].

She got her chance in *The Moonlighter* because "As I recall we did have a stunt woman but she was not available at the precise time we wanted to shoot that scene." "That scene" found Stanwyck sliding down a waterfall into a fast-moving river in the High Sierras. There were a lot of rocks on the way down, and she hit every one of them—on her back, on her side, on her stomach. Stanwyck's comment on the experience: "It hurt!" Rowland's comment: "She received bruises, but she never complained or held up the picture in any way."

Quality has always been something that mattered to Stanwyck in a role. Size is something else. As she once put it, "Size has never bothered me. If it had, I would not have done *Executive Suite*. I liked the role

Warners. General publicity—1953

and I wanted to do it, no matter how short it was. I think I worked all of seven days."

Executive Suite—a battle for the presidency of a big furniture company after the sudden death of the incumbent—was fitted out with as heavy a cast of pros as its director, Robert Wise, could have wished for. He says:

> Once [Barbara and I] had an understanding together of the script and of the character she was playing and had agreed on the approach to the character, it was a matter of [her] coming in day after day with just the right things to bring to the scenes—no fuss, no bother, no nonsense —and that is marvelous to work with. I've always been sorry that, for one reason or another, [we] never worked together again after *Executive Suite.*

William Holden adds: "Everybody was so good— so on his toes—that when you went in there in the morning you had to put on your best. It was a great experience." Holden thinks they finished filming in 37 days instead of the allotted 48–50.

Stanwyck—with very few speeches and scenes— makes a remarkably vivid impression. She is the bitter mistress of the man who died—a man who cared more for the company than for her but, still, the man who was her only reason for living. When his death is reported to her over the phone, she is sitting in a high-backed chair smoking. Wise shoots from the back of the chair, showing an indifferent hand reaching out for the receiver. There are no words. As the message is conveyed, a close-up of her face shows what she hears. She says nothing, puts the phone down, closes her eyes. One woman's life— and death—in a few seconds.

As an important stockholder whose vote for the next president is crucial (and who couldn't care less who is chosen) she must subsequently be handled with skill. It is Holden who gets to her through her vulnerability—and saves her from herself in the process. Their scene together has all the fire they exhibited in *Golden Boy.* Holden strips her down to her nerve endings—and she responds like the wounded thing she is.

This performance won Stanwyck her third "Laurel," the film was cited as one of the ten best of the year by both *Film Daily* and the National Board of Review, and George Folsey's photography was nominated for an Academy Award.

Witness to Murder called for plenty of endurance on the part of its star. Stanwyck's observation of a murder committed by George Sanders prompts her to notify police. By the time they arrive, he has covered all clues, and they decide she was mistaken. She spends the rest of the film in a tight spot because Sanders now has reason to kill her. She tries to prove he is guilty; he tries to convince the police she is a mental case. This lands her in a psychiatric ward for observation, puts doubts in her own mind, and leads to the confrontation with Sanders which she had predicted.

Mentally, she is driven almost to distraction. Her fears—and her attempts to rationalize her way out of them—call for some highly seasoned acting, which they get. When, for instance, she is subjected to the questions of a psychiatrist with an impersonal and even insulting approach, she balances the character's doubts in herself with an awareness of what she must do to convince him of her sanity—showing that she understands him far better than he does her (and showing how many facets of character Stanwyck can convey at one time).

Physically, she is chased through streets and up a skeleton skyscraper into the film's cliff-hanging climax—where pursuit by Sanders causes her to fall off the roof and onto a platform that gives way just as she is pulled to safety.

Speaking to the *Toronto Telegram* in 1965, Stanwyck said of her 83 films:

> That total sometimes amazes people, but what is a lot MORE amazing is the fact that I've managed to SURVIVE some of them. I've been in some bad ones in my day.

Interviewer Clyde Gilmour suggested that *Cattle Queen of Montana* and *Escape to Burma* "belong in any definitive list of stinkers in which [her] talents have been squandered," and she replied:

> Awful! Dreadful! You might wonder how such a thing could happen. The answer is simply that you make a horrible mistake. You get taken in by what seems like a basically good idea and a sort of rough, temporary screenplay and you sign on to do the picture without ever having seen a completed script.
>
> Within one week after the start of shooting, everybody on the set knows that the thing is just

Blowing Wild, *with Gary Cooper*

Blowing Wild, *with Anthony Quinn*

The Moonlighter

The Moonlighter

The Moonlighter, *with Fred MacMurray*

Witness to Murder

Executive Suite, *with Fredric March and Nina Foch*

254

*Listening to the translation of the speech
in which she was adopted by the Blackfeet Indians*

Cattle Queen of Montana, *with Ronald Reagan*

not jelling. But by that time you're hooked. So you do the best you can—and you privately hope that nobody goes to see it.

Concerning *Cattle Queen, The New York Times* stated:

> Barbara Stanwyck, an intrepid citizen who has shown no fear of man, terrain or scripts over a long and illustrious career, is tackling all three in *Cattle Queen of Montana,* [a] highly improbable Technicolored adventure. . . .
>
> Accoutered in split skirts and off-the-face Stetson, she is as photogenic as any lady pioneer has a right to be. But it is her misfortune to discover that there are dastardly cattle men among the decent settlers in the old Montana territory, and that there are villainous, whiskey-slugging Blackfeet braves among the upstanding warriors who want to be at peace with the white man.
>
> Miss Stanwyck manages to hold her own with both the men and terrain, but she definitely drops the decision to the script.

As the *Times* implies, both Stanwyck and the film are well-photographed. Cinematographer John Alton says: "She has a face that is a pleasure to light." Stanwyck, and the Glacier National Park area of Montana where they were shooting, gave him inspiration if the script did not.

About the only good thing that came out of *Cattle Queen* was Stanwyck's adoption by the Blackfeet Indians, who had worked in the picture and were impressed by her physical endurance and the fact that she did her own stunts. She was given the tribe's most revered name: Princess Many Victories III. And the braves—the men who are braves themselves—made her a member of their Brave Dog Society. In a ceremony which she has described as "quite beautiful" she received a big eagle feather with a claw on it. And speeches accompanying this declared:

> Princess Many Victories III. She rides. She shoots. She has bathed in waters from our glaciers. She has done very hard work—rare for a white woman. To be a member of our Brave Dog Society is to be known as one of our brave people. Princess Many Victories III is one of us.

Ronald Reagan, Stanwyck's co-star on the film, speaks of the sort of thing that caught the Blackfeet's admiration:

> There is a scene where she is bathing in a mountain lake. The director was prepared to shoot this with a double because the temperature of the water was in the mid-forties. Naturally, the scene would not be as good if the camera had to play far enough away for use of a double. She insisted on doing [it] herself.

John Alton adds: "She came out blue, but did not hesitate to do another take."

The Violent Men, Stanwyck's first film in Cinema-Scope, shows her as an avaricious wife, described by the *New York Herald Tribune* as "a sort of Lady Macbeth of the plains." The script gives her a clear direction in which to work—and she goes after what she wants smoothly. This means Edward G. Robinson, as the husband she would like to discard for his brother, Brian Keith, is in trouble.

Robinson is a tough guy himself—but no match for the ruthless Stanwyck who robs him of his crutches and leaves him to die in a flaming ranch house. She doesn't succeed in doing away with him, or in obtaining the land or the man that she wants—but it is not for lack of trying. And her attempts, reminiscent of her approach in *Double Indemnity*, have class. The *Tribune* saw that the film was "a better-than-average Western" because "the characters are interesting. Robinson and Miss Stanwyck have both been twisted by cupidity into villains of more than routine blackness."

The less said about *Escape to Burma*, the better. It was a disaster—although a visually lovely one thanks to art director Van Nest Polglase and cameraman John Alton. Producer Benedict Bogeaus had dug up a 1936 *Collier's* story that should have been allowed to rest in peace. Just why writers Talbot Jennings and Hobart Donavan used the dialogue they did eludes speculation. Exchanges like the following are typical:

> Murvyn Vye: There is a small trouble, but it is a small trouble several times. Thus it becomes a large trouble.
> Stanwyck: If we face it together, it will only be half as large. Tell me about it.

The Violent Men, *with Brian Keith*

The Violent Men, *with Brian Keith
and Edward G. Robinson*

The Violent Men

Escape to Burma, *with Robert Ryan*

Escape to Burma, *with "Roger"*

As mistress of a teak forest in the Burmese jungle, Stanwyck is described in a program accompanying the film as "wise about elephants and men." Robert Ryan, who becomes her lover, is a " 'jungle salt,' courageous but a realist." David Farrar, who almost breaks this up, is a "Security Officer, very determined." That should be enough to put things in their proper perspective. But *The New York Times*, unable to resist, went a step further:

> Even the monkeys seem bewildered. One little simian, called upon to pick up a revolver dropped in a fight, holds it, looks silly and walks out the back door. Whereupon Mr. Ryan says happily, "There goes the evidence." Yes, siree!

AND, as Stanwyck points out: "The animals were better than the picture!"

Director Allan Dwan, despite his vast experience, couldn't make much out of it all. But, even under such circumstances as these, he was pleased to have the opportunity to direct Stanwyck. He says:

> A director's greatest pleasure is the cooperation of a dedicated star. My sixty years of work would have been blessed by a longer association with her.
> To know Barbara is to love her. Her graceful transition from age to age is proof of her genius and dedication.

Dwan was "particularly impressed by her compassion for the crew. Nothing upset her more than to see a member of the staff mistreated or abused. She not only resented it, but let the management know her feelings." And he marveled at her touch with the animals. He says: "The animals loved and obeyed her. The gigantic elephants were like kittens in her presence. She could have been a great animal trainer had she wished."

There's Always Tomorrow was looked upon by critics with disdain. As the *New York Herald Tribune* put it:

> Married Man falls for Other Woman, and somebody has to suffer. The same formula has been selling soap in this country for years.

Director Douglas Sirk was interested in projecting not just a stock situation—but a couple of interesting people, genuinely trying to straighten out lives that—

up to then—hadn't been doing very well. Stanwyck and Fred MacMurray play with charm, but since they are faced—as *Film Daily* put it—with "routine material and dialogue," they can do little more than give their characters "a competent surface coating."

Producer-director Joe Kane explains that *The Maverick Queen*, Stanwyck's next, "was one of those partly completed novels left by Zane Grey when he died. His son finished it." In this one, Stanwyck is the prosperous owner of a hotel, who works with a notorious outlaw gang headed by Scott Brady, and loses her life when she falls for Pinkerton detective Barry Sullivan. The film, Republic's first in the widescreen process, was shot in color around Silverton, Colorado, in 1955.

Stanwyck is in fine form. Her composure is flawless, and so are her riding and stunt work, as Kane's comments will show. He says:

> It was pretty high up [in Silverton] and the weather was a little unstable but, rain or shine, Barbara was within call and went in there and played her part intelligently and without making a lot of "suggestions." When she did have an idea, it was well worth listening.
> She didn't make the fast ride down the canyon, but did most of the other riding. I couldn't take a chance on my star, but she would have done it if I'd been crazy enough to suggest it. A stunt girl did the ride and fall and I didn't even want her to do that. I preferred a young man, Whitey Hughes, who was there and, if I remember correctly, we finally split it up some way between them. But Barbara took over, clambering up the side of the cliff, pushing off the log and the whole bit. I can imagine some stars would have balked completely, but then there are stars and stars.

Scott Brady adds:

> Working with [Stanwyck] was a delight all the way. In fact, it was a little like on-the-job training for me—earn as you learn I've heard it called. I particularly remember one long angry scene we had together. The writer somehow had not put a finish to it and, after one rehearsal, I said: "Now what?" Missy said, "You exit, pal, pronto." I thought at first, well—the star is calling the shots. But when I saw the film, she proved dead right. My exit then was just what the scene needed.

All I can say is I would love to have the pleasure of being kicked out of a scene again by Barbara Stanwyck. That gal is dynamite and I love her.

Two pros who had never had a chance to work together enriched *These Wilder Years* as much as they could. James Cagney plays a business tycoon who wants the one thing money cannot give him: an illegitimate son he put up for adoption twenty years ago. Stanwyck, as the head of an adoption agency, stands in his way in order to protect the son. The *New York Daily News* said:

Although the veterans are incapable of inadequate performances, they are not at their best in this dramatization. A major handicap is the static presentation of a story already devitalized by excess padding.

and *The New York Times* added:

The intent of this little drama is lofty enough . . . and Mr. Cagney and Miss Stanwyck go at it with becoming restraint and good-will. But the story is hackneyed and slushy and Roy Rowland's direction is so slow and pictorially uninteresting that the picture is mawkish and dull.

In *Crime of Passion*, Stanwyck is a worldly newspaper columnist who marries an easy-going detective (Sterling Hayden) and finds herself smothered in domestic boredom. Her frustration with the monotony of their life and the irritating circle of friends that inhabits it leads her to look for an outlet. Since she no longer has a career of her own, she turns to advancing her husband's. And the overpowering ambition that results when her efforts are blocked causes her to commit murder.

The film is built upon a logical premise: that the person Stanwyck was before marriage—an aggressive career woman—cannot settle into doing, as the picture puts it, "only what every other wife does"— and that "strange offenses" can be "committed by seemingly normal people" because "frustration can lead them quickly to violence."

Stanwyck presents this believably. She balances her devotion to Hayden with an increasingly uncontrollable desire to push him into a better job. There are hints throughout that she is being driven, and she builds these until it is obvious she is in the grip of something over which she has no control. When she holds a gun on the man who stands in the way of what she wants, she hovers between rationality and obsession for a moment—making it clear that what follows is the result of stress which gives her no choice.

The heavy moments that Stanwyck played in the picture were accompanied by some light ones on the set. Director Gerd Oswald says that, after Sterling Hayden had been decided upon for the male lead, Stanwyck

. . . was in full agreement with the choice, but had one small reservation—namely, the way Sterling dresses.

Even though she was well aware that a low-income Los Angeles detective would not wear tailor-made suits, Missy felt that Sterling should wear neat and well-fitting clothes—a stock-in-trade he was not known for.

Her reasoning was that a sophisticated San Francisco newspaper columnist wouldn't fall head over heels in love at first sight with a guy wearing ill-fitting, sloppy clothes. She asked me to talk Sterling into buying himself a couple of new suits for his role. I talked to him in diplomatic language and he got the message.

One day, while we were in the middle of production, Sterling's trousers got caught on some equipment—resulting in a large rip on one of the trouser legs. Missy, who witnessed the mishap, said dryly: "There goes Jack Clinton's best suit."

Sterling replied: "*Jim* Clinton. I have an extra pair of trousers. I'll go change." Needless to say the entire set broke up. However, the joke is only funny if you are familiar with the Clinton story.

Jim Clinton, like Robert Hall and a few others, was a chain of men's clothing stores throughout Los Angeles. They offered bargain suits with two pairs of trousers for thirty-odd dollars in those days—hardly a clothier catering to movie stars. So Sterling kept his promise by buying a couple of new suits, but Missy's wish that he wore neat and well-fitting attire remained unfulfilled.

Anyway, anyone connected with the making of *Crime of Passion* had a ball. Everyone, including myself, loved working with Missy.

Having directed such great ladies of the screen as Bette Davis, Jo Van Fleet, Miriam Hopkins and Joanne Woodward, I can truthfully say that Barbara Stanwyck ranks as one of the greatest.

*There's Always Tomorrow,
with Fred MacMurray*

The Maverick Queen

During the first seventeen minutes of her next film—despite the fact that she appears in most of them—Stanwyck does not speak. *Trooper Hook*'s dramatic opening introduces the problem on which the movie will focus: that of a white woman whose love for the son she has had while prisoner of an Apache chief makes her an outcast with her own people. Her refusal to respond to questions and insults from those who have rescued her makes her most interesting. Withdrawal to the point of stoicism contrasts with a sequence that follows in which she is left alone with her child. Here—still silent—she begins a return to the world she once knew. Her touch with it is as fragile as the Indian theme that floats through the scenes. And her reaction to her image in the mirror, to the sound of her name voiced softly for the first time, and to an outfit left for her outside the door by one of the women, shows the strangeness she feels along with the attraction. All of this builds anticipation for the moment when she does talk.

From there, she and Joel McCrea (as a cavalry sergeant who befriends her, escorts her back to the husband from whom she was kidnapped and—when circumstances eliminate the husband—teams up with her himself) work smoothly together. Or, as *The New York Times* said:

> Armed with some good blunt dialogue, Miss Stanwyck and Mr. McCrea deliver a pair of easy, restrained and natural performances typical of two screen veterans. Is anyone surprised?

Director Charles Marquis Warren says of Stanwyck: "She is the most magnificent actress I ever worked with and, I think, the finest actress Hollywood has ever turned out." In working with her, he would "tell her what I wanted. Watch in wonder." She got it in "one take always." Although she was not involved in any stunt work in this film, Warren observes that "she could have done some of the Indians' stunts better than they did."

And Joel McCrea, on his sixth picture with Stanwyck, sums up his work with her over the years by saying "She is, with no reservations, the best I ever met. Every crew we ever worked with loved and admired her and so did I. She taught me a lot and I shall be ever grateful to her."

Forty Guns had Stanwyck working with Samuel Fuller in a story he wrote, produced and directed. The toughest character she had yet played in a Western ("I was born upset"), she was described at the time as the "stallion-riding leader of a band of hired gunmen—and the sister of a gun-happy ne'er-do-well—who rides roughshod over the countryside and the sheriff in a section of Arizona to which Barry Sullivan comes to establish law and order." Needless to say, Sullivan has his hands full.

Violence fills the screen in the Fuller tradition, and there would have been more if he had had his way. The film would have been called *Woman With a Whip* (Stanwyck puts one to good use) and she would have been killed in the end instead of wounded. The studio interfered on both counts.

However, there's plenty of action—as well as a couple of major stunts for Stanwyck. These occur while she and Sullivan are out riding, when a storm comes up and she is thrown from her horse and dragged along the ground with her foot caught in the stirrup. Fuller says:

> The storm, if memory serves, was shot in the purlieus of Death Valley, controlled by a number of giant fans (mammoth Liberty props) with truckloads of tumbleweeds. The twister, as far as Stanwyck was concerned, could have been dangerous since the gut of the prop wind was aimed directly at her to give the scene complete authenticity for the birth of a fast twister.
>
> The stunt men refused to do the [horse drag] unless they controlled it—meaning the stunt man would be able to unhitch his foot from the stirrup when he thought the horse's hoof was coming too damned close to his head. I refused. Stanwyck volunteered to do the stunt herself and to be "shook-off" naturally from the stirrup hold, instead of controlling the release.

Stanwyck did the drag three times before Fuller got what he wanted.

He also recalls that

> There was a scene loaded with a page of monologue and she knew it perfectly. I asked her, before the take, to eliminate the gibble-gabble and show the words in her face. Her eyes did it superbly.

Fuller—who says he "always wanted [Stanwyck] for the role despite the fact that Marilyn Monroe wanted so badly to play it"—continues:

These Wilder Years, *with James Cagney*

Crime of Passion, *with Sterling Hayden*

To work with Stanwyck is to work with the happy pertinence of professionalism and emotion. She's superb as a queen, slut, matriarch, con girl or on a horse—a viable criterion of dramatic impact because she naturally (bless her) eschews aspects of forced emotion. Her form or class or appeal or whatever you want to call it stems from tremendous sensitivity and thousands of closeted thoughts she can select at will, at the right moment, for the exact impact.

Once I toyed with the idea of making a film of Evita Perón with Stanwyck, but my fault I never did saddle myself down to that project and see it through. She would have made, and still could, a great character out of that role.

Forty Guns (filming in 1957) would be Stanwyck's last movie until she began *Walk On the Wild Side* in 1961. Asked by the *San Francisco Examiner* (while she was starring in *The Big Valley*) why she had done no films during those four years, Stanwyck replied: "Because nobody asked me. They don't normally write parts for women my age because America is now a country of youth."

Speaking of the kind of films Hollywood had made prior to this, she said:

> Something is gone. They were beautiful, romantic films, not as stark and realistic as today's, and I loved doing and watching them. Now we've matured and moved on. The past belongs to the past. But don't get me wrong. Just because I'm over 50 doesn't mean I'm dead or in a wheelchair. I go with these new trends and enjoy them and respect them for their own values.

At "over 50"—although she couldn't know it at the time—Barbara Stanwyck was just beginning what would be a major part of her career: one which would contribute a unique excitement to the screen, and result in a popularity for her with viewers perhaps greater than she had ever known. Such was the power of her talent and personality and a medium which could bring it into the homes of millions.

Trooper Hook, *with Terry Lawrence*

Forty Guns, *with John Ericson*

Forty Guns, *with Barry Sullivan*

Part IV

The Bandwagon

Photo by John Engstead

Of course I like TV. I'd be in it right now except that the Brain Boys [her agent] can't make up their minds what I should do. I wanted a Western series. But the Brain Boys said no, Westerns were on the way out.

Way out? Not around my house they're not. From 6 o'clock on it sounds like the last frontier around there. On Monday it's Restless Gun *and* Wells Fargo; *Tuesday,* Cheyenne, Sugarfoot *and* Earp; *Wednesday —. Don't I ever get tired? Hell, no! I love it. I don't care what anybody says, I have a ball.*

What she spoke of to *TV Guide* in 1958, Barbara Stanwyck had been trying to put across—to those who lacked her foresight—since 1956. She had dropped one agent who thought she was crazy for wanting a woman's Western. The one she took on had agreed to give the idea a try, but was having trouble selling it.

Stanwyck wanted to portray a rugged role. One of her inspirations for this was James D. Horan's book *Desperate Women*, which contains biographies of daring women from the Western frontier. She told the *Los Angeles Times* in 1958:

> The title of the book is a misnomer. The women weren't desperate. They were just real. Some were good and some were bad. In all the Westerns these days—and I love Westerns—the women are always left behind with the kids and the cows while the men do the fighting.
>
> Nuts to the kids and the cows. There were women who went out and fought, too. That's what I want to do. People say it's not feminine. It isn't. Sure, those women wore guns and breeches. But, don't kid yourself, they were female!

It would be seven years before "those in power" saw the light and starred Stanwyck in *The Big Valley*. In the meantime, she would become thoroughly familiar with the medium of television through guest appearances and an anthology show.

Stanwyck's early television appearances included dramas for the *Ford Theatre* and the *Alcoa-Goodyear Playhouse*. But probably her most interesting work was done on the *Zane Grey Theatre* where four episodes that starred her in 1958–59 clearly illustrated what a woman's Western could offer. One of these, "The Freighter," she persuaded Dick Powell (whose company produced the show) to "take back east to the boys on Madison Avenue" as a pilot. It didn't sell.

Another and even more exciting one is a direct ancestor to what she would eventually do in *The Big Valley*. Called "Trail to Nowhere," it was written by Aaron Spelling and presented Stanwyck in a couple of beautifully staged—and executed—battles. In one of them, she hits her opponent over the head with a lamp, runs for the door where he throws a knife at her, belts him on the jaw and in the stomach, and closes his hand in the door. Later, pursued by another would-be murderer (David Janssen) she shoots it out from behind some bales of hay, trips him with a rope, and runs outside where she falls into a mass of mud. Janssen follows and they tackle each other in a free-for-all of mud and blows. This was the kind of stuff Stanwyck delighted in doing (because she loves physical action) and could handle superbly. The portrayal of a frontier woman different from the gingham-skirted stereotype (backed up by Stanwyck's ability to ride, shoot and fight) could be a unique contribution to television. But Madison Avenue didn't see it.

NBC did, however, want her to do an anthology show. *The Barbara Stanwyck Show*—which premiered in 1960—had been suggested as early as 1956. But Stanwyck would not agree to it then—partly because she was holding out for a Western, and partly because there was talk of her portraying "history's noble women." ("If someone wants me noble, he'll have to do it on his own time. That anthology I'll never do.") She finally gave in when the Western was rejected, the characters became less noble, and "I wasn't working and I wanted to work."

Once she had taken on the series, she gave it everything. Its format was similar to that of *The Loretta Young Show* and others of this type, with Stanwyck acting as hostess and starring in most of the half-hour segments. (As it turned out, she starred in 32 of the show's 36.) She worked hard to obtain good stories ("The foundation of any good show is the story, not the star"). She did not give up on her desire "to play an Annie Oakley-type character" and managed to include a few Westerns in the package ("I sort of slipped them in"). And she was equally concerned about having fine male stars with her.

The opening and closing of *The Barbara Stanwyck Show* is not its strongest point. Appearing as herself, Stanwyck had to deliver an introduction in which she set the scene for what was to come. Even worse, she had to make silly comments on it when it was over.

This was awkward for several reasons. First of all, as she put it, the whole thing was "nonsense. Me

Zane Grey Theatre—"Trail to Nowhere"

swooping in and out of an elegant drawing room in those flourishing gowns. That wasn't me for a second. And I knew it." The elegant gowns were by Werlé and she wore them superbly. But, instead of being allowed to move as she delivered her lines (which would have put her at ease and drawn attention away from the phony setup) she was confined to a rigid model's pose: one foot slightly in front of the other, and her body in a three-quarter turn toward the camera.

Second, she often had to plug the sponsor's product—an artificiality for both performer and audience. And last, she was forced to read her lines from a teleprompter. She has explained:

> You couldn't learn them because of not knowing the star or story for the next week. We were sometimes five or six weeks behind with the intros. Sometimes, the story hadn't been written. It was too expensive to do these—so we did them six, seven or eight at a time. Sometimes, they had to be done over again. Now, of course, they have voice-overs.

However, the show's unsteady introductions are a minor thing. Barbara Stanwyck won an Emmy for her work in this series, and with good reason. Of the 32 segments in which she stars, maybe 15 have really good stories and dialogue. Despite her search for fine scripts, she wasn't able to find 36 of them. It was Stanwyck who, ultimately, became the "foundation" of the show—softening all of its problems by pulling things up to her level.

The Barbara Stanwyck Show had good directors—among them Robert Florey, David Lowell Rich, Jacques Tourneur and Richard Whorf. It was exquisitely photographed—mostly by Hal Mohr and Nicholas Musuraca. And it was loaded with top guest stars. But it also had an enemy: time. Time is always a hindrance to perfection in the fast-paced medium of television but, on a half-hour show, it poses special problems. Robert Florey states that the segments were shot in three days—sometimes prepared in one. And writer Albert Beich (who did a number of scripts for the series) points out that "to tell a decent story in half an hour is not easy."

One of the most successful of the show's segments involved a little borrowing from a sure-fire plot. Called "Confession" (with a teleplay by Ellis St. Joseph from a story by Gavin Lambert) it was a melodrama "in the manner of *Double Indemnity*" and allowed Stanwyck and Lee Marvin to have a great time with familiar roles.

This time it is Stanwyck who does the narrating. The film opens with a shot of her legs (no anklet) as she sits in the police station in her widow's weeds, telling how she killed Marvin. Marvin was a crooked lawyer—"an ambulance chaser"—and their motives for getting rid of Stanwyck's husband were, of course, greed and lust.

Flashbacks show the classic scenes on the sofa of Marvin's cheap apartment—but there is one wonderful surprise. The apartment is built over a merry-go-round. Hiding out from the police, Stanwyck is about ready to go up the wall anyway when, with a crash, the merry-go-round opens—subjecting her to a never-ending blare of music. Shots of her torture—and of the merry-go-round in full swing—are a macabre little touch that will not be forgotten by anyone who has seen them.

About those Westerns that Stanwyck "slipped in." One is called "A Man's Game" (written by David Harmon and Albert Beich) and Stanwyck introduces it with the words

> Tonight we place our tongue in cheek and present a gentle spoof of the old West. You know the West I mean. Where every man is a fast-draw gunslinger, and every lady works in a saloon. My role? Well, believe it or not, I play the sheriff—but don't take it all too seriously.

The show pokes plenty of fun—with freeze-frame photography and a dry Stanwyck narrating. Seems the town has trouble keeping sheriffs. Stanwyck refers to one who walks into her saloon: "That's our star-crossed sheriff—agile, but marked for tragedy." He is gunned down in short order and a character announces: "That's the third sheriff in six months. Job's open again." A challenge, and the fact that no one else will take it, throws the job Stanwyck's way. She emerges, properly dressed, with a "How d'ya like *that* outfit, hah? That's how *all* lady sheriffs dressed in those days" and rides off to take a jujitsu lesson. Her sense of humor—and everyone else's—has a ball. But there is undoubtedly method in her madness. She may be kidding about a lady playing a rugged role, but she *is* playing one—and well.

Jacques Tourneur, who directed the largest number of segments of *The Barbara Stanwyck Show*, says:

The Barbara Stanwyck Show—"The Triple C"

The Barbara Stanwyck Show—*as Little Joe in* "Dragon By the Tail," *with George Givot*

◄ The Barbara Stanwyck Show—"Good Citizen"

The Barbara Stanwyck Show—"The Secret of Mrs. Randall," *with Bruce Gordon*

The Barbara Stanwyck Show—"Confession"▷

Outstanding Actress in an Anthology Series.
Emmy Award for The Barbara Stanwyck Show—*1961*

I can give you no details, as I have forgotten all those pictures.

But I can tell you that Barbara is one hell of a hard worker, an artisan, a driver. She lives only for two things, and both of them are work.

We were both of the same mold. I, too, am a person who lives only for his work. We had a mutual admiration society going. We never met socially, but every day on the set at seven in the morning she would say, "Hey, you big fat Frenchman, get your big fanny (?) over here. Get the lead out . . ."

I am wearing a pair of tasteful gold cufflinks, properly inscribed, which she gave me in a moment of weakness. I told her I always wear short sleeves, but that—since they were a present from her—I would have my wrists pierced.

B. S. is quite a gal, and I am proud to have known her.

Many pros who had worked with Stanwyck earlier joined her on this show. Joan Blondell was delighted to be one of them. As she puts it, Stanwyck is "a special lady who knows what she is doing. She gives everything that she has to give."

Ralph Bellamy remembers that

She had finished another story in the series the day before, and she had had an unpleasant experience with a guest star—the details of which I never knew. It had been a blow and a disappointment which she and the director discussed at length between scenes. But when it came time to do a scene on the new one, on which I was working, all her problems and emotional upsets disappeared, and her concentration was completely on the scene at hand.

An anthology show (which requires different actors for each segment) is not all roses for its star, as Bellamy's comment indicates. And Stanwyck had her share of frustrations. She recalled one for the *Toronto Telegram* in 1965—concerning a performer from The Actors' Studio who

. . . kept mumbling away and I just didn't know what the hell he was talking about. I finally told him, "Look, apparently you're pleasing the director, but do me just one favor. LET ME HEAR MY CUE! That's not too much to ask, is it? Just so I won't have to stand around like an idiot and people think I've forgotten MY lines!"

As Albert Beich, who witnessed the incident, puts it: "He obeyed with alacrity."

Beich created a character (used in three segments of the show) that was an excellent one for Stanwyck. This was "Little Joe"—an American importer-exporter in the Orient who "gambles with everything except her American passport." Stanwyck and the producers wanted Little Joe for a series, and Beich explains:

The idea for the character came from life. I was on a freighter trip around the world working on a play, *The Man In The Dog Suit*, when I wandered into a bar in Manila. Concealed behind some innocent-looking mahogany paneling was a high-class gambling room. In it was an attractive, self-assured, hard-eyed American girl in her twenties, working for the house, dealing blackjack. She was all business and very very good at her trade. Later, while I was writing some of the Stanwyck shows and the producers were looking for spin-offs, the image of the girl under the overhead lights came back to me. I named her Little Joe. She had style and authority, and the idea of a lady adventurer wandering around the Orient getting into all sorts of melodrama seemed a good one.

Stanwyck was delightful as Little Joe. The setup allowed her to be capable, shrewd and fast-moving, to use her sense of humor, and to function in an atmosphere charged with excitement. She seemed very much at home. But the show never made it—for a number of reasons which Beich quotes from the producers involved:

One said it was a question of economics—anthology shows being expensive, requiring different sets and casts each week. *Little Joe* was, in effect, an anthology-type show, since Stanwyck would be the only continuing player, more or less. To do it right, not only would Stanwyck and a director have to go to Hong Kong, but actors would have to be flown there as well, since no pool of talent existed in the Orient. At the time the logistics of the whole thing just seemed to NBC to be too formidable. They'd much prefer a three-camera show in Hollywood. There was also the question of editing, scoring and dubbing. Who was to do that, and where?

Another said that NBC felt that a half-hour show was not good enough for Stanwyck. That she was the kind of actress who needed an hour or an hour and a half. Acting room, as he put it.

Expansion of the show's running time would only have added to its cost. And thus a project with really good potential for Stanwyck never got off the ground.

The Barbara Stanwyck Show was cancelled at the end of its first season—despite the fact that Stanwyck won an Emmy as "Outstanding Actress in an Anthology Series." Concerning the executives who had made the decision, Stanwyck told columnist Joe Hyams:

> I don't know who "they" are, but they've decreed no more women on television. The only woman who will be left next year is Donna Reed. The rest of us have been dropped—Loretta Young, June Allyson, Dinah Shore, Ann Sothern and myself. And we all had good ratings.
>
> As I understand it "they" want action shows and have a theory that women don't do action. The fact is I'm the best action actress in the world. I can do horse drags and jump off buildings, and I have the scars to prove it.

At this point, fortunately, a good screen role came her way and, as she has put it: "It was a chance to go back to pictures and see what would happen." Concerning *Walk On the Wild Side*, Stanwyck "always felt it could have been a damn good picture but it just didn't work out."

The film's failure to be a huge success was in no way the fault of its actors. It seemed to be in the writing—or rather all of the rewriting that took place. Laurence Harvey told *Variety* at the time that "the original script was excellent and had the force of the book" but that the producer "called in new writers" who watered it down. As the *New York Herald Tribune* phrased it:

> The movie has over-simplified and over-stated [Nelson] Algren's novel. . . . The compassion, the sense of personal waste, that could make the film unusual and penetrating . . . is crowded out by constant underlining [and] melodramatic clichés.

In any event, Stanwyck's work doesn't suffer from any of this. As the madam of the "Doll House," a high-class New Orleans bordello (She said at the time: "Chalk up another first for Stanwyck!") it is her job to see that anything that comes between her and one of her beautiful girls (Capucine) is removed swiftly and by whatever method is necessary.

There are a lot of things for Stanwyck to play here: attraction to the girl, aversion to a legless husband, impatience and frustration when she is crossed. She is a power figure: intelligent, capable, cruel and—in less guarded moments—vulnerable. The role is a meaty one and Stanwyck makes it exciting. It brought her back to the screen in fine form.

Anne Baxter, working with Stanwyck for the first time, became very fond of her and stated in *Portrait: Barbara Stanwyck:*

> We had very little to do together. But we talked on the set and that sort of thing, and I happened—which was a secret—to be very pregnant at the time with my second child, Melissa. I was in agony because I had a 22-inch belt and kept calling the doctor to say "Will I hurt the child?" And I unburdened to Barbara. She's that kind of person. You feel that you can trust her always. And she didn't tell anyone, but she thought it was awfully funny, and was terribly interested. She loves children.

Speaking today, Anne Baxter adds:

> I was in one scene with Miss Stanwyck, which was a retake of a retake of a retake: the last scene in the picture where Laurence Harvey is in bed. The one thing I can remember that specifically had to do with Miss Stanwyck's professionalism—which is of the highest caliber—was her utter fury at Laurence Harvey's late arrival on the set. She tongue-lashed him without mercy and, from that moment on, he was on time!

Laurence Harvey apparently remembers the incident well, for his recollection of working with Barbara Stanwyck—quoted in its entirety—is:

> Miss Stanwyck is one of the most startling and professional women I have ever worked with.
>
> She had a great air of honesty and directness about her, and her relationship with cast and crew was totally unpretentious . . . in fact I could never quite decide what side of the camera she was working on!

Photo by John Engstead

Walk On the Wild Side, *with Richard Rust,*
Donald Barry and Anne Baxter

◄ Walk On the Wild Side

Walk On the Wild Side, *with Richard Rust*
and Donald Barry

Roustabout, *with Elvis Presley*

Roustabout

◁ Roustabout

Returning to television, Stanwyck guest-starred on a number of shows—among them *Rawhide, The Untouchables* and *Wagon Train. Wagon Train* was a special favorite. She loved doing it and appeared in four segments—three of which were directed by Virgil Vogel (who would later be *The Big Valley*'s top director). In "The Molly Kincaid Story," she was more than a little impressive cracking a bullwhip— not an easy thing for a small person to do. Vogel states: "She became quite proficient with the bull-whip." But accidents happen, and he adds: "On the third day of shooting, the tip of the whip caught her eyelid. When we finished shooting six days later, her eye was almost swollen shut from infection."

In 1963, Stanwyck was given a Special Award by The Professional Photographers of California who named her "The First Lady of the Camera." The award was for still work and she has said: "I guess they just got to the S's—I never knew how I got it." A look at the photographs in this book ought to give some indication of how she got it.

Back at Paramount in 1964, Stanwyck was out-fitted for *Roustabout* in blue jeans by Edith Head. Columnist Dave Smith, visiting the set, was impressed with her youthful appearance—then told himself:

> Come off it, bub. Miss Stanwyck's no pullet any more, and she'd be the last to deny it. But she's a long way from the moulting season, too.

This led him to come up with a pretty good observation:

> Somewhere in between is a woman who is 56 and doesn't hide it, who has covered plenty of mileage but doesn't show it, who has had some rough breaks and doesn't crab about it, and who knows the score and doesn't forget it.

She also knew a good opportunity when it presented itself. Stanwyck is a smart business woman, and she realized that doing a picture with Elvis Presley would expose her to a younger group of fans who might not have seen her before. As it turned out, she had a good time too. She discussed the experience with Bill Hahn for WNAC in Boston:

> Hahn: You worked with Elvis Presley in *Roustabout*. Did this have an influence on your musical tastes at all?

> Stanwyck: (laughing) As a matter of fact, I had never seen Elvis Presley in a picture. But I had worked for Hal Wallis, the producer, many times. And when he called me up and said that he had a part in a picture, and mentioned Elvis Presley—I thought, well, for heaven's sake, what would I do in an Elvis Presley film? I can't sing. I can't dance.

> Hahn: What do you mean, you can't dance?

> Stanwyck: Ohhhhh, no. Oh, no. But he said let me send you a script because it's the owner of a broken-down carnival and so forth. Well, I liked it. And the idea of working with Mr. Presley intrigued me because that would bring me into a younger audience than I'm accustomed to. And I thought this would be rather fun. Mr. Wallis said that he was a wonderful person to work with and, by golly, he is. His manners are impeccable, he is on time, he knows his lines, he asks for nothing—nothing outside of what any other actor or actress wants.

> Hahn: That's an interesting comment.

> Stanwyck: Yes, it is. Because so many people expect the other—the swelled head and all that sort of thing. As a matter of fact, very honestly, so did I. It is *not* the case.

As for the film, *The New York Times* said:

> It has three assets. One is Mr. Presley, perfectly cast and perfectly at ease, as a knockabout, leathery young derelict who links up with a small-time transient midway. It also has, as the carnival owner, the professional seasoning of Barbara Stanwyck. Welcome back, Miss Stanwyck, and where on earth have you been? And while the carnival canvas yields little in the way of dramatic substance, it does cue in 11 songs.

When producer-director William Castle signed his stars for *The Night Walker*, he announced:

> I consider this one of the most dramatic castings of many years. I couldn't be more pleased that these two great stars consented to do this drama for me.

As Stanwyck explained the casting of the film to Bill Hahn:

> I heard from Mr. Castle—'round about March or

The Night Walker, with Robert Taylor

April—and he said, "I have a good screenplay. At least, I think it's good. Would you read it?" I said, "I would be delighted to read it." He had just returned from Australia where he had purchased the property. And I read it and was rather fascinated by it.

A few days later he called and said, "I had a wonderful idea and I want to throw it at you and see what you think. What do you think of Robert Taylor in the part of the attorney?" And I said, "Well *I* think it's wonderful but you'd better ask Mr. Taylor how he feels about it." And so he called Bob and sent him the script and Bob said the same thing—so it was as simple as that.

Stanwyck went on to say that the film was "a shocker suspense story. It is not a horror film, because [she was laughing] even I would be too scared to do a horror film!" It's the story of "a woman who lives between dreams and reality and becomes so confused she doesn't know which is which." Fortunately, although there are elements of horror *in* the film, Stanwyck is not asked for anything in this vein herself. The worst she must do is scream her lungs out.

Stanwyck is excellent in *The Night Walker*. Her role is a highly emotional one and she is deeply involved in it—but the fact that the character is confused and unable to orient herself to what is happening allows Stanwyck to play with a fragility and softness which set her apart from her surroundings. She works with grace, dignity and restraint.

Harold E. Stine, who photographed the picture, says:

In 1964 I photographed *A House Is Not a Home* with Shelley Winters. Robert Taylor was her leading man, and we became good friends. He liked my work and told me he was going to do another picture right away and would like me to film it. He talked to Bill Castle and, with this recommendation, I was practically hired by telephone. Mr. Castle set up a meeting with Miss Stanwyck and that's when we met for the first time.

Arrangements were made to shoot some tests of her. She said this would be a good way for us to get acquainted. She was most cooperative. She gave me the feeling that she was working for me.

During the production we got along just great. I had talked to a lot of people in time past and they had nothing but praise for her and I now join them.

William Castle, equally happy about the whole thing, says:

Her very presence on a set inspired. Her feeling of camaraderie toward everyone she worked with—and the love of the entire crew, as they called her Missy, was something to behold. I used to watch in awe and amazement as the electricians, high up in the rafters, shouted down, "Hi, Missy!" She would look up and shout back with warmth.

In our work, I felt we were simpatico—something I rarely experienced with an actress, and I have worked with the best. It is a privilege to say I knew, loved and directed Barbara Stanwyck.

In late 1964, Stanwyck began an extensive promotion tour with Castle for the film. The *Toronto Telegram*'s direct question "Why?" got a direct answer: "Because I own a percentage of this picture, along with Bob and Mr. Castle. I hope it does well at the box office." Her visits to various cities were heralded by another "appearance" that she had agreed to earlier—for similar reasons—her coffee commercial. As she explained the latter to Vernon Scott for the March 1965 issue of *McCall's*:

One day, Norman Brokaw, my agent, called to tell me of the offer. And I answered as though I were Catherine of Russia or Bette Davis in *Elizabeth and Essex*—"Do a COMMERCIAL?"

"Think about it," Brokaw said.

"Why?" I demanded. . . . "What for?" I meant, he needn't bother. But, as he is a practical, literal man—and my agent—my "What for?" got a practical answer. He quoted a very tidy sum—real folding money. And once more he added, "Think about it."

Next day, he called with an even bigger offer! I said, "You're kidding!"

This was getting monotonous. But I said to myself, let's face it. . . . Sponsors obviously care more about a ninety-second commercial and *want* to pay you more than any guest star gets for a ninety-minute *acting* performance. And if you don't do it, somebody else will. Why let someone else laugh all the way to the bank?

When Brokaw called the next day, he said, "They'll even remodel your kitchen."

The Night Walker

I needed my kitchen remodeled as much as I need another hole in my head, but—don't ask me why—that did it.

Stanwyck then remembered Billy Wilder's challenge to her when she had held back on another first: the heavy in *Double Indemnity* ("What are you, an actress or a mouse?") and pointed out that she had "felt it was safe to assume I wasn't a mouse. I felt the same way about the commercial."

Photo by John Engstead

CHAPTER SEVENTEEN

This was to be the big season for comedy. Everybody was to fall on the floor laughing. Well, everybody fell on the floor, but they weren't laughing. So we're falling back on Westerns.

Stanwyck's comment to the *New York Journal-American* in 1965 concerned the pilot she had made for *The Big Valley*. The time was right at last for her to play the "blood and guts" matriarch of the Western series she had wanted. She said:

When I was a little girl nothing fascinated me more than the history of our West. I loved the cowboy and Indian stories, but more than that, I marveled at the pioneers. The real people who went into the wilderness with little other than their courage. I still love everything about the West—the people, the land, everything.

Some producers think women did nothing in those days except keep house and have children. But, if you read your history, they did a lot more than that. They were in cattle drives. They were *there*.

I try to make Victoria Barkley as human as possible. She doesn't come waltzing down the staircase in calico to inquire as to the progress of the cattle. She's an old broad who combines elegance with guts.

The Big Valley was created for Barbara Stanwyck in 1961, right after her anthology show. As she told it:

Lou Edelman, my producer [for the anthology] and a writer, A. I. Bezzerides, developed the idea but they couldn't sell the show because it had a woman star. That was the year women went out of style on television.

Later, the idea was sold to Four-Star Productions, and we made a pilot late in 1964. The original cast, idea and theme [stayed] the same.

As is well known, the series centers around the wealthy and powerful Barkley family running their ranch in the San Joaquin Valley in the 1870s and helping settlers about them. Linda Evans, Richard Long and Peter Breck play Stanwyck's children, and Lee Majors is the illegitimate son of her late husband. (Another son, Charles Brilles—generally away at college—was cut from the show during the first season.) Stanwyck said:

I thought it would be much more interesting to have Lee play the *widow's* illegitimate son, but the network was horrified at the idea.

In its four-year run, *The Big Valley* piled up 112 segments. Stanwyck appeared in all but seven—through an arrangement which had her either carrying an episode completely, sharing it with a guest star or other member of the family, or appearing briefly when someone else carried it.

The show got off to a weak start and was slammed by critics. But, as Stanwyck told columnist Bob Thomas:

Bad reviews don't hurt. By the time the review appears in print, the viewer has seen the show already. And he's just as liable to be defensive about a rap, figuring "That show wasn't as bad as all that."

In the end, it's the viewers themselves who decide whether a show is a hit or not. They don't need any help to make up their minds.

And that's exactly what happened. The audience loved the show—and continues to love it in syndication, four years after "those in power" dropped it.

However, early critical comment that referred to a female *"Bonanza"* and called Stanwyck "a Lorne Greene with skirts" did gripe her—and she threw a number of comments back. She made it clear that the show was "not patterned after *Bonanza* at all," and that she played a strong Victoria because pioneer women *were* strong and because "I don't want to become the Loretta Young of the West. I don't mean that to be nasty but just as a quick description." As to any comparison of the Barkley and Cartwright families, she said:

Our family is much tougher. My sons are strong. They're real men. This is not one of those "Mother Knows Best" things. Hell, I wouldn't play one. Our family behaves like any normal family. We fight, argue, discuss things. We're not like some of the TV families today. I don't know where the hell these people are. I never see anybody like them in real life. The woman I'm playing has plenty of battles with her boys. She's a very vital person. So are her sons. They all have minds of their own.

This is what makes the show interesting. The characters are part of a family, but they are individuals. Fights, humor, warmth—and a philosophy holding it all together—are presented realistically and with spirit. The actors have strong personalities. They adjusted to each other and shaped their roles quickly. And they continued to grow in them.

Heading things with a firm and vivid portrayal, Stanwyck was very much in her glory. She was playing a woman she could admire, she understood her thoroughly, and she developed her into a person. Victoria Barkley is a character that will remain as strongly associated with Stanwyck as any she has ever created. Not because she played her for so long, but because she did her so well.

There is a danger in playing one role for four years. *The Big Valley* is cut to a pattern. There are repetitious scenes and situations. And it would have been possible to get in a rut—to lose the spark that keeps a character fresh. Study of Stanwyck's performances shows how skillfully she avoided this. She is full of surprises. Just when you think you've seen them all, she tosses you a new reading or reaction. She makes them—as she has all her life—just a bit different from what you might have expected. And, always, they are right.

Stanwyck was able to tackle a little of everything in this series: humorous episodes like "The Great Safe Robbery"; moving ones such as "Boots With My Father's Name," "Teacher of Outlaws" and "The Disappearance"; terrific fights such as those in "The Challenge" and "The Emperor of Rice"; and perils to rival any of Pearl White's in "Four Days to Furnace Hill," "Alias Nellie Handly," "Earthquake," "The Long Ride" and "Ambush." These are only a few of her high points. And—whether she is carrying an episode or not—her superb blending of compassion, "elegance and guts" brightens a scene whenever she appears.

A television series is not easy work. Outlining her schedule in 1968, Stanwyck said:

> If we're shooting inside the studio, I get up at 4:30 in the morning and we start shooting at 8 and I get home maybe 7:30 or 8 o'clock at night. If we're on location, which we are two days a week, that's 3:30 in the morning and maybe I get home around 8:30.

Weekends, she added, were reserved for studying scripts. She was always prepared a week in advance. While she was filming one show, she would have learned the next. The discipline required for this was recognized and adhered to. She explained:

> I prepare for a part. I don't try to "get by." You can't fool those damned cameras. If I'm exhausted at the end of the day, I go home and rest up for the next one.

And she had no complaints about any of the demands. As she put it:

> We do 26 shows in 26 weeks and no one bothers to count the hours. In a television series such as ours, you are actually making 26 very fast movies. The script is there, the cameras are there and you are there.

One of the greatest delights for Stanwyck on this show was the physical action. *Portrait: Barbara Stanwyck* showed her riding the camera car as it followed the action of a performer because

> It's very exciting. As many years as I've been in pictures, I still get a big kick out of watching all these stunts being done. I still enjoy it.

"Doing" was even more exciting for her than "watching." And rarely could a director hold her back. Virgil Vogel, who directed 45 episodes of *The Big Valley* (Stanwyck says in *Portrait:* "I guess Mr. Vogel knows as much about making Westerns as the old master, John Ford") states:

> As all directors who have worked with Miss Stanwyck, I fell in love with her, and no one likes to see a loved one in danger. Many times I wished she would let me double her, but she knew the camera would have to be farther away and the stunt wouldn't be as good, so Barbara did it. Even though at all times there was a stunt person standing by.

Vogel speaks of Stanwyck's ability to handle stunts:

> To be a good stunt person you first have to be courageous. No physical action ever frightened Barbara. She has as much courage as any person I have ever known. She also had great confidence I would give her all the protection possible. I checked each stunt carefully, but in her extreme dedication to her work she always gave a little more than she was instructed to do. If I asked her to jump eight feet she would do ten.

As Victoria Barkley in The Big Valley

The Big Valley—"By Force and Violence"

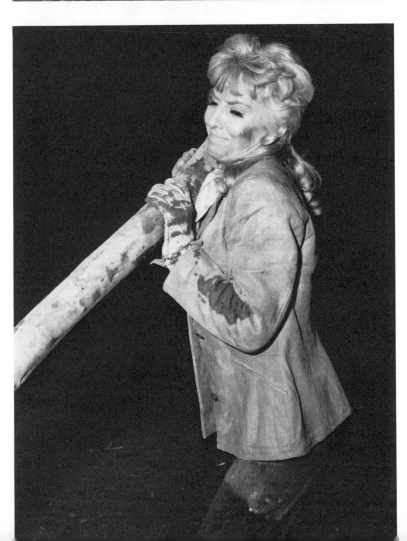

The Big Valley, *with Linda Evans*

The Big Valley, *with Peter Breck
and Richard Long*

◁ The Big Valley, *with Lee Majors*

The most dangerous stunt that Stanwyck did for Vogel was the waist drag. In "Four Days to Furnace Hill," she is lassoed around her waist, pulled to the ground, and dragged by the horse of the man who has captured her. Vogel says:

> I didn't know until the shooting day was over that she was ill with the flu. The ground was very rough with buried sharp, jagged rocks that were difficult to dig out. The crew prepared about fifty feet of it as well as they could. I checked it very carefully and explained to her that under no circumstances was she to hold on after she passed the cleared area. Of course Barbara dragged *150 feet.* Lucky we had two cameras on it. I ran in front of one yelling for her to let go—it was a great shot.

Stanwyck fought a lot of battles in this series and, although illusion helped them, she did undergo a fair amount of roughing up—which she gave back with vigor. Vogel explains:

> Generally she fought with stunt men who are very tough. She gave them all they could handle. The crew always enjoyed this and would encourage Barbara to "get him"—this would spur her to greater effort and if the stunt man wasn't very careful, he couldn't even get a draw.

As for her riding, Vogel says: "Barbara is an excellent horsewoman." She did use a double for fast mounting but this is "because she is so tiny it is difficult for her to do a fast mount." (For anyone who's wondering how tiny: 5'4" and 110 pounds.)

Although, fortunately, Stanwyck was never seriously injured by a stunt, she did not come away without some uneasy experiences. Stunts are a gamble no matter how capable you are or how carefully they are planned. In "Earthquake"—an episode in which she is buried in the rubble of a collapsing church—the building was rigged with cut beams that would break loose at the touch of a finger, and chutes loaded with "rock" —a material that is light but not so light that you would want it to fall on you. Stanwyck said she would like to do the scene herself if they were sure it was safe. The chutes were high above the set and—at a signal—one of them was to bring rocks down between her and the camera. Something went wrong and a rock hit her on the head and she passed out. Since she was supposed to fall to the ground, nobody thought much about it until one of her co-stars real-

ized she'd been there longer than she should have and rushed in to get her. Although Stanwyck did not like the hairpiece she wore in the show's first season, it's a good thing she had not yet gotten rid of it, because it was a help to her that day.

There were other accidents. Stanwyck knows, for instance, what it is like to be thrown from a horse. But, in general, such occurrences were rare. She was capable; animals and setups were carefully selected and checked out; and she battled successfully with man and beast for four years.

A much more common situation—and one that may have bothered her more—was the lowly retake, described in a light treatment by writer John Stanley in the *San Francisco Sunday Examiner & Chronicle* after a 1968 visit to the set:

> Breakfast scenes [Stanwyck had told him earlier] are eternally painful because you must keep eating over and over for retakes. And this morning . . . are there retakes.
>
> Dish out the eggs, chew the ham. Cut! Replace the eggs on the silver platter, fetch fresh ham. Roll 'em!
>
> [The reason for all the trouble on this particular morning is the condition of Stanwyck's co-stars.] The night before they were honorary guests at a raucous celebration where liquids flowed freely. . . . They're still in a state of semi-euphoria.
>
> Scene 410, Take Four. Which means the breakfast has already been interrupted three times. Once, because Long got his line twisted: "You could have been shot stone dead cold" instead of "stone cold dead."
>
> Then, because someone noticed Majors' fly was unzipped and decided to add that little observation to the dialogue. Again, when Long began his line "Hell hath no fury like a . . ." and then broke down guffawing.
>
> Nobody, however, is too disturbed, including the director. He's laughing too. The good humor is contagious because, says a publicity man, "this is a happy set." Long caps it with "What do we care? Jules (referring to a producer) is money." More rollicking.
>
> Barbara, who didn't attend the party and got a good night's rest, has been pretty straight-faced through most of this. With Take Four, however . . . "Why don't we all let Heath eat his breakfast in peace" is her line, but she says it in such a manner that she must conclude with a fit of laughter.

The Big Valley—"Alias Nellie Handly"

The Big Valley, *with James Gregory*

A much-needed break is called. Barbara scrapes the eggs back on the platter and hands it to Bud Hollis, the property manager. . . . "Sometimes if the retakes get heavy on eating scenes he has to leave the studio to buy more eggs and ham," she explains.

[After the break] a bell rings. A stagehand hustles [her] back to the set. Hopefully, everyone has quieted down enough so the scene can now be finished. Barbara dishes herself some eggs and ham while inquiring as to how everyone feels this morning. Peter Breck starts to say he's fine but blows his line, sputtering into his raised glass of orange juice. Barbara dutifully scrapes the eggs and ham back onto their respective platters.

On Take 6 of Scene 410, all goes perfectly. Nobody sputters, quips or breaks down laughing. The director places his hands on his hips. "Well," he says.

"Thank God," says Barbara, pushing her chair back from the table. "One more piece of ham and I swear, I would have choked to death."

Four years together is a long time and, for the most part, cast and crew found it a pleasant one. Peter Breck said in *Portrait*: "There's no conflict on this set. Miss Stanwyck has a great rapport with all of us, as we do with her, because she is a pro." And Richard Long continued:

When you have a star of Barbara's proportion that has stayed a *major* star for as long as she has and as deservedly as she has, you're dealing with quite a human being. It's a treat to work with her, and I say that most sincerely. But there's more to it than that. She not only has great strength and stamina and is vitally interested in what she's doing. She's vitally interested in other people. [There are performers who] hog the camera or the moment to the detriment of the scene or the story—in other words, reduce it to their personality rather than play it honestly as it should be done. Barbara has *never* been guilty of this in our association. She believes in the scene, and she believes in the quality of other people's performances and strives to help those come about.

Guest stars were a large part of the show and James Gregory, who starred opposite Stanwyck in four episodes, says:

The set was always relaxed when we worked together—and it was quite a day when Kent, the wardrobe man, put a life-like dummy in her dressing room bathroom (we had used it in a shot) propped on the "commode," do we say? It was discovered by Barbara's companion, Harriett, who almost had a heart attack. Kent disappeared for the rest of the day, or Barbara might've murdered him. But the next day we all had a good laff about it.

About her insisting on doing most of her own stunts: ripped her leg open in one scene while riding horseback through a narrow rock pass. Gave us all some anxious moments.

Never any big "star complex"—always the common touch. Knew the first names of all the crew and the smallest bit actor.

Yeah, she's a "great broad" and I sure hope to get the chance to work with her again.

Recognition for what she has given to the entertainment industry began coming thick and fast to Barbara Stanwyck following *The Big Valley*'s first season. In 1959, *Photoplay* magazine had presented her with a Special Gold Medal Award: "For meeting, with simplicity, honesty, and superb craftsmanship, the challenges of starring roles in 75 motion pictures; for giving wise and sympathetic counsel to newcomers." In 1966, they added their Editors' Award: "To the 'Eternal Star' whose glamour, talent and professionalism both on and off the screen have thrilled millions of fans throughout the years." And in 1967 and 1968, fans voted her two more Gold Medals as *Photoplay*'s "Most Popular Female Star." *TV-Radio Mirror*'s National Television Critics' Poll named her 1966's "Best Dramatic Actress in Television."

Once again, the coveted Emmy was hers. She won it in 1966—the first year of *The Big Valley*—as "Outstanding Actress in a Dramatic Series." And she was nominated again in 1967 and 1968.

The Big Valley was cancelled prematurely in 1969 (mostly because of bad ratings caused by a wrong time slot)—but syndication has kept it on the screen ever since with a popularity that astounds even its producers who "knew it was a good show." In 1969, Four Star International announced that *The Big Valley* was directly attributable to their more than doubling their income during that year. In 1971, the show's producers thought it would "probably break the huge gross records of our other series *The Rifleman*." And, at the end of 1972, *Variety* reported that *The Big Valley* was being recycled for another syndication run because "it is consistently at the top of the list of ALL the off network hour shows in syndication."

The Big Valley, *with Linda Evans, Lee Majors,*
Peter Breck, Richard Long

Barbara Stanwyck has won a lot of awards and she is, rightly, proud of them all. But one that holds a special meaning for her is the Screen Actors Guild Award presented in 1966. It is an award for excellence not only as an actress but as a human being.

Governor Ronald Reagan (then Governor-elect) who made the presentation, says:

Nothing illustrates more her personality and attitude. Those who knew her were concerned that if she suspected she was getting an award she wouldn't be there, so they invited her to come down and present the award to me. She was standing off-stage, fully expecting to come out and make the presentation of the award to me, when she heard me making the presentation to her.

In his speech, Reagan said:

The Screen Actors Guild Award is not presented just for longtime excellence on screen. It should be called, perhaps, an above-and-beyond award, because it is given for outstanding achievement in fostering the finest ideals of the acting profession.

The individual to be honored has given of herself in unpublished works of charity and good citizenship. I think there are few among us of her fellow performers or in the public who have any comprehension of the extent of this artist's devotion to those who are handicapped by blindness, human misery and poverty, both here and abroad. . . .

So for performance of [our] craft, as well as for performance as a citizen, this . . . award is [being] presented from actors to an actor, and I am very proud to present someone whom so many of us have worked with; we have known her in this profession as truly a professional and an exponent of our art and craft of the best. Barbara Stanwyck.

A much-moved Stanwyck, who had listened to the speech from the wings, walked on stage—where Reagan embraced her—and managed, through her tears, to say: "This is the first time I have been kissed by a Governor." After accepting the award, she said:

I am very, very proud at this moment. I love our profession very much. I love our people in it. I always have and I always will. And whatever little contribution I can make to the profession, or to anything, for that matter, I am very proud to do so.

It is a long road. There are a lot of bumps and rocks in it, but this kind of evens it all out, when an event like this happens in your life. From a very proud and grateful heart, thank you very much.

Outstanding Actress in a Dramatic Series.
Emmy Award for **The Big Valley**—*1966*

The Screen Actors Guild Annual Award—1966

Barbara Stanwyck's reaction when she learned
the award was being given to her

Ronald Reagan's presentation of the award

I've been in this business since Noah built the ark. But television is not like motion pictures. It requires much more professionalism. You've got to know what you're doing or you'll be trampled to death. And the hours are much tougher. You have to be some kind of a nut to enjoy it.

Few film stars have made the adjustment from the large to the small screen as successfully as Barbara Stanwyck. The hours and pace she speaks of don't bother her. And, since she is a one-take actress, she is able to make the quality of her acting as good on TV as it is in films. In fact, those who have been lucky enough to have her accept a television role know she has been its life's blood.

As of this writing, Stanwyck has made three TV movies. The first was aired in 1970, the second in 1971, and the third in 1973, shortly before this book went to press.

Her first, *The House That Wouldn't Die,* is a simple and effectively handled ghost story. An old house that Stanwyck has inherited gives trouble to her and niece Katherine Winn, who becomes possessed by an uneasy spirit that roams it. Richard Egan and Michael Anderson Jr. join them in seances, attic and cellar investigations, and battles with mysterious forces.

The film is very much an ensemble one. Characters are dependent on each other and governed by the situation. Stanwyck plays a combination of softness and strength, charm and capability. Her velvet voice, intelligence and understanding produce a warm and interesting person. And her flawless technical polish deals easily with the script's requirements.

John Llewellyn Moxey, directing Stanwyck in this and her second TV movie, speaks of filming with her:

It has always been my practice to arrive on the set at least half an hour before the official crew call—to walk around it and think out my day's work. Not a day passed but that, when I arrived, there would be Barbara fully made-up, costumed, hair done, sitting on the set with a mug of black coffee, the inevitable cigarette between her teeth, lines all well learned, raring to go. When the crew arrived, she would greet them by name and have a joke or something pleasant or funny to say to each one. Needless to say, the crews *adored* her. I remember her stand-in on *The House That Wouldn't Die* saying to me that

it was hardly worth her while to be on the set, because for the last five to ten minutes of lighting (a boring, tedious process) Barbara would insist on standing in herself so that the cinematographer could get his lighting *absolutely* perfect.

One of the outstanding memories I have of her on that particular picture was her kindness to Kitty Winn. It was Kitty's second picture I think, and certainly her first TV movie. On the first day of shooting, Barbara insisted that her own make-up man and hairdresser take care of Kitty, and that Kitty ride with her in her limousine to the location. She took the time to explain some of the technicalities and tricks of the trade of film making to Kitty that I, because of the tightness of the 12 day schedule, didn't have the time to explain.

When it came to the fight sequences [the possessed niece attacks Stanwyck and tries to strangle her] again Barbara gave Kitty many tips. Of course Barbara did all the fight stuff herself, demanding to be hurled roughly into the shot from off camera. On one occasion she missed her timing and really bashed her face against a cupboard. [But] in spite of [this], there she was the next morning when I arrived on the set—made-up and ready to go as usual. When I asked how her face felt, she said: "It hurts a bit, but as long as it looks OK, let's get on with the job!"

A Taste of Evil, Stanwyck's second TV movie, shows her trying to drive daughter Barbara Parkins insane, have her confined, and collect the inheritance left to Parkins by a husband that preferred his daughter to his wife.

Throughout the first two-thirds of the film, Stanwyck is pleasant, helpful and infinitely patient. You never doubt that she loves her daughter, and this is part of the build-up. However, the minute she has shed her last tears as Parkins is taken away, a change occurs that rivals Jekyll and Hyde. Stanwyck completely reverses her character, or—rather—reveals it for the first time. The last 25 minutes of the film give her plenty of acting room—and she makes the most of it.

This is a role *made* for Stanwyck, and she rides the crest of the wave all the way. Working with Arthur O'Connell, a servant whom she has forced to help her get rid of the girl, she flares up into glorious malevolence—revealing how she hated Parkins and how she

will be equally merciless with O'Connell if he crosses her. There is anger; there is justification in a moving speech about the love she had for a husband who turned against her; and there is a woman fully enjoying power and revenge. Stanwyck comes up with brilliant line readings, alternating assurance and agitation with lightning speed.

She continues the excitement when, hounded by strange phone calls and events, she loads a shotgun and braves a storm in search of her tormentor. After she has shot O'Connell, been trapped into a confession, and lost out to the daughter, she tops the proceedings with a spectacular cross down a staircase and outside to a waiting police car where—in a last look up at the house—her composure is unruffled and her hate unchanged. It's a moment one remembers.

John Llewellyn Moxey, recalling the filming of the storm sequence, says:

Barbara was to run out of her house through the garden, carrying a shotgun, on a frantic search for the character who was trying to scare her. We were working in the grounds and house of a privately owned estate in Beverly Hills on a warm California night. The special effects man was having a field day with rain, lightning and wind. On the first take, Barbara ran out of the house along a winding path to an outbuilding—clad only in a dressing gown and slippers. I was quite happy with the shot and shouted "Cut!" A very rain-sodden Barbara came up to me and said: "You know, John, I think it would look a lot better if I took a fall in my frantic hurry—right when I pass in front of the camera." After some hemming and hawing from the producer, Aaron Spelling (who was concerned for her safety) she—much to my delight—got her way. She was given knee pads and was stomping about scraping the soles of the new slippers and walking through the fall she planned to do. The wind, rain, and lightning all started up again and off we went. She executed a realistic stumble right on the mark, and it did indeed help build suspense and drama in the scene.

After each shot she was bundled up with towels to keep her warm, and fortified with mugs of steaming hot chocolate. After the fall bit, we still had a fair amount of coverage to do—all in the pouring rain—and there she was, dripping wet—laughing and joking—until midnight when we finally wrapped for the day.

Photo by John Engstead

Barbara Stanwyck was three days into production on another TV movie—*Fitzgerald and Pride*—when circumstances brought her an experience unlike any she had known. *Fitzgerald and Pride* had been written to present her as a lawyer—a woman of intelligence and principles—and Stanwyck was enthusiastic about it. But cameras came to a halt in November of 1971 when she was suddenly hospitalized for removal of a kidney. So close was her brush with death that, after her recovery, she said: "For two days I was on the other side. It's very cold there and it's very dark. Thank God I came back."

When it was realized that she would need several months to recuperate, changes were made in the script of *Fitzgerald and Pride* and it was released under the title *Heat of Anger*, with Susan Hayward as its star.

By mid-1972, Stanwyck had bounced back, feeling and looking better than ever, as her next TV movie would show. This one—filmed in January of 1973 and called *The Letters*—is a trilogy of separate but connected stories dealing with letters lost in a plane crash and delivered a year late. John Forsythe heads the first story, Stanwyck the second, and Ida Lupino the third.

Variety called the film "1930s women's mag stuff with no attempt at real involvement" and said "Romanticism runs rampant with Barbara Stanwyck and Ida Lupino as only performers able to rise above the soapsuds."

Having dealt with her share of soapy scripts in the past, Stanwyck had no trouble with this one—which shows her as the overpowering sister of Dina Merrill, and the person who controls the fortune left to them. When ambitious concert pianist Leslie Nielsen learns who is in charge of the money, he switches his attentions from Merrill (who loves him) to Stanwyck (who sees through him, but enjoys tormenting her sister). Stanwyck and Nielsen are married. But she then falls in love with him herself and refuses to finance a concert tour that will separate them. Deprived of what he was after, he kills her. Retribution follows when a letter Stanwyck wrote, before her apparent suicide, shows Merrill he is guilty.

The story is a study in sibling rivalry based on childhood deprivation. Unloved by their father, Stanwyck developed a hatred of Merrill who *was* loved, and now uses her powerful personality to dominate her sister and deprive her of male attention. Crushing

The House That Wouldn't Die

A Taste of Evil, *with William Windom*

A Taste of Evil ▷

Merrill gives her satisfaction, as does the manner in which she chooses to do it. She treats Merrill like a child, savoring every indignity she thrusts upon her. And she is devious—working around and up to a blow before delivering it.

Stanwyck shows a woman whose pleasure comes from inflicting pain, whose nature is devoid of pity, and whose manner is at once sarcastic, indifferent, and magnetically fascinating. But there is another side to this character and, unfortunately, the audience saw very little of what Stanwyck did with it. When filming was completed, the movie ran 25 minutes over its allotted time, and cutting left some important scenes on the floor. Character development was sacrificed to exposition, making Stanwyck's Geraldine Parkington something of an enigma.

Despite her ability to "buy whatever I want" (and that includes men) this woman is an unhappy one. She has attempted suicide three times. Love for Nielsen brings about a change. Three key scenes—which would have shown her temperament before she knows love, and the softness in her after she has found it—were dropped. So clumsy was the editing that examination of the film shows lines like Stanwyck's "Darling, you are wonderful. After what happened yesterday—well, you're just wonderful" referring to nothing—because the scene between her and Nielsen that "happened yesterday" is missing.

The first omitted scene (valuable as embellishment which the movie badly needed) shows the similarities between Stanwyck and Nielsen as they begin their relationship. Both know what they are going into and why. In a concert hall, after she has bought out the house and he has played for her alone, she applauds. He, in turn, applauds as she bangs discordantly on the piano. Musical ability is not what either is praising.

The second scene is a transitional one, revealing a contented Stanwyck sailing with Nielsen on their honeymoon. And the third and most important is a love scene with Nielsen in which Stanwyck explains her previous behavior. It is this moment that is needed to justify her hardness. A softened Stanwyck does appear briefly toward the end of the film, and the origin of the change in her is explained in the letter she writes—but hearing about it is not the same as seeing it happen. The film's editing presented an uneven portrait of a character that—as written and acted—was properly balanced.

What came through in the footage that *was* shown was a new and revitalized Stanwyck who seemed to be experimenting with different techniques. There was an abundance of energy—of powers which the film drew upon only in part. There was a freer, less guarded interpretation than some she has used in past roles. There was a searching in her approach for the unusual, the startling, the complex. And, certainly, there was an actress who had fought a battle in her personal life, won out over difficult odds, and entered what may be an entirely new phase of her career. You have the feeling that there are unlimited depths in her—powers that have never been tapped. And this brief glimpse of them only leaves you wanting to see more.

The Letters was followed by an event of major importance for Stanwyck—one that was a fitting tribute to her achievements in a unique area. On April 28th, she was elected to the Hall of Fame of Great Western Performers in the National Cowboy Hall of Fame.

The Hall of Fame and Western Heritage Center in Oklahoma City is a museum sponsored by the 17 Western states. Along with paintings, artifacts and other items connected with the West, it contains commemorative exhibits honoring outstanding Western stars.

Each year, Wrangler awards (statuettes of a cowboy on a horse, copied from a Charles Russell sculpture) are given to actors, writers, musicians, etc., whose work has contributed to maintaining the heritage of the West.

The 13th annual presentation of the awards took place at twilight, with candlelight adding to the beauty of a black-tie dinner. The last artist to be honored was Stanwyck, whose introduction began with a showing of clips from her Western films and from *The Big Valley*. As she later described the footage: "It started out in the forties when I was young and it went bang—bang—bang—very fast, with still photos and a man narrating. Then it moved into the film clips. Whoever edited this did a sensational job because, when they started showing the stunts, it looked as if I was breaking my ass and my neck. The people oohed and aahed. It was quite stirring."

Stanwyck mounted the platform to a standing ovation and was presented with her award by Joel Mc-

The Letters, with Leslie Nielsen

Crea, president of the Center's board of directors. Struck by the dignity of the ceremony, she commented later on the sincerity and warmth that prevailed—and said the evening would remain in her memory as one of the finest of her life.

The Center's recognition for Stanwyck's devotion to the West, and for the pride she has taken in depicting it honestly, will culminate in a portrait painted of her, at a future date, to hang permanently in the Hall of Fame.

What can one add about Stanwyck that hasn't already been said? Maybe one thing. When Stanwyck was asked the "secret of her durable popularity" in 1967, she answered: "You have to learn to adjust. And the American public had a helluva lot to do with it. They're the ones who buy the tickets or tune in the TV."

It's true that the American public has stayed with Barbara Stanwyck. And her ability to adjust, as well as the completeness with which she gives herself to her work, is partly responsible. As Allan Dwan put it: "Her graceful transition from age to age is proof of her genius and dedication."

But there is one thing more that should be noted.

The reason people originally took to her—or are discovering her now for the first time—lies simply in what she is.

BARBARA
A Quick Impression on a Drunken Christmas Night
by David O. Selznick

Without guile . . .
O. Henry Style . . .
Evening prayers at home . . .
Corned Beef and Cabbage at the Court of
    Rome . . .
Minsky learns emotion . . .
Devotion . . .
Grant Wood on 48th Street . . .
Salome's Vine Street Beat . . .
Guff . . .
Helen Hayes gets tough . . .
Situation found . . .
Talent on a merry-go-round . . .
Rhapsody in Blue . . .
Spangles for Sunbonnet Sue . . .
The Manhattan Nation . . .
Appreciation . . .

Photo by John Engstead

AWARDS AND HONORS

The National Cowboy Hall of Fame and Western Heritage Center—Wrangler Award

1973 — For Outstanding Contribution To The West Through Motion Pictures. Elected to The Hall of Fame of Great Western Performers.

The Screen Actors Guild Award

1966 — For Outstanding Achievement in Fostering the Finest Ideals of the Acting Profession.

Television Academy of Arts and Sciences—Emmy

Awards
1966 — Outstanding Actress–Dramatic Series—*The Big Valley*
1961 — Outstanding Actress–Anthology Series—*The Barbara Stanwyck Show*
Nominations
1968 — Outstanding Actress–Dramatic Series—*The Big Valley*
1967 — Outstanding Actress–Dramatic Series—*The Big Valley*

Motion Picture Academy of Arts and Sciences—Oscar

Nominations
1948 — *Sorry, Wrong Number*
1944 — *Double Indemnity*
1941 — *Ball of Fire*
1937 — *Stella Dallas*

Photoplay Magazine Readers' Poll—Gold Medal Award

1968 — Most Popular Female Star
1967 — Most Popular Female Star

Hollywood Foreign Press Correspondents—Golden Globe Award

Nominations
1967 — Outstanding TV Personality—Female
1966 — Favorite Female Star—Television

American Cinema Editors' Award

1966 — Best Dramatic Actress in a Television Film ("Boots With My Father's Name"—*The Big Valley*)

Photoplay Magazine—Editors' Award

1966 — To the "Eternal Star" whose glamour, talent and professionalism both on and off the screen have thrilled millions of fans throughout the years.

TV-Radio Mirror—National Television Critics' Poll

1966 — Best Dramatic Actress in Television

Japan

1966 — Most Popular Television Actress

The City of Hope Biennial Awards

1965 — Heart Of The World Award
1963 — Golden Anniversary Award

Motion Picture Costumers' Award

1964 — For Artistry . . . and Unfailing Cooperation
1957 — For Artistry in the Use and Interpretation of Costumes

Professional Photographers of California—Special Award
1963 — The First Lady Of The Camera

Junior Philharmonic Orchestra Award
1963 — The World-Wide Star

Los Angeles Advertising Women's Award
1962 — The Woman Of The Year
1953 — The Woman Of The Year

Hollywood Women's Press Club—Golden Apple Award
1961 — Most Cooperative Actress

National Association of Women Lawyers Award
1961 — For Exceptional Performance in a Teleplay of *The Barbara Stanwyck Show* (as Little Joe in "Dragon By the Tail") and for her Patriotism.

Note: During this episode, Stanwyck departed from the script in one scene and became emotional in her defense of the United States against threats from a Red Chinese agent. Representative Francis E. Walter (D-Pa.) called the incident "encouraging, heart warming and inspiring" and read her ad-libbed speech into the *Congressional Record* for Jan. 16, 1961.

Radio and Television Women of Southern California Award
1961 — The Woman Most Outstanding on Television

B'nai B'rith Plaque
1961 — Most Consistently Outstanding Television Actress

Limelight Magazine
1961 — Best Actress in a Dramatic Series

Assistance League of Southern California Mannequins
1960 — Best Dressed Woman

Photoplay Magazine—Special Gold Medal Award
1959 — For meeting, with simplicity, honesty, and superb craftsmanship, the challenges of starring roles in 75 motion pictures; for giving wise and sympathetic counsel to newcomers.

Motion Picture Exhibitor—Laurel Award
1955 — *Executive Suite*
1954 — *Clash By Night*
1953 — *Titanic*

Browning, Montana
1954 — Full ceremonial adoption by the Blackfeet Indians. Induction into their Brave Dog Society.

Primer Plano Award—Estrella De Oro (Madrid)
1950 — Best Actress of Foreign Motion Pictures

FILMOGRAPHY

The following are listed by New York release date. Their order of production is given in the text.

1927. BROADWAY NIGHTS. *Producer:* Robert Kane. *Director:* Joseph C. Boyle. *Screenplay:* Forrest Halsey from a story by Norman Houston. *Photography:* Ernest Haller. *Cast:* Lois Wilson, Sam Hardy, Louis John Bartels, Philip Strange, Barbara Stanwyck (Dancer), Bunny Weldon. (First Nat, 6765 ft.)

1930. THE LOCKED DOOR. *Producer-director:* George Fitzmaurice. *Screenplay:* C. Gardner Sullivan from the play "The Sign on the Door" by Channing Pollock. *Dialogue:* George Scarborough. *Photography:* Ray June. *Editor:* Hal Kern. *Cast:* Rod La Rocque, Barbara Stanwyck (Ann Carter), William [stage] Boyd, Betty Bronson, Harry Stubbs, Harry Mestayer, Mack Swain, ZaSu Pitts, George Bunny. (UA, 74 min.)

1930. MEXICALI ROSE. *Producer:* Harry Cohn. *Director:* Erle C. Kenton. *Screenplay:* Gladys Lehman. *Continuity:* Norman Houston. *Photography:* Ted Tetzlaff. *Editor:* Leon Barsha. *Cast:* Barbara Stanwyck (Mexicali Rose), Sam Hardy, William Janney, Louis Natheaux, Arthur Rankin, Harry Vejar, Louis King, Julia Beharano. (Col, 62 min.)

1930. LADIES OF LEISURE. *Producer:* Harry Cohn. *Director:* Frank Capra. *Screenplay:* Jo Swerling from the play "Ladies of the Evening" by Milton Herbert Gropper. *Photography:* Joseph Walker. *Editor:* Maurice Wright. *Cast:* Barbara Stanwyck (Kay Arnold), Lowell Sherman, Ralph Graves, Marie Provost, Nance O'Neil, George Fawcett, Juliette Compton, Johnnie Walker. (Col, 98 min.)

1931. ILLICIT. *Director:* Archie Mayo. *Screenplay:* Harvey Thew from the play by Edith Fitzgerald and Robert Riskin. *Photography:* Robert Kurrle. *Editor:* William Holmes. *Costumes:* Earl Luick. *Cast:* Barbara Stanwyck (Anne Vincent), James Rennie, Ricardo Cortez, Natalie Moorhead, Charles Butterworth, Joan Blondell, Claude Gillingwater. (WB, 81 min.)

1931. TEN CENTS A DANCE. *Producer:* Harry Cohn. *Director:* Lionel Barrymore. *Screenplay:* Jo Swerling. *Continuity:* Dorothy Howell. *Photography:* Ernest Haller, Gil Warrenton. *Editor:* Arthur Huffsmith. *Music:* Abe Lyman and his band. *Music director:* Bakaleinikoff. *Cast:* Barbara Stanwyck (Barbara O'Neil), Ricardo Cortez, Monroe Owsley, Sally Blane, Blanche Friderici, Martha Sleeper, David Newell, Victor Potel, Sidney Bracey. (Col, 80 min.)

1931. NIGHT NURSE. *Director:* William A. Wellman. *Screenplay:* Oliver H. P. Garrett from the novel by Dora Macy. *Additional dialogue:* Charles Kenyon.

Photography: Barney McGill. *Editor:* Edward M. McDermott. *Art director:* Max Parker. *Costumes:* Earl Luick. *Cast:* Barbara Stanwyck (Lora Hart), Ben Lyon, Joan Blondell, Clark Gable, Blanche Friderici, Charlotte Merriam, Charles Winninger, Edward Nugent, Vera Lewis, Ralf Harolde, Walter McGrail, Allan Lane, Marcia Mae Jones, Betty Jane Graham. (WB, 73 min.)

1931. THE MIRACLE WOMAN. *Producer:* Harry Cohn. *Director:* Frank Capra. *Screenplay:* Jo Swerling from the play "Bless You Sister" by John Meehan and Robert Riskin. *Continuity:* Dorothy Howell. *Photography:* Joseph Walker. *Editor:* Maurice Wright. *Cast:* Barbara Stanwyck (Florence Fallon), David Manners, Sam Hardy, Beryl Mercer, Russell Hopton, Charles Middleton, Eddie Boland, Thelma Hill. (Col, 90 min.)

1932. FORBIDDEN. *Producer:* Harry Cohn. *Director:* Frank Capra. *Story:* Frank Capra. *Adaptation and dialogue:* Jo Swerling. *Photography:* Joseph Walker. *Editor:* Maurice Wright. *Cast:* Barbara Stanwyck (Lulu Smith), Adolphe Menjou, Ralph Bellamy, Dorothy Peterson, Thomas Jefferson, Myrna Fresholt, Charlotte V. Henry, Oliver Eckhardt. (Col, 85 min.)

1932. SHOPWORN. *Director:* Nicholas Grinde. *Story:* Sarah Y. Mason. *Dialogue:* Jo Swerling and Robert Riskin. *Photography:* Joseph Walker. *Editor:* Gene Havlick. *Cast:* Barbara Stanwyck (Kitty Lane), Regis Toomey, ZaSu Pitts, Lucien Littlefield, Clara Blandick, Robert Alden, Oscar Apfel, Maude Turner Gordon, Albert Conti. (Col, 72 min.)

1932. SO BIG. *Director:* William A. Wellman. *Screenplay:* J. Grubb Alexander and Robert Lord from the novel by Edna Ferber. *Photography:* Sid Hickox. *Editor:* William Holmes. *Art director:* Jack Okey. *Cast:* Barbara Stanwyck (Selina Peake), George Brent, Dickie Moore, Guy Kibbee, Bette Davis, Mae Madison, Hardie Albright, Robert Warwick, Arthur Stone, Earle Foxe, Alan Hale, Dorothy Peterson, Dawn O'Day, Dick Winslow, Harry Beresford, Eulalie Jensen, Elizabeth Patterson, Rita LeRoy, Blanche Friderici, Willard Robertson, Harry Holman, Lionel Belmore. (WB, 80 min.)

1932. THE PURCHASE PRICE. *Director:* William A. Wellman. *Screenplay:* Robert Lord from a story "The Mud Lark" by Arthur Stringer. *Photography:* Sid Hickox. *Editor:* William Holmes. *Art director:* Jack Okey. *Cast:* Barbara Stanwyck (Joan Gordon), George Brent, Lyle Talbot, Hardie Albright, David Landau, Murray Kinnell, Leila Bennett, Matt McHugh, Clarence Wilson, Lucille Ward, Dawn O'Day, Victor Potel, Adele Watson, Snub Pollard. (WB, 68 min.)

1933. THE BITTER TEA OF GENERAL YEN. *Producer:* Walter Wanger. *Director:* Frank Capra. *Screenplay:* Edward Paramore from the story by Grace Zaring Stone. *Photography:* Joseph Walker. *Editor:* Edward Curtis. *Costumes:* Edward Stevenson. *Music:* W. Frank Harling. *Cast:* Barbara Stanwyck (Megan Davis), Nils Asther, Toshia Mori, Walter Connolly, Gavin Gordon, Lucien Littlefield, Richard Loo, Helen Jerome Eddy, Emmett Corrigan. (Col, 90 min.)

1933. LADIES THEY TALK ABOUT. *Directors:* Howard Bretherton, William Keighley. *Screenplay:* Sidney Sutherland and Brown Holmes from the play "Women in Prison" by Dorothy Mackaye and Carlton Miles. *Photography:* John Seitz. *Editor:* Basil Wrangel. *Art director:* Esdras Hartley. *Costumes:* Orry-Kelly. *Cast:* Barbara Stanwyck (Nan Taylor), Preston Foster, Lyle Talbot, Dorothy Burgess, Lillian Roth, Maude Eburne, Harold Huber, Ruth Donnelly, Robert Warwick, Helen Ware, DeWitt Jennings, Robert McWade, Cecil Cunningham, Helen Mann, Grace Cunard, Mme. Sul-Te-Wan, Harold Healy, Harry Gribbon. (WB, 69 min.)

1933. BABY FACE. *Director:* Alfred E. Green. *Screenplay:* Gene Markey and Kathryn Scola from a story by Mark Canfield. *Photography:* James Van Trees. *Editor:* Howard Bretherton. *Art director:* Anton Grot. *Costumes:* Orry-Kelly. *Cast:* Barbara Stanwyck (Lily Powers), George Brent, Donald Cook, Alphonse Ethier, Henry Kolker, Margaret Lindsay, Arthur Hohl, John Wayne, Robert Barrat, Douglas Dumbrille, Theresa Harris. (WB, 70 min.)

1933. EVER IN MY HEART. *Director:* Archie Mayo. *Screenplay:* Bertram Milhauser from a story by Milhauser and Beulah Marie Dix. *Photography:* Arthur Todd. *Editor:* Owen Marks. *Art director:* Anton Grot. *Costumes:* Earl Luick. *Cast:* Barbara Stanwyck (Mary Archer), Otto Kruger, Ralph Bellamy, Ruth Donnelly, Frank Albertson, George Cooper, Wallis Clark, Florence Roberts, Laura Hope Crews, Ronnie Crosby, Frank Reicher, Clara Blandick, Elizabeth Patterson, Willard Robertson, Nella Walker, Harry Beresford, Virginia Howell, Ethel Wales. (WB, 68 min.)

1934. GAMBLING LADY. *Director:* Archie Mayo. *Screenplay:* Ralph Block and Doris Malloy from a story by Malloy. *Photography:* George Barnes. *Editor:* Harold McLernon. *Art director:* Anton Grot. *Costumes:* Orry-Kelly. *Cast:* Barbara Stanwyck (Lady Lee), Joel McCrea, Pat O'Brien, Claire Dodd, C. Aubrey Smith, Robert Barrat, Arthur Vinton, Phillip Reed, Philip Faversham, Robert Elliott, Ferdinand Gottschalk, Willard Robertson, Huey White. (WB, 66 min.)

1934. A LOST LADY. *Director:* Alfred E. Green. *Screenplay:* Gene Markey and Kathryn Scola from the novel by Willa Cather. *Photography:* Sid Hickox. *Editor:* Owen Marks. *Art director:* Jack Okey. *Costumes:* Orry-Kelly. *Cast:* Barbara Stanwyck (Marian Ormsby), Frank Morgan, Ricardo Cortez, Lyle Talbot, Phillip Reed, Hobart Cavanaugh, Henry Kolker, Rafaela Ottiano, Edward McWade, Walter Walker, Samuel Hinds, Willie Fung, Jameson Thomas. (First Nat, 61 min.)

1935. THE SECRET BRIDE. *Director:* William Dieterle. *Screenplay:* Tom Buckingham, F. Hugh Herbert, Mary McCall Jr. from the play by Leonard Ide. *Photography:* Ernest Haller. *Editor:* Owen Marks. *Art director:* Anton Grot. *Costumes:* Orry-Kelly. *Cast:* Barbara Stanwyck (Ruth Vincent), Warren William, Glenda Farrell, Grant Mitchell, Arthur Byron, Henry O'Neill, Douglas Dumbrille, Arthur Aylesworth, Willard Robertson, William Davidson. (WB, 64 min.)

1935. THE WOMAN IN RED. *Director:* Robert Florey. *Screenplay:* Mary McCall Jr. and Peter Milne from the novel "North Shore" by Wallace Irwin. *Photography:* Sol Polito. *Editor:* Terry Morse. *Art director:* Esdras Hartley. *Costumes:* Orry-Kelly. *Cast:* Barbara Stanwyck (Shelby Barret), Gene Raymond, Genevieve Tobin, John Eldredge, Phillip Reed, Dorothy Tree, Russell Hicks, Nella Walker, Claude Gillingwater, Doris Lloyd, Hale Hamilton, Arthur Treacher. (First Nat, 68 min.)

1935. RED SALUTE. *Producer:* Edward Small. *Director:* Sidney Lanfield. *Screenplay:* Humphrey Pearson and Manuel Seff from a story by Pearson. *Photography:* Robert Planck. *Editor:* Grant Whytock. *Art director:* John Ducasse Schulze. *Cast:* Barbara Stanwyck (Drue Van Allen), Robert Young, Hardie Albright, Cliff Edwards, Ruth Donnelly, Gordon Jones, Paul Stanton, Purnell Pratt, Nella Walker, Arthur Vinton, Edward McWade, Henry Kolker, Henry Otho. (UA, 78 min.)

1935. ANNIE OAKLEY. *Assoc. producer:* Cliff Reid. *Director:* George Stevens. *Screenplay:* Joel Sayre and John Twist from a story by Joseph A. Fields and Ewart Adamson. *Photography:* J. Roy Hunt. *Editor:* Jack Hively. *Art director:* Van Nest Polglase. *Associate:* Perry Ferguson. *Music director:* Alberto Columbo. *Cast:* Barbara Stanwyck (Annie Oakley), Preston Foster, Melvyn Douglas, Moroni Olsen, Pert Kelton, Andy Clyde, Chief Thunder Bird, Margaret Armstrong, Delmar Watson, Adeline Craig. (RKO, 90 min.)

1936. A MESSAGE TO GARCIA. *Producer:* Darryl F. Zanuck. *Assoc. producer:* Raymond Griffith. *Di-*

rector: George Marshall. *Screenplay:* W. P. Lipscomb and Gene Fowler, suggested by Elbert Hubbard's essay and Lieut. Andrew S. Rowan's book. *Photography:* Rudolph Maté. *Editor:* Herbert Levy. *Art director:* William Darling. *Associate:* Rudolph Sternad. *Set decorator:* Thomas Little. *Music director:* Louis Silvers. *Cast:* Wallace Beery, Barbara Stanwyck (Senorita Raphaelita Maderos), John Boles, Alan Hale, Herbert Mundin, Mona Barrie, Enrique Acosta, Juan Torena, Martin Garralaga, Blanca Vischer, Jose Luis Tortosa. (20th, 86 min.)

1936. THE BRIDE WALKS OUT. *Producer:* Edward Small. *Director:* Leigh Jason. *Screenplay:* P. J. Wolfson and Philip G. Epstein from a story by Howard Emmett Rogers. *Photography:* J. Roy Hunt. *Editor:* Arthur Roberts. *Art director:* Van Nest Polglase. *Associate:* Al Herman. *Costumes:* Bernard Newman. *Music director:* Roy Webb. *Cast:* Barbara Stanwyck (Carolyn Martin), Gene Raymond, Robert Young, Ned Sparks, Helen Broderick, Willie Best, Robert Warwick, Billy Gilbert, Wade Boteler, Hattie McDaniel, Irving Bacon. (RKO, 81 min.)

1936. HIS BROTHER'S WIFE. *Producer:* Lawrence Weingarten. *Director:* W. S. Van Dyke. *Screenplay:* Leon Gordon and John Meehan from a story by George Auerbach. *Photography:* Oliver T. Marsh. *Editor:* Conrad A. Nervig. *Art director:* Cedric Gibbons. *Associates:* Harry McAfee, Edwin B. Willis. *Costumes:* Dolly Tree. *Music:* Franz Waxman. *Cast:* Barbara Stanwyck (Rita Wilson), Robert Taylor, Jean Hersholt, Joseph Calleia, John Eldredge, Samuel S. Hinds, Leonard Mudie, Jed Prouty, Pedro De Cordoba, Rafael Corio, William Stack, Edgar Edwards. (M-G-M, 90 min.)

1936. BANJO ON MY KNEE. *Producer:* Darryl F. Zanuck. *Assoc. producer:* Nunnally Johnson. *Director:* John Cromwell. *Screenplay:* Nunnally Johnson from the novel by Harry Hamilton. *Photography:* Ernest Palmer. *Editor:* Hansen Fritch. *Art director:* Hans Peters. *Set decorator:* Thomas Little. *Costumes:* Gwen Wakeling. *Music and lyrics:* Jimmy McHugh, Harold Adamson. *Music director:* Arthur Lange. *Cast:* Barbara Stanwyck (Pearl), Joel McCrea, Walter Brennan, Buddy Ebsen, Helen Westley, Walter Catlett, Anthony Martin, Katherine de Mille, Victor Kilian, Minna Gombell, Spencer Charters, Hall Johnson Choir. (20th, 95 min.)

1937. THE PLOUGH AND THE STARS. *Assoc. producers:* Cliff Reid, Robert Sisk. *Director:* John Ford. Assisted by Arthur Shields of the Abbey Theatre. *Screenplay:* Dudley Nichols from the play by Sean O'Casey. *Photography:* Joseph August. *Editor:* George Hively. *Art director:* Van Nest Polglase.

Associate: Carroll Clark. *Set decorator:* Darrell Silvera. *Costumes:* Walter Plunkett. *Music:* Roy Webb. *Music director:* Nathaniel Shilkret. *Cast:* Barbara Stanwyck (Nora Clitheroe), Preston Foster, Barry Fitzgerald, Denis O'Dea, Eileen Crowe, F. J. McCormick, Arthur Shields, Una O'Connor, Moroni Olsen, J. M. Kerrigan, Bonita Granville, Erin O'Brien-Moore. (RKO, 72 min.)

1937. INTERNES CAN'T TAKE MONEY. *Producer:* Benjamin Glazer. *Director:* Alfred Santell. *Screenplay:* Rian James and Theodore Reeves from a story by Max Brand. *Photography:* Theodor Sparkuhl. *Editor:* Doane Harrison. *Art directors:* Hans Dreier, Roland Anderson. *Costumes:* Travis Banton. *Music:* Gregory Stone. *Music director:* Boris Morros. *Cast:* Barbara Stanwyck (Janet Haley), Joel McCrea, Lloyd Nolan, Stanley Ridges, Lee Bowman, Barry Macollum, Irving Bacon, Gaylord Pendleton, Pierre Watkin, Charles Lane, Priscilla Lawson, James Bush, Nick Lukats, Anthony Nace, Fay Holden, Frank Bruno, Sarah Padden. (Para, 75 min.)

1937. THIS IS MY AFFAIR. *Producer:* Darryl F. Zanuck. *Assoc. producer:* Kenneth Macgowan. *Director:* William A. Seiter. *Screenplay:* Allen Rivkin, Lamar Trotti. *Photography:* Robert Planck. *Editor:* Allen McNeil. *Art director:* Rudolph Sternad. *Costumes:* Royer. *Music and lyrics:* Mack Gordon, Harry Revel. *Music director:* Arthur Lange. *Dance director:* Jack Haskell. *Cast:* Robert Taylor, Barbara Stanwyck (Lil Duryea), Victor McLaglen, Brian Donlevy, Sidney Blackmer, John Carradine, Alan Dinehart, Douglas Fowley, Robert McWade, Frank Conroy, Sig Rumann, Marjorie Weaver, J. C. Nugent. (20th, 100 min.)

1937. STELLA DALLAS. *Producer:* Samuel Goldwyn. *Assoc. producer:* Merritt Hulburd. *Director:* King Vidor. *Screenplay:* Sarah Y. Mason and Victor Heerman from the novel by Olive Higgins Prouty. *Dramatization:* Harry Wagstaff Gribble and Gertrude Purcell. *Photography:* Rudolph Maté. *Editor:* Sherman Todd. *Art director:* Richard Day. *Costumes:* Omar Kiam. *Music director:* Alfred Newman. *Cast:* Barbara Stanwyck (Stella Dallas), John Boles, Anne Shirley, Barbara O'Neil, Alan Hale, Marjorie Main, George Walcott, Ann Shoemaker, Tim Holt, Nella Walker, Bruce Satterlee, Jimmy Butler, Jack Egger, Dickie Jones, Al Shean. (UA, 105 min.)

1937. BREAKFAST FOR TWO. *Producer:* Edward Kaufman. *Director:* Alfred Santell. *Screenplay:* Charles Kaufman, Paul Yawitz and Viola Brothers Shore from a story by David Garth. *Photography:* J. Roy Hunt. *Editor:* George Hively. *Art director:* Van Nest Polglase. *Associate:* Al Herman. *Set decorator:* Darrell Silvera. *Costumes:* Edward Stevenson. *Cast:*

Barbara Stanwyck (Valentine Ransom), Herbert Marshall, Glenda Farrell, Eric Blore, Donald Meek, Etienne Girardot, Frank M. Thomas, Pierre Watkin. (RKO, 65 min.)

1938. ALWAYS GOODBYE. *Producer:* Darryl F. Zanuck. *Assoc. producer:* Raymond Griffith. *Director:* Sidney Lanfield. *Screenplay:* Kathryn Scola and Edith Skouras from a story by Gilbert Emery and Douglas Doty. *Photography:* Robert Planck. *Editor:* Robert Simpson. *Art directors:* Bernard Herzbrun, Hans Peters. *Set decorator:* Thomas Little. *Costumes:* Royer. *Music director:* Louis Silvers. *Cast:* Barbara Stanwyck (Margot Weston), Herbert Marshall, Ian Hunter, Cesar Romero, Lynn Bari, Binnie Barnes, Johnnie Russell, Mary Forbes, Albert Conti, Marcelle Corday, Franklyn Pangborn, George Davis, Ben Welden (20th, 75 min.)

1938. THE MAD MISS MANTON. *Producer:* Pandro S. Berman. *Assoc. producer:* P. J. Wolfson. *Director:* Leigh Jason. *Screenplay:* Philip G. Epstein from a story by Wilson Collison. *Photography:* Nicholas Musuraca. *Editor:* George Hively. *Art director:* Van Nest Polglase. *Associate:* Carroll Clark. *Set decorator:* Darrell Silvera. *Costumes:* Edward Stevenson. *Music:* Roy Webb. *Cast:* Barbara Stanwyck (Melsa Manton), Henry Fonda, Sam Levene, Frances Mercer, Stanley Ridges, Whitney Bourne, Vicki Lester, Ann Evers, Catherine O'Quinn, Linda Terry, Eleanor Hansen, Hattie McDaniel, James Burke, Paul Guilfoyle, Penny Singleton, Leona Maricle, Kay Sutton, Miles Mander, John Qualen, Grady Sutton, Olin Howland. (RKO, 80 min.)

1939. UNION PACIFIC. *Producer-director:* Cecil B. DeMille. *Assoc. producer:* William H. Pine. *Second unit director:* Arthur Rosson. *Screenplay:* Walter DeLeon, C. Gardner Sullivan and Jesse Lasky Jr. from an adaptation by Jack Cunningham of a story by Ernest Haycox. *Photography:* Victor Milner, Dewey Wrigley. *Editor:* Anne Bauchens. *Art directors:* Hans Dreier, Roland Anderson. *Costumes:* Natalie Visart. *Music:* Sigmund Krumgold, John Leipold. *Cast:* Barbara Stanwyck (Mollie Monahan), Joel McCrea, Akim Tamiroff, Lynne Overman, Robert Preston, Brian Donlevy, Anthony Quinn, Evelyn Keyes, Stanley Ridges, Regis Toomey, Syd Saylor, J. M. Kerrigan, William Haade, Harry Woods, Fuzzy Knight, Francis MacDonald, Henry Kolker, Richard Lane, Hugh McDonald. (Para, 135 min.)

1939. GOLDEN BOY. *Producer:* William Perlberg. *Director:* Rouben Mamoulian. *Screenplay:* Lewis Meltzer, Daniel Taradash, Sarah Y. Mason, Victor Heerman from the play by Clifford Odets. *Photography:* Nicholas Musuraca, Karl Freund. *Editor:* Otto

Meyer. *Art director:* Lionel Banks. *Montage effects:* D. W. Starling. *Costumes:* Kalloch. *Music:* Victor Young. *Music director:* M. W. Stoloff. *Cast:* Barbara Stanwyck (Lorna Moon), Adolphe Menjou, William Holden, Lee J. Cobb, Joseph Calleia, Sam Levene, Edward S. Brophy, Beatrice Blinn, William H. Strauss, Don Beddoe. (Col, 99 min.)

1940. REMEMBER THE NIGHT. *Producer-director:* Mitchell Leisen. *Screenplay:* Preston Sturges. *Photography:* Ted Tetzlaff. *Editor:* Doane Harrison. *Art directors:* Hans Dreier, Roland Anderson. *Stanwyck costumes:* Edith Head. *Music:* Frederick Hollander. *Cast:* Barbara Stanwyck (Lee Leander), Fred MacMurray, Beulah Bondi, Elizabeth Patterson, Sterling Holloway, Willard Robertson, Charles Waldron, Paul Guilfoyle, Charlie Arnt, John Wray, Thomas W. Ross, Snowflake, Tom Kennedy, Georgia Caine, Virginia Brissac, Spencer Charters. (Para, 94 min.)

1941. THE LADY EVE. *Producer:* Paul Jones. *Director:* Preston Sturges. *Screenplay:* Preston Sturges from a story by Monckton Hoffe. *Photography:* Victor Milner. *Editor:* Stuart Gilmore. *Art directors:* Hans Dreier, Ernst Fegté. *Costumes:* Edith Head. *Music director:* Sigmund Krumgold. *Cast:* Barbara Stanwyck (Jean Harrington), Henry Fonda, Charles Coburn, Eugene Pallette, William Demarest, Eric Blore, Melville Cooper, Martha O'Driscoll, Janet Beecher, Robert Greig, Dora Clement, Luis Alberni. (Para, 97 min.)

1941. MEET JOHN DOE. *Producer-director:* Frank Capra. *Screenplay:* Robert Riskin from a story by Richard Connell and Robert Presnell. *Photography:* George Barnes. *Editor:* Daniel Mandell. *Art director:* Stephen Goosson. *Montage effects:* Slavko Vorkapich. *Special effects:* Jack Cosgrove. *Costumes:* Natalie Visart. *Music:* Dimitri Tiomkin. *Music director:* Leo F. Forbstein. *Choral arrangements:* Hall Johnson. *Cast:* Gary Cooper, Barbara Stanwyck (Ann Mitchell), Edward Arnold, Walter Brennan, Spring Byington, James Gleason, Gene Lockhart, Rod La Rocque, Irving Bacon, Regis Toomey, J. Farrell MacDonald, Warren Hymer, Harry Holman, Andrew Tombes, Pierre Watkin, Stanley Andrews, Mitchell Lewis, Charles Wilson, Vaughan Glaser, Sterling Holloway, Mike Frankovich, Knox Manning, John B. Hughes, Hall Johnson Choir. (Produced at Warner Brothers Studios by Frank Capra Productions, Inc., 123 min.)

1941. YOU BELONG TO ME. *Producer-director:* Wesley Ruggles. *Screenplay:* Claude Binyon from a story by Dalton Trumbo. *Photography:* Joseph Walker. *Editor:* Viola Lawrence. *Art director:* Lionel Banks. *Costumes:* Edith Head. *Music:* Frederick Hollander. *Music director:* M. W. Stoloff. *Cast:* Barbara Stanwyck (Helen Hunt), Henry Fonda, Edgar Buchanan, Roger Clark, Ruth Donnelly, Melville Cooper, Ralph Peters, Maude Eburne, Renie Riano, Ellen Lowe, Mary Treen, Gordon Jones. (Col, 94 min.)

1942. BALL OF FIRE. *Producer:* Samuel Goldwyn. *Director:* Howard Hawks. *Screenplay:* Charles Brackett and Billy Wilder from a story "From A to Z" by Wilder and Thomas Monroe. *Photography:* Gregg Toland. *Editor:* Daniel Mandell. *Art director:* Perry Ferguson. *Assistant:* McClure Capps. *Set decorator:* Howard Bristol. *Stanwyck costumes:* Edith Head. *Music:* Alfred Newman. *Cast:* Gary Cooper, Barbara Stanwyck (Sugarpuss O'Shea), Oscar Homolka, Henry Travers, S. Z. Sakall, Tully Marshall, Leonid Kinskey, Richard Haydn, Aubrey Mather, Allen Jenkins, Dana Andrews, Dan Duryea, Ralph Peters, Kathleen Howard, Mary Field, Charles Lane, Charles Arnt, Elisha Cook, Alan Rhein, Eddie Foster, Aldrich Bowker, Addison Richards, Pat West, Kenneth Howell, Tommy Ryan, Tim Ryan, Will Lee, Gene Krupa and his orchestra. (RKO, 111 min.)

1942. THE GREAT MAN'S LADY. *Producer-director:* William A. Wellman. *Screenplay:* W. L. River. Original story by Adela Rogers St. Johns and Seena Owen from a short story by Viña Delmar. *Photography:* William C. Mellor. *Editor:* Thomas Scott. *Art directors:* Hans Dreier, Earl Hedrick. *Special effects:* Gordon Jennings. *Costumes:* Edith Head. *Music:* Victor Young. *Cast:* Barbara Stanwyck (Hannah Sempler), Joel McCrea, Brian Donlevy, Katharine Stevens, Thurston Hall, Lloyd Corrigan, Etta McDaniel, Frank M. Thomas, William B. Davidson, Lillian Yarbo, Helen Lynd, Lucien Littlefield, John Hamilton. (Para, 90 min.)

1942. THE GAY SISTERS. *Producer:* Henry Blanke. *Director:* Irving Rapper. *Screenplay:* Lenore Coffee from the novel by Stephen Longstreet. *Photography:* Sol Polito. *Editor:* Warren Low. *Art director:* Robert Haas. *Stanwyck costumes:* Edith Head. *Music:* Max Steiner. *Music director:* Leo F. Forbstein. *Orchestration:* Hugo Friedhofer. *Cast:* Barbara Stanwyck (Fiona Gaylord), George Brent, Geraldine Fitzgerald, Donald Crisp, Gig Young, Nancy Coleman, Gene Lockhart, Larry Simms, Donald Woods, Grant Mitchell, William T. Orr, Anne Revere, Helene Thimig, George Lessey, Charles D. Waldron, Frank Reicher, David Clyde, Mary Thomas, Hank Mann. (WB, 110 min.)

1943. LADY OF BURLESQUE. *Producer:* Hunt Stromberg. *Director:* William A. Wellman. *Screenplay:* James Gunn from the novel "The G-String Murders" by Gypsy Rose Lee. *Photography:* Robert De Grasse. *Editor:* James E. Newcome. *Art director:* Bernard Herzbrun. *Stanwyck costumes:* Edith Head. *Others:* Natalie Visart. *Music:* Arthur Lange. *Songs:* Sammy Cahn, Harry Akst. *Dance director:* Danny Dare. *Cast:* Barbara Stanwyck (Dixie Daisy), Michael O'Shea, J. Edward Bromberg, Iris Adrian, Gloria Dickson, Victoria Faust, Stephanie Bachelor, Charles Dingle, Marion Martin, Eddie Gordon, Frank Fenton, Pinky Lee, Frank Conroy, Lew Kelly, Claire Carleton, Janis Carter, Gerald Mohr, Bert Hanlon, Sid Marion, Lou Lubin. (UA, 91 min.)

1943. FLESH AND FANTASY. *Producers:* Charles Boyer, Julien Duvivier. *Director:* Julien Duvivier. *Screenplay:* Ernest Pascal, Samuel Hoffenstein, Ellis St. Joseph from stories by St. Joseph, Oscar Wilde and Laslo Vadnay. *Photography:* Paul Ivano, Stanley Cortez. *Editor:* Arthur Hilton. *Art directors:* John B. Goodman, Richard Riedel, Robert Boyle. *Set decorators:* R. A. Gausman, E. R. Robinson. *Stanwyck costumes:* Edith Head. *Others:* Vera West. *Music:* Alexandre Tansman. *Music director:* Charles Previn. *Cast:* Edward G. Robinson, Charles Boyer, Barbara Stanwyck (Joan Stanley), Betty Field, Robert Cummings, Thomas Mitchell, Charles Winninger, Anna Lee, Dame May Whitty, C. Aubrey Smith, Robert Benchley, Edgar Barrier, David Hoffman. (Univ, 93 min.)

1944. DOUBLE INDEMNITY. *Producer:* Joseph Sistrom. *Director:* Billy Wilder. *Screenplay:* Billy Wilder and Raymond Chandler from a James M. Cain short story in his book "Three Of a Kind." *Photography:* John Seitz. *Editor:* Doane Harrison. *Art directors:* Hans Dreier, Hal Pereira. *Process photography:* Farciot Edouart. *Set decorator:* Bertram Granger. *Costumes:* Edith Head. *Music:* Miklos Rozsa. *Cast:* Fred MacMurray, Barbara Stanwyck (Phyllis Dietrichson), Edward G. Robinson, Porter Hall, Jean Heather, Tom Powers, Byron Barr, Richard Gaines, Fortunio Bonanova, John Philliber, Betty Farrington. (Para, 107 min.)

1944. HOLLYWOOD CANTEEN. *Producer:* Alex Gottlieb. *Director and screenplay:* Delmer Daves. *Photography:* Bert Glennon. *Editor:* Christian Nyby. *Art director:* Leo Kuter. *Set decorator:* Casey Roberts. *Music adapter:* Ray Heindorf. *Music director:* Leo F. Forbstein. *Cast:* Joan Leslie, Robert Hutton, Dane Clark, Janis Paige. Guest appearances by Barbara Stanwyck and many other Warner stars. (WB, 123 min.)

1945. CHRISTMAS IN CONNECTICUT. *Producer:* William Jacobs. *Director:* Peter Godfrey. *Screenplay:* Lionel Houser and Adele Commandini from a story by Aileen Hamilton. *Photography:* Carl Guthrie. *Editor:* Frank Magee. *Art director:* Stanley Fleischer. *Set decorator:* Casey Roberts. *Costumes:* Edith Head. *Music:* Frederick Hollander. *Music director:* Leo F. Forbstein. *Orchestration:* Jerome Moross. *Cast:* Barbara Stanwyck (Elizabeth Lane), Dennis Morgan, Sydney Greenstreet, Reginald Gardiner, S. Z. Sakall, Robert Shayne, Una O'Connor, Frank Jenks, Joyce Compton, Dick Elliott, Charles Arnt. (WB, 101 min.)

1946. MY REPUTATION. *Producer:* Henry Blanke. *Director:* Curtis Bernhardt. *Screenplay:* Catherine Turney from the novel "Instruct My Sorrows" by Clare Jaynes. *Photography:* James Wong Howe. *Editor:* David Weisbart. *Art director:* Anton Grot. *Special effects:* Roy Davidson. *Set decorator:* George James Hopkins. *Stanwyck costumes:* Edith Head. *Others:* Leah Rhodes. *Music:* Max Steiner. *Music director:* Leo F. Forbstein. *Cast:* Barbara Stanwyck (Jessica Drummond), George Brent, Warner Anderson, Lucile Watson, John Ridgely, Eve Arden, Jerome Cowan, Esther Dale, Scotty Beckett, Bobby Cooper, Leona Maricle, Mary Servoss, Cecil Cunningham, Janis Wilson, Ann Todd. (WB, 96 min.)

1946. THE BRIDE WORE BOOTS. *Producer:* Seton I. Miller. *Director:* Irving Pichel. *Screenplay:* Dwight Mitchell Wiley from a story by Wiley and a play by Harry Segall. *Photography:* Stuart Thompson. *Editor:* Ellsworth Hoagland. *Art directors:* Hans Dreier, John Meehan. *Special effects:* Gordon Jennings. *Set decorators:* Sam Comer, Jerry Welch. *Costumes:* Edith Head. *Music:* Frederick Hollander. *Cast:* Barbara Stanwyck (Sally Warren), Robert Cummings, Diana Lynn, Patric Knowles, Peggy Wood, Robert Benchley, Willie Best, Natalie Wood, Gregory Muradian, Mary Young. (Para, 86 min.)

1946. THE STRANGE LOVE OF MARTHA IVERS. *Producer:* Hal B. Wallis. *Director:* Lewis Milestone. *Screenplay:* Robert Rossen from a story by Jack Patrick (see text, page 195, on this). *Photography:* Victor Milner. *Editor:* Archie Marshek. *Art directors:* Hans Dreier, John Meehan. *Process photography:* Farciot Edouart. *Set decorators:* Sam Comer, Jerry Welch. *Costumes:* Edith Head. *Music:* Miklos Rozsa. *Cast:* Barbara Stanwyck (Martha Ivers), Van Heflin, Lizabeth Scott, Kirk Douglas, Judith Anderson, Roman Bohnen, Darryl Hickman, Janis Wilson, Ann Doran, Frank Orth, James Flavin, Mickey Kuhn, Charles D. Brown. (Para, 116 min.)

1947. CALIFORNIA. *Producer:* Seton I. Miller. *Director:* John Farrow. *Screenplay:* Frank Butler and Theodore Strauss from a story by Boris Ingster. *Photography:* Ray Rennahan (Technicolor). *Editor:* Eda Warren. *Art directors:* Hans Dreier, Roland Anderson. *Special effects:* Gordon Jennings. *Set decorators:* Sam Comer, Ray Moyer. *Women's costumes:* Edith Head. *Men's costumes:* Gile Steele. *Music:* Victor Young. *Songs:* E. Y. Harburg, Earl Robinson. *Cast:* Ray Milland, Barbara Stanwyck (Lily Bishop), Barry Fitzgerald, George Coulouris, Albert Dekker, Anthony Quinn, Frank Faylen, Gavin Muir, James Burke, Eduardo Ciannelli, Roman Bohnen, Argentina Brunetti, Howard Freeman, Julia Faye. (Para, 98 min.)

1947. THE TWO MRS. CARROLLS. *Producer:* Mark Hellinger. *Director:* Peter Godfrey. *Screenplay:* Thomas Job from the play by Martin Vale. *Photography:* Peverell Marley. *Editor:* Frederick Richards. *Art director:* Anton Grot. *Special effects:* Robert Burks. *Set decorator:* Budd Friend. *Stanwyck costumes:* Edith Head. *Others:* Milo Anderson. *Music:* Franz Waxman. *Music director:* Leo F. Forbstein. *Orchestration:* Leonid Raab. *Cast:* Humphrey Bogart, Barbara Stanwyck (Sally), Alexis Smith, Nigel Bruce, Isobel Elsom, Pat O'Moore, Ann Carter, Anita Bolster, Barry Bernard, Colin Campbell, Peter Godfrey. (WB, 99 min.)

1947. THE OTHER LOVE. *Producer:* David Lewis. *Director:* Andre de Toth. *Screenplay:* Harry Brown and Ladislas Fodor from the short story "Beyond" by Erich Maria Remarque. *Photography:* Victor Milner. *Editor:* Walter Thompson. *Art director:* Nathan Juran. *Special scenic effects:* Robert H. Moreland. *Set decorator:* Edward G. Boyle. *Stanwyck costumes:* Edith Head. *Others:* Edward P. Lambert. *Music:* Miklos Rozsa. *Music director:* Rudolph Polk. *Cast:* Barbara Stanwyck (Karen Duncan), David Niven, Richard Conte, Gilbert Roland, Joan Lorring, Lenore Aubert, Maria Palmer, Natalie Schafer, Edward Ashley, Richard Hale, Michael Romanoff, Jimmy Horne, Mary Forbes, Ann Codee, Kathleen Williams. (UA, 96 min.)

1947. CRY WOLF. *Producer:* Henry Blanke. *Director:* Peter Godfrey. *Screenplay:* Catherine Turney from the novel by Marjorie Carleton. *Photography:* Carl Guthrie. *Editor:* Folmar Blangsted. *Art director:* Carl Jules Weyl. *Special effects:* William McGann, Robert Burks. *Set decorator:* Jack McConaghy. *Stanwyck costumes:* Edith Head. *Others:* Travilla. *Music:* Franz Waxman. *Music director:* Leo F. Forbstein. *Orchestration:* Leonid Raab. *Cast:* Errol Flynn, Barbara Stanwyck (Sandra Demarest), Geraldine Brooks, Richard Basehart, Jerome Cowan, John Ridgely, Patricia White, Rory Mallinson, Helen Thimig, Paul Stanton, Barry Bernard. (WB, 84 min.)

1947. VARIETY GIRL. *Producer:* Daniel Dare. *Director:* George Marshall. *Screenplay:* Edmund Hartmann, Frank Tashlin, Robert Welch, Monte Brice.

Photography: Lionel Lindon, Stuart Thompson. *Editor:* LeRoy Stone. *Art directors:* Hans Dreier, Robert Clatworthy. *Special effects:* Gordon Jennings. *Process photography:* Farciot Edouart. *Set decorators:* Sam Comer, Ross Dowd. *Stars' costumes:* Edith Head. *Music and direction:* Joseph J. Lilley. *Associate:* Troy Sanders. *Orchestration:* Van Cleave. *Cast:* Brief appearances by Bing Crosby, Bob Hope, Gary Cooper, Ray Milland, Alan Ladd, Barbara Stanwyck, Paulette Goddard, Dorothy Lamour and most of the Paramount lot. (Para, 93 min.)

1948. B. F.'S DAUGHTER. *Producer:* Edwin H. Knopf. *Director:* Robert Z. Leonard. *Screenplay:* Luther Davis from the novel by John P. Marquand. *Photography:* Joseph Ruttenberg. *Editor:* George White. *Art directors:* Cedric Gibbons, Daniel B. Cathcart. *Special effects:* Warren Newcombe. *Montage:* Peter Ballbusch. *Set decorators:* Edwin B. Willis, Jack D. Moore. *Women's costumes:* Irene. *Music:* Bronislau Kaper. *Music director:* Charles Previn. *Cast:* Barbara Stanwyck (Polly Fulton), Van Heflin, Charles Coburn, Richard Hart, Keenan Wynn, Margaret Lindsay, Spring Byington, Marshall Thompson, Barbara Laage, Thomas E. Breen, Fred Nurney. (M-G-M, 108 min.)

1948. SORRY, WRONG NUMBER. *Producers:* Hal B. Wallis, Anatole Litvak. *Director:* Anatole Litvak. *Screenplay:* Lucille Fletcher from her radio play. *Photography:* Sol Polito. *Editor:* Warren Low. *Art directors:* Hans Dreier, Earl Hedrick. *Special effects:* Gordon Jennings. *Process photography:* Farciot Edouart. *Set decorators:* Sam Comer, Bertram Granger. *Costumes:* Edith Head. *Stanwyck's jewels:* Ruser. *Music:* Franz Waxman. *Cast:* Barbara Stanwyck (Leona Stevenson), Burt Lancaster, Ann Richards, Wendell Corey, Harold Vermilyea, Ed Begley, Leif Erickson, William Conrad, John Bromfield, Jimmy Hunt, Dorothy Neumann, Paul Fierro. (Para, 89 min.)

1949. THE LADY GAMBLES. *Producer:* Michel Kraike. *Director:* Michael Gordon. *Screenplay:* Roy Huggins. *Adaptation:* Halsted Welles. *Story:* Lewis Meltzer, Oscar Saul. *Photography:* Russell Metty. *Editor:* Milton Carruth. *Art director:* Alexander Golitzen. *Special photography:* David S. Horsley. *Set decorators:* Russell A. Gausman, Ruby R. Levitt. *Stanwyck costumes:* Orry-Kelly. *Music:* Frank Skinner. *Cast:* Barbara Stanwyck (Joan Boothe), Robert Preston, Stephen McNally, Edith Barrett, John Hoyt, Elliott Sullivan, John Harmon, Phil Van Zandt, Leif Erickson, Curt Conway, Houseley Stevenson, Don Beddoe, Nana Bryant, Anthony Curtis, Peter Leeds. (Univ, 99 min.)

1949. EAST SIDE, WEST SIDE. *Producer:* Voldemar Vetluguin. *Director:* Mervyn LeRoy. *Screenplay:* Isobel Lennart from the novel by Marcia Davenport. *Photography:* Charles Rosher. *Editor:* Harold F. Kress. *Art directors:* Cedric Gibbons, Randall Duell. *Special effects:* A. Arnold Gillespie. *Set decorator:* Edwin B. Willis. *Associate:* Arthur Krams. *Women's costumes:* Helen Rose. *Music:* Miklos Rozsa. *Cast:* Barbara Stanwyck (Jessie Bourne), James Mason, Van Heflin, Ava Gardner, Cyd Charisse, Nancy Davis, Gale Sondergaard, William Conrad, Raymond Greenleaf, Douglas Kennedy, Beverly Michaels, William Frawley, Lisa Golm, Tom Powers. (M-G-M, 108 min.)

1950. THE FILE ON THELMA JORDAN. *Producer:* Hal B. Wallis. *Director:* Robert Siodmak. *Screenplay:* Ketti Frings from a story by Marty Holland. *Photography:* George Barnes. *Editor:* Warren Low. *Art directors:* Hans Dreier, Earl Hedrick. *Special effects:* Gordon Jennings. *Process photography:* Farciot Edouart. *Set decorators:* Sam Comer, Bertram Granger. *Costumes:* Edith Head. *Music:* Victor Young. *Cast:* Barbara Stanwyck (Thelma Jordan), Wendell Corey, Paul Kelly, Joan Tetzel, Stanley Ridges, Richard Rober, Minor Watson, Barry Kelley, Laura Elliot, Basil Ruysdael, Jane Novak, Gertrude W. Hoffman, Harry Antrim, Geraldine Wall. (Para, 100 min.)

1950. NO MAN OF HER OWN. *Producer:* Richard Maibaum. *Director:* Mitchell Leisen. *Screenplay:* Sally Benson, Catherine Turney from the novel "I Married a Dead Man" by William Irish (see text, page 222, on this). *Photography:* Daniel L. Fapp. *Editor:* Alma Macrorie. *Art directors:* Hans Dreier, Henry Bumstead. *Special effects:* Gordon Jennings. *Process photography:* Farciot Edouart. *Set decorators:* Sam Comer, Ray Moyer. *Costumes:* Edith Head. *Music:* Hugo Friedhofer. *Cast:* Barbara Stanwyck (Helen Ferguson, Patrice Harkness), John Lund, Jane Cowl, Phyllis Thaxter, Lyle Bettger, Henry O'Neill, Richard Denning, Carole Mathews, Harry Antrim, Catherine Craig, Esther Dale, Milburn Stone, Griff Barnett, Georgia Backus. (Para, 98 min.)

1950. THE FURIES. *Producer:* Hal B. Wallis. *Director:* Anthony Mann. *Screenplay:* Charles Schnee from a novel by Niven Busch. *Photography:* Victor Milner. *Editor:* Archie Marshek. *Art directors:* Hans Dreier, Henry Bumstead. *Special effects:* Gordon Jennings. *Process photography:* Farciot Edouart. *Set decorators:* Sam Comer, Bertram Granger. *Costumes:* Edith Head. *Music:* Franz Waxman. *Cast:* Barbara Stanwyck (Vance Jeffords), Wendell Corey, Walter Huston, Judith Anderson, Gilbert Roland, Thomas Gomez, Beulah Bondi, Albert Dekker, John Bromfield,

Wallace Ford, Blanche Yurka, Louis Jean Heydt, Frank Ferguson. (Para, 109 min.)

1950. TO PLEASE A LADY. *Producer-director:* Clarence Brown. *Screenplay:* Barré Lyndon and Marge Decker. *Photography:* Harold Rosson. *Editor:* Robert J. Kern. *Art directors:* Cedric Gibbons, James Basevi. *Special effects:* A. Arnold Gillespie, Warren Newcombe. *Montage:* Peter Ballbusch. *Set decorators:* Edwin B. Willis, Ralph S. Hurst. *Costumes:* Helen Rose. *Music:* Bronislau Kaper. *Cast:* Clark Gable, Barbara Stanwyck (Regina Forbes), Adolphe Menjou, Will Geer, Roland Winters, William C. McGaw, Lela Bliss, Emory Parnell, Frank Jenks, Helen Spring, Bill Hickman, Lew Smith, Ted Husing. (M-G-M, 91 min.)

1951. THE MAN WITH A CLOAK. *Producer:* Stephen Ames. *Director:* Fletcher Markle. *Screenplay:* Frank Fenton from a story by John Dickson Carr. *Photography:* George Folsey. *Editor:* Newell P. Kimlin. *Art directors:* Cedric Gibbons, Arthur Lonergan. *Set decorators:* Edwin B. Willis, Arthur Krams. *Women's costumes:* Walter Plunkett. *Men's costumes:* Gile Steele. *Music:* David Raksin. *Cast:* Joseph Cotten, Barbara Stanwyck (Lorna Bounty), Louis Calhern, Leslie Caron, Joe DeSantis, Jim Backus, Margaret Wycherly, Richard Hale, Nicholas Joy, Roy Roberts, Mitchell Lewis. (M-G-M, 81 min.)

1952. CLASH BY NIGHT. *Executive producers:* Jerry Wald, Norman Krasna. *Producer:* Harriet Parsons. *Director:* Fritz Lang. *Screenplay:* Alfred Hayes from the play by Clifford Odets. *Photography:* Nicholas Musuraca. *Editor:* George J. Amy. *Art directors:* Albert S. D'Agostino, Carroll Clark. *Special effects:* Harold Wellman. *Set decorators:* Darrell Silvera, Jack Mills. *Costumes:* Michael Woulfe. *Music:* Roy Webb. *Music director:* C. Bakaleinikoff. *Cast:* Barbara Stanwyck (Mae Doyle), Paul Douglas, Robert Ryan, Marilyn Monroe, J. Carrol Naish, Keith Andes, Silvio Minciotti. (RKO, 105 min.)

1953. JEOPARDY. *Producer:* Sol Baer Fielding. *Director:* John Sturges. *Screenplay:* Mel Dinelli from a story by Maurice Zimm. *Photography:* Victor Milner. *Editor:* Newell P. Kimlin. *Art directors:* Cedric Gibbons, William Ferrari. *Set decorators:* Edwin B. Willis, Fred MacLean. *Costumes:* Helen Rose. *Music and direction:* Dimitri Tiomkin. *Cast:* Barbara Stanwyck (Helen Stilwin), Barry Sullivan, Ralph Meeker, Lee Aaker. (M-G-M, 69 min.)

1953. TITANIC. *Producer:* Charles Brackett. *Director:* Jean Negulesco. *Screenplay:* Charles Brackett, Walter Reisch, Richard Breen. *Photography:* Joe MacDonald. *Editor:* Louis Loeffler. *Art directors:* Lyle Wheeler, Maurice Ransford. *Set decorator:* Stuart

Reiss. *Costumes:* Dorothy Jeakins. *Music:* Sol Kaplan. *Music director:* Lionel Newman. *Orchestration:* Herbert Spencer. *Cast:* Clifton Webb, Barbara Stanwyck (Julia Sturges), Audrey Dalton, Harper Carter, Robert Wagner, Brian Aherne, Thelma Ritter, Richard Basehart, Allyn Joslyn, James Todd, Frances Bergen, William Johnstone. (20th, 98 min.)

1953. ALL I DESIRE. *Producer:* Ross Hunter. *Director:* Douglas Sirk. *Screenplay:* James Gunn, Robert Blees from the novel "Stopover" by Carol Brink. *Adaptation:* Gina Kaus. *Photography:* Carl Guthrie. *Editor:* Milton Carruth. *Art directors:* Bernard Herzbrun, Alexander Golitzen. *Set decorators:* Russell A. Gausman, Julia Heron. *Costumes:* Rosemary Odell. *Music director:* Joseph Gershenson. *Cast:* Barbara Stanwyck (Naomi Murdoch), Richard Carlson, Lyle Bettger, Marcia Henderson, Lori Nelson, Maureen O'Sullivan, Richard Long, Billy Gray, Lotte Stein, Dayton Lummis, Fred Nurney. (Univ, 79 min.)

1953. THE MOONLIGHTER. *Producer:* Joseph Bernhard. *Director:* Roy Rowland. *Screenplay:* Niven Busch. *Photography:* Bert Glennon (Natural Vision 3-D). *Editor:* Terry Morse. *Art director:* Dan Hall. *Set decorator:* Fred MacLean. *Costumes:* Joe King, Ann Peck. *Music and direction:* Heinz Roemheld. *Cast:* Barbara Stanwyck (Rela), Fred MacMurray, Ward Bond, William Ching, John Dierkes, Morris Ankrum, Jack Elam, Charles Halton, Norman Leavitt, Sam Flint, Myra Marsh. (WB, 77 min.)

1953. BLOWING WILD. *Producer:* Milton Sperling. *Director:* Hugo Fregonese. *Screenplay:* Philip Yordan. *Photography:* Sid Hickox. *Editor:* Alan Crosland Jr. *Art director:* Al Ybarra. *Set decorator:* William Wallace. *Music:* Dimitri Tiomkin. *Music director:* Ray Heindorf. *Cast:* Gary Cooper, Barbara Stanwyck (Marina), Ruth Roman, Anthony Quinn, Ward Bond, Ian MacDonald, Richard Karlan. (WB, 90 min.)

1954. WITNESS TO MURDER. *Producer:* Chester Erskine. *Director:* Roy Rowland. *Screenplay:* Chester Erskine. *Photography:* John Alton. *Editor:* Robert Swink. *Art director:* William Ferrari. *Set decorator:* Alfred E. Spencer. *Costumes:* Jack Masters, Irene Caine. *Music:* Herschel Burke Gilbert. *Cast:* Barbara Stanwyck (Cheryl Draper), George Sanders, Gary Merrill, Jesse White, Harry Shannon, Claire Carleton, Lewis Martin, Dick Elliott, Harry Tyler, Juanita Moore, Joy Hallward, Adeline DeWalt Reynolds, Gertrude Graner. (UA, 83 min.)

1954. EXECUTIVE SUITE. *Producer:* John Houseman. *Director:* Robert Wise. *Screenplay:* Ernest Lehman from the novel by Cameron Hawley. *Photog-*

raphy: George Folsey. *Editor:* Ralph E. Winters. *Art directors:* Cedric Gibbons, Edward Carfagno. *Special effects:* A. Arnold Gillespie, Warren Newcombe. *Set decorators:* Edwin B. Willis, Emile Kuri. *Women's costumes:* Helen Rose. *Cast:* William Holden, June Allyson, Barbara Stanwyck (Julia Tredway), Fredric March, Walter Pidgeon, Shelley Winters, Paul Douglas, Louis Calhern, Dean Jagger, Nina Foch, Tim Considine, William Phipps, Lucille Knoch, Edgar Stehli, Mary Adams, Virginia Brissac, Harry Shannon. (M-G-M, 104 min.)

1955. CATTLE QUEEN OF MONTANA. *Producer:* Benedict Bogeaus. *Director:* Allan Dwan. *Screenplay:* Howard Estabrook and Robert Blees from a story by Thomas Blackburn. *Photography:* John Alton (Technicolor). *Editor:* Carl Lodato. *Art director:* Van Nest Polglase. *Set decorator:* John Sturtevant. *Costumes:* Gwen Wakeling. *Music:* Louis Forbes. *Cast:* Barbara Stanwyck (Sierra Nevada Jones), Ronald Reagan, Gene Evans, Lance Fuller, Anthony Caruso, Jack Elam, Yvette Dugay, Morris Ankrum, Chubby Johnson, Myron Healey, Rod Redwing. (RKO, 88 min.)

1955. THE VIOLENT MEN. *Producer:* Lewis J. Rachmil. *Director:* Rudolph Maté. *Screenplay:* Harry Kleiner from a novel by Donald Hamilton. *Photography:* Burnett Guffey, W. Howard Greene (Technicolor, CinemaScope). *Editor:* Jerome Thoms. *Art director:* Carl Anderson. *Set decorator:* Louis Diage. *Costumes:* Jean Louis. *Music:* Max Steiner. *Music director:* Morris Stoloff. *Orchestration:* Murray Cutter. *Cast:* Glenn Ford, Barbara Stanwyck (Martha Wilkison), Edward G. Robinson, Dianne Foster, Brian Keith, May Wynn, Warner Anderson, Basil Ruysdael, Lita Milan, Richard Jaeckel, James Westerfield, Jack Kelly, Willis Bouchey, Harry Shannon. (Col, 96 min.)

1955. ESCAPE TO BURMA. *Producer:* Benedict Bogeaus. *Director:* Allan Dwan. *Screenplay:* Talbot Jennings and Hobart Donavan from a story "Bow Tamely To Me" by Kenneth Perkins. *Photography:* John Alton (Technicolor, SuperScope). *Editor:* James Leicester. *Art director:* Van Nest Polglase. *Set decorator:* Fay Babcock. *Costumes:* Gwen Wakeling. *Music:* Louis Forbes. *Cast:* Barbara Stanwyck (Gwen Moore), Robert Ryan, David Farrar, Murvyn Vye, Lisa Montell, Robert Warwick, Reginald Denny, Peter Coe, Alex Montoya, Robert Cabal, Anthony Numkema, Lala Chand Mehra. (RKO, 88 min.)

1956. THERE'S ALWAYS TOMORROW. *Producer:* Ross Hunter. *Director:* Douglas Sirk. *Screenplay:* Bernard C. Schoenfeld from a story by Ursula Parrott. *Photography:* Russell Metty. *Editor:* William M. Morgan. *Art directors:* Alexander Golitzen, Eric Orbom. *Set decorators:* Russell A. Gausman, Julia Heron. *Costumes:* Jay Morley Jr. *Music:* Herman Stein, Heinz Roemheld. *Cast:* Barbara Stanwyck (Norma Miller), Fred MacMurray, Joan Bennett, Pat Crowley, William Reynolds, Gigi Perreau, Judy Nugent, Jane Darwell. (Univ, 84 min.)

1956. THE MAVERICK QUEEN. *Assoc. producer-director:* Joe Kane. *Screenplay:* Kenneth Gamet and DeVallon Scott from the novel by Zane Grey. *Photography:* Jack Marta (Naturama, Trucolor). *Editor:* Richard L. Van Enger. *Art director:* Walter Keller. *Special effects:* Howard and Theodore Lydecker. *Set decorators:* John McCarthy Jr., Fay Babcock. *Costumes:* Adele Palmer. *Music:* Victor Young. *Cast:* Barbara Stanwyck (Kit Banion), Barry Sullivan, Scott Brady, Mary Murphy, Wallace Ford, Howard Petrie, Jim Davis, Emile Meyer, Walter Sande, George Keymas, John Doucette, Taylor Holmes, Pierre Watkin. (Republic, 92 min.)

1956. THESE WILDER YEARS. *Producer:* Jules Schermer. *Director:* Roy Rowland. *Screenplay:* Frank Fenton from a story by Ralph Wheelwright. *Photography:* George Folsey. *Editor:* Ben Lewis. *Art directors:* Cedric Gibbons, Preston Ames. *Set decorators:* Edwin B. Willis, Edward G. Boyle. *Costumes:* Helen Rose. *Music:* Jeff Alexander. *Cast:* James Cagney, Barbara Stanwyck (Ann Dempster), Walter Pidgeon, Betty Lou Keim, Don Dubbins, Edward Andrews, Basil Ruysdael, Grandon Rhodes. (M-G-M, 91 min.)

1957. CRIME OF PASSION. *Executive producer:* Bob Goldstein. *Producer:* Herman Cohen. *Director:* Gerd Oswald. *Screenplay:* Joe Eisinger. *Photography:* Joseph La Shelle. *Editor:* Marjorie Fowler. *Art director:* Leslie Thomas. *Set decorator:* Morris Hoffman. *Costumes:* Grace Houston. *Music:* Paul Dunlap. *Cast:* Barbara Stanwyck (Kathy), Sterling Hayden, Raymond Burr, Fay Wray, Royal Dano, Virginia Grey, Dennis Cross, Robert Griffin, Jay Adler, Malcolm Atterbury, John S. Launer. (UA, 84 min.)

1957. TROOPER HOOK. *Producer:* Sol Baer Fielding. *Director:* Charles Marquis Warren. *Screenplay:* Warren, David Victor and Herbert Little Jr. from a story by Jack Schaefer. *Photography:* Ellsworth Fredericks. *Editor:* Fred Berger. *Art director:* Nick Remisoff. *Women's costumes:* Voulee Giokaris. *Music and direction:* Gerald Fried. *Cast:* Joel McCrea, Barbara Stanwyck (Cora), Earl Holliman, Edward Andrews, John Dehner, Susan Kohner, Royal Dano, Terry Lawrence, Celia Lovsky, Rudolfo Acosta. (UA, 81 min.)

1957. FORTY GUNS. *Producer, director, screenplay:* Samuel Fuller. *Photography:* Joseph Biroc (CinemaScope). *Editor:* Gene Fowler Jr. *Art director:* John

Mansbridge. *Set decorators:* Walter M. Scott, Chester Bayhi. *Costumes:* Charles LeMaire, Leah Rhodes. *Music and direction:* Harry Sukman. *Cast:* Barbara Stanwyck (Jessica Drummond), Barry Sullivan, Dean Jagger, John Ericson, Gene Barry, Robert Dix, Jidge Carroll, Paul Dubov, Gerald Milton, Ziva Rodann, Hank Worden, Neyle Morrow, Eve Brent. (20th, 80 min.)

1962. WALK ON THE WILD SIDE. *Producer:* Charles K. Feldman. *Director:* Edward Dmytryk. *Screenplay:* John Fante and Edmund Morris from the novel by Nelson Algren. *Photography:* Joe MacDonald. *Editor:* Harry Gerstad. *Art director:* Richard Sylbert. *Set decorator:* William Kiernan. *Costumes:* Charles LeMaire. *Music:* Elmer Bernstein. *Orchestration:* Leo Shuken, Jack Hayes. *Cast:* Laurence Harvey, Capucine, Jane Fonda, Anne Baxter, Barbara Stanwyck (Jo Courtney), Joanna Moore, Richard Rust, Karl Swenson, Donald Barry, Juanita Moore, John Anderson, Ken Lynch, Todd Armstrong, Lillian Bronson, Adrienne Marden, Sherry O'Neil, John Bryant, Kathryn Card. (Col, 114 min.)

1964. ROUSTABOUT. *Producer:* Hal B. Wallis. *Director:* John Rich. *Screenplay:* Anthony Lawrence and Allan Weiss from a story by Weiss. *Photography:* Lucien Ballard (Technicolor, Techniscope). *Editor:* Warren Low. *Art directors:* Hal Pereira, Walter Tyler. *Special effects:* Paul K. Lerpae. *Process photography:* Farciot Edouart. *Set decorators:* Sam Comer, Robert Benton. *Costumes:* Edith Head. *Music and direction:* Joseph J. Lilley. *Cast:* Elvis Presley, Barbara Stanwyck (Maggie Morgan), Joan Freeman, Leif Erickson, Sue Ane Langdon, Pat Buttram, Joan Staley, Dabbs Greer, Steve Brodie, Norman Grabowski, Jack Albertson, Jane Dulo. (Para, 101 min.)

1965. THE NIGHT WALKER. *Producer-director:* William Castle. *Screenplay:* Robert Bloch. *Photography:* Harold E. Stine. *Editor:* Edwin H. Bryant. *Art directors:* Alexander Golitzen, Frank Arrigo. *Set decorators:* John McCarthy, Julia Heron. *Costumes:* Helen Colvig. *Music:* Vic Mizzy. *Music director:* Joseph Gershenson. *Cast:* Robert Taylor, Barbara Stanwyck (Irene Trent), Judith Meredith, Hayden Rorke, Rochelle Hudson, Marjorie Bennett, Jess Barker, Tetsu Kumal, Ted Durant, Lloyd Bochner. (Univ, 86 min.)

1970. THE HOUSE THAT WOULDN'T DIE. *Producer:* Aaron Spelling. *Director:* John Llewellyn Moxey. *Teleplay:* Henry Farrell from the novel "Ammie, Come Home" by Barbara Michaels. *Photography:* Fleet Southcott (Color). *Editor:* Art Seid. *Art director:* Tracy Bousman. *Stanwyck costumes:* Nolan Miller. *Music:* Laurence Rosenthal. *Music director:* George Duning. *Cast:* Barbara Stanwyck (Ruth Bennett), Richard Egan, Michael Anderson Jr., Katherine Winn, Doreen Lang, Mabel Albertson. (ABC Movie of the Week, 73 min.)

1971. A TASTE OF EVIL. *Producer:* Aaron Spelling. *Director:* John Llewellyn Moxey. *Teleplay:* Jimmy Sangster. *Photography:* Arch Dalzell (Color). *Editor:* Art Seid. *Art director:* Paul Sylos. *Stanwyck costumes:* Nolan Miller. *Music:* Robert Drasnin. *Cast:* Barbara Stanwyck (Miriam Jennings), Barbara Parkins, Roddy McDowall, William Windom, Arthur O'Connell, Bing Russell, Dawn Frame. (ABC Movie of the Week, 74 min.)

1973. THE LETTERS. *Executive producers:* Aaron Spelling, Leonard Goldberg. *Producer:* Paul Junger Witt. Credits for Stanwyck story: *Director:* Gene Nelson. *Teleplay:* Ellis Marcus, Hal Sitowitz from a story by Marcus. *Photography:* Tim Southcott (Color). *Editor:* Carroll Sax. *Art director:* Tracy Bousman. *Stanwyck costumes:* Nolan Miller. *Music supervisor:* Rocky Moriana. *Cast:* Story 1—John Forsythe, Jane Powell, Lesley Warren. Story 2—Barbara Stanwyck (Geraldine Parkington), Leslie Nielsen, Dina Merrill. Story 3—Ida Lupino, Ben Murphy, Pamela Franklin. (ABC Movie of the Week, 74 min.)

INDEX

Aaker, Lee, 237
Academy Award, 50, 110, 147, 162, 177, 212, 229, 242, 248
Alcoa-Goodyear Playhouse, 271
Algren, Nelson, 280
All I Desire, 241–42
Allyson, June, 280
Alton, John, 255
Always Goodbye, 115
Ameche, Don, 134
American Society of Cinematographers, 32, 200
Anderson, Judith, 229
Anderson, Michael Jr., 311
Annie Oakley, 75–77, 93, 229, 237, 271
Anybody's Girl, 27
Arliss, George, 27
Arnold, Edward, 138
Asther, Nils, 50, 54
Astor, Mary, 100
Atkinson, Brooks, 11
Baby Face, 47, 54–55, 62
Back Street, 39
Ball of Fire, 83, 93, 99, 147, 155–62, 185
Banjo On My Knee, 90, 93
Barbara Frietchie, 5
Barbara Stanwyck Show, The, 68, 185, 271–80, 293
Barnes, George, 215
Barnes, Howard, 125
Barnett, S. H., 212
Barrymore, John, 27
Barrymore, Lionel, 27–29
Baxter, Anne, 280
Beebe, Lucius, 125–28
Beery, Wallace, 77
Beich, Albert, 273, 279–80
Bellamy, Ralph, 39, 279
Bennett, Belle, 99, 110
Benny, Jack, 83
Benson, Sally, 222
Bernhardt, Curtis, 181
Bettger, Lyle, 222, 227
Bezzerides, A. I., 293
B. F.'s Daughter, 203–7
Big Valley, The, 1, 99, 185, 237, 265, 271, 287, 293–304, 317
Bitter Tea of General Yen, The, 47–54
Bless You Sister, 32
Blondell, Joan, 27, 29, 279
Blore, Eric, 113
Blowing Wild, 47, 247
Boehnel, William, 42, 55
Bogart, Humphrey, 185, 215
Bogeaus, Benedict, 255
Boles, John, 77, 99, 100, 103, 110
Bonanza, 293

Bondi, Beulah, 133
Bond, Ward, 247
Boyd, William, 13
Boyer, Charles, 165, 169
Brackett, Charles, 155, 242
Brady, Scott, 259–60
Breakfast for Two, 113–15
Breck, Peter, 293, 304
Breen, Richard, 242
Brennan, Walter, 90, 138
Brent, George, 41–42, 47, 116, 165, 181
Bretherton, Howard, 54
Bride Walks Out, The, 77–80
Bride Wore Boots, The, 185–92
Brilles, Charles, 293
British Agent, 62
Broadway Nights, 8
Broderick, Helen, 80
Brokaw, Norman, 288
Brook, Clive, 115
Brown, Harry, 202
Burdett, Winston, 125
Burke, James, 116
Burlesque, 8–11, 13, 14, 27
Busch, Niven, 247
Butterworth, Charles, 27
Byington, Spring, 138
Cagney, James, 260
Cain, James M., 170, 177
Calhern, Louis, 232
California, 14, 93, 198–200
Capra, Frank, 1, 5, 14–24, 29, 32–39, 47–50, 110, 134–38
Capucine, 280
Caron, Leslie, 232
Castle, William, 287–88
Cather, Willa, 62, 68
Cattle Queen of Montana, 248–55
Chandler, Raymond, 170
Chatterton, Ruth, 8, 100
Christmas in Connecticut, 181–85
Christmas in July, 145
Clarke, Mae, 4, 11
Clash By Night, 233–37
Coburn, Charles, 145
Cohan, George M., 4
Cohn, Harry, 14, 17, 29, 34, 128
Colbert, Claudette, 134
Coleman, Nancy, 165
Concealment, 68
Conte, Richard, 200, 202
Cooper, Gary, 109, 138, 155, 162, 247
Coray, Harriett, 191, 304
Corey, Wendell, 215, 222, 229
Cortez, Ricardo, 27–29, 62
Cortez, Stanley, 169
Cotten, Joseph, 232
Cowl, Jane, 5
Crime of Passion, 260

Cromwell, John, 13, 90
Cry Wolf, 200
Cummings, Bob, 185, 191–92

Dance of Life, The, 13
Dark Victory, 83
Daves, Delmer, 181
Davis, Bette, 68, 115, 215, 241, 260, 288
Davis, Nancy, 227
Dawn, Hazel, 4
Death Comes for the Archbishop, 68
DeMille, Cecil B., 83, 99, 125, 128, 133, 237
DeSantis, Joe, 232
Desperate Women, 271
DeSylva, Buddy, 170
De Toth, Andre, 202–3
Devine, Andy, 215
Dieterle, William, 68
Dodd, Claire, 62
Donaldson, Walter, 4
Donavan, Hobart, 255
Donlevy, Brian, 93, 151
Dooley, Johnny, 4
Dorfman, Ania, 202
Double Indemnity, 54, 55, 99, 169–77, 181, 195, 212, 247, 255, 273, 290
Douglas, Kirk, 177, 195, 198
Douglas, Paul, 233, 237
Dreier, Hans, 90, 170
Dress Doctor, The, 147, 151, 212
Duel in the Sun, 247
Duvivier, Julien, 169
Dwan, Allan, 259, 318

East Side, West Side, 203, 227
Ebsen, Buddy, 90
Eburne, Maude, 54
Edelman, Louis F., 293
Egan, Richard, 311
Emmy Award, 273, 280, 304
Epstein, Phil, 77
Escape to Burma, 248, 255–59
Evans, Linda, 293
Everglades Café, 4
Ever In My Heart, 27, 58, 62
Executive Suite, 233, 247–48
Exploits of Elaine, The, 1

Farrar, David, 259
Farrow, John, 198
Fay, Frank, 11, 14–17, 77
Ferber, Edna, 41
File on Thelma Jordan, The, 215–22
Film Daily Award, 138, 248
Fitzgerald and Pride, 313
Fitzgerald, Barry, 198–200
Flesh and Fantasy, 165–69
Fletcher, Lucille, 211
Florey, Robert, 68–73, 273

Flynn, Errol, 200
Fodor, Ladislas, 202
Folsey, George, 233, 248
Fonda, Henry, 116, 120, 145, 147, 155
Forbidden, 29, 34–39
Ford, John, 83–90, 294
Ford Theatre, 271
Forsythe, John, 313
Forty Guns, 241, 263–65
Foster, Preston, 54, 75, 83
Fox, William, 202
Foxworth, Robert, 241
Frings, Ketti, 215
From A to Z, 155
Fuller, Samuel, 1, 263–65
Furies, The, 229, 237, 247

Gable, Clark, 29–32, 54, 94, 109, 229–32
Gabriel, Gilbert, 8–11
Gallant Lady, 115
Gambling Lady, 62
Gardiner, Reginald, 185
Gay Paree, 4
Gay Sisters, The, 47, 83, 165
Gemora, Charles, 151
Gilbert, Billy, 80
Gilbert, John, 104
Gillette, Ruth, 4
Gilmour, Clyde, 248
Gleason, James, 138
Godfrey, Peter, 181, 185, 200
Golden Boy, 125, 128–33, 248
Goldwyn, Samuel, 93–94, 100, 109, 155
Good Earth, The, 110
Gordon, Michael, 215
Granville, Bonita, 100
Graves, Ralph, 21–24
Great Man's Lady, The, 29, 83, 93, 147–55
Great McGinty, The, 145
Green, Alfred E., 62
Greene, Lorne, 293
Greenstreet, Sidney, 185
Gregory, James, 304
Grey, Zane, 259
Grinde, Nick, 41
G-String Murders, The, 169

Hahn, Bill, 211, 287
Hale, Alan, 100, 103, 104, 110
Harding, Ann, 115
Hardy, Sam, 8, 13, 32, 34
Harmon, David, 273
Hart, Lorenz, 27
Hart, Richard, 207
Harvey, Laurence, 280
Hawks, Howard, 155, 162
Hayden, Sterling, 260
Hayes, Alfred, 233

Hayes, Bernadine, 100
Hayward, Susan, 313
Head, Edith, 145, 147, 151, 198, 212, 287
Heat of Anger, 313
Heflin, Van, 195–98, 203–7, 227
Hellman, Lillian, 241
Hersholt, Jean, 80
Hickox, Sidney, 47
High Noon, 247
His Brother's Wife, 80–83
Holden, William, 128–33, 248
Hollis, Bud, 304
Holloway, Sterling, 133
Hollywood Canteen, 181
Hollywood Star Playhouse, 215
Hopkins, Arthur, 8, 11, 17
Hopkins, Miriam, 260
Hopper, Hedda, 4, 185, 242
Hopwood, Avery, 4
Horan, James D., 271
House Is Not a Home, A, 288
House That Wouldn't Die, The, 311
Housman, A. E., 242
Howard, Leslie, 62
Hughes, Whitey, 259
Hunter, Ross, 242
Hurst, Fannie, 39
Huston, John, 229
Huston, Walter, 109, 229
Hyams, Joe, 280

Illicit, 27
I Married a Dead Man, 222
Internes Can't Take Money, 90–93
Irene, 203
Irish, William, 222
Irwin, Wallace, 68
It Happened One Night, 75
Ivano, Paul, 169

James, Kent, 304
Janssen, David, 271
Jason, Leigh, 77, 80, 115–16, 120
Jeffers, William, 128
Jennings, Talbot, 255
Jeopardy, 237–41

Kane, Bob, 5
Kane, Joe, 259
Keep Kool, 1–4
Keighley, William, 54, 212, 215
Keith, Brian, 255
Kenton, Erle C., 14
Kiam, Omar, 100
King, Charles, 4
Korda, Sir Alexander, 14, 17
Kruger, Otto, 58

Ladies of Leisure, 1, 5, 14–24, 27, 110, 115
Ladies of the Evening, 21
Ladies They Talk About, 54
Lady Eve, The, 83, 99, 116, 145–47, 155, 185
Lady Gambles, The, 215
Lady of Burlesque, 93, 169
LaHiff, Billy, 4
Lambert, Gavin, 273
Lancaster, Burt, 212
Lang, Fritz, 233–37
La Rocque, Rod, 13
Lee, Gypsy Rose, 169
Le Gallienne, Eva, 34
Leisen, Mitchell, 133, 134, 222–27
Leonard, Robert Z., 203–7
Letters, The, 313–17
Levant, Oscar, 11
Levene, Sam, 115, 116
Lightner, Winnie, 4
Lindsay, Earl, 1–4
Little Joe, 279–80
Litvak, Anatole, 211, 212
Locked Door, The, 8, 13
Lombard, Carole, 134
Long, Richard, 293, 301, 304
Longstreet, Stephen, 165
Lord, Pauline, 8
Loretta Young Show, The, 271
Lost Lady, A, 47, 62–68
Lund, John, 222
Lupino, Ida, 313
Lux Radio Theatre, 83, 109, 115, 120, 134, 212–15

Mack, Willard, 4–5, 17
MacMurray, Fred, 133, 134, 170, 177, 247, 259
Macy, Dora, 29
Madden, Owney, 198
Mad Miss Manton, The, 115–20
Main Street, 83
Majors, Lee, 293, 301
Mamoulian, Rouben, 133
Man in the Dog Suit, The, 279
Mann, Anthony, 229
Manners, David, 32, 34
Mansfield, Walda, 4
Man With a Cloak, The, 93, 232–33
Markey, Gene, 62
Markle, Fletcher, 232, 233
Marquand, John P., 203
Marshall, George, 77
Marshall, Herbert, 113
Martin, Tony, 90
Marvin, Lee, 273
Mason, James, 227

Mason, Sarah Y., 41
Maté, Rudolph, 77, 109
Maverick Queen, The, 241, 259–60
Mayo, Archie, 27, 58, 62
McCrea, Joel, 62, 90, 93–94, 125, 151, 155, 263, 317–18
McPherson, Aimee Semple, 32
Meehan, John, 32
Meeker, Ralph, 237, 241
Meet John Doe, 134–38
Menjou, Adolph, 39
Mercer, Frances, 116
Merrill, Dina, 313, 317
Message to Garcia, A, 77
Mexicali Rose, 13–14, 80
Midnight, 134
Milestone, Lewis, 195–98
Milland, Ray, 198, 215
Miller, Arthur, 241
Milner, Victor, 145, 155, 229
Miracle Woman, The, 32–34
Mohr, Hal, 273
Monroe, Marilyn, 233, 263
Monroe, Thomas, 155
Moonlighter, The, 247
Moore, Colleen, 41
Moore, Dickie, 41
Moorehead, Agnes, 211
Morgan, Dennis, 181, 185
Morgan, Frank, 62, 68
Morning Glory, 83, 120
Morse, Wilbur Jr., 5–8
Motion Picture Costumers' Award, 147
Motion Picture Exhibitor Award, 237, 242, 248
Moxey, John Llewellyn, 311, 313
Musuraca, Nicholas, 115, 128, 233, 273
My Reputation, 47, 181

Name Above the Title, The, 1, 14–17, 20, 21, 32, 34, 39, 50, 110, 138
National Board of Review Award, 147, 248
National Cowboy Hall of Fame Award, 317–18
Negulesco, Jean, 242
Nelson, Ralph, 1, 211
Nielsen, Leslie, 313, 317
Night Nurse, 29–32, 47
Night of January 16th, The, 134
Night Walker, The, 211, 287–88
Niven, David, 200, 202
Nolan, Lloyd, 90
No Man of Her Own, 134, 222–27
Noose, The, 4–5, 8, 13, 14, 17, 20, 90
North Shore, 68

O'Brien, Pat, 62
O'Casey, Sean, 83

O'Connell, Arthur, 311–13
O'Connor, Una, 185
Odets, Clifford, 128, 233
O'Neil, Barbara, 100, 103, 109, 110
O'Neill, Eugene, 4
Only Yesterday, 83
Orry-Kelly, 55
Oswald, Gerd, 260
Other Love, The, 200–203
Owsley, Monroe, 27

Parkins, Barbara, 311, 313
Parsons, Harriet, 233–37
Patterson, Elizabeth, 133
Peck, Gregory, 215
Penny Serenade, 83
Pereira, Hal, 170
Perils of Pauline, The, 1, 125
Photoplay Magazine Awards, 304
Pichel, Irving, 185, 191–92
Pickford, Mary, 200
Pine, Bill, 128
Pioneer Woman, 151
Plough and the Stars, The, 83–90
Pola, Eddie, 232
Polglase, Van Nest, 115, 255
Polito, Sol, 211
Pollock, Channing, 13
Portrait: Barbara Stanwyck, 1, 93, 169, 191, 211, 280, 294, 304
Powell, Dick, 271
Presley, Elvis, 287
Presnell, Robert, 134
Preston, Robert, 125, 215
Princess Many Victories III, 255
Professional Photographers of California Award, 287
Prouty, Olive Higgins, 110
Purchase Price, The, 47

Quinn, Anthony, 247

Raft, George, 170
Rainer, Luise, 110
Raksin, David, 233
Rapper, Irving, 165
Rawhide, 287
Raymond, Gene, 68, 77–80
Reagan, Governor Ronald, 255, 307
Red Salute, 75
Reed, Donna, 280
Reisch, Walter, 242
Remarque, Erich Maria, 200
Remember the Night, 83, 133–34, 145, 147, 227
Rennahan, Ray, 14, 198–200
Rennie, James, 27
Rich, David Lowell, 273

Ridges, Stanley, 222
Rifleman, The, 304
Riskin, Robert, 32, 41, 134
Robinson, Edward G., 170, 177, 255
Rodgers, Richard, 27
Rogers, Ginger, 215
Roland, Gilbert, 229
Roseland, 27
Rossen, Robert, 195
Rosson, Arthur, 125
Roustabout, 287
Rowland, Roy, 247, 260
Rozsa, Miklos, 170, 195, 200, 202
Ruggles, Wesley, 155
Russell, Johnnie, 115
Ruttenberg, Joseph, 203–7
Ryan, Robert, 233, 237, 259
Ryder, Loren, 177

St. Joseph, Ellis, 273
Sakall, S. Z., 185
Sanders, George, 248
Santell, Alfred, 90–93, 113–15
Schenck, Joseph, 13
Scola, Kathryn, 62
Scott, George C., 241
Scott, Vernon, 288
Screen Actors Guild Award, 307–9
Screen Guild Players, 83, 215
Secret Bride, The, 68
Seitz, John, 54, 170, 177
Selznick, David O., 318
Sennett, Mack, 113
Shanghai Gesture, 169
Shirley, Anne, 47, 94, 99, 100, 103, 104,
   109, 110
Shopworn, 39–41
Shore, Dinah, 280
Sign on the Door, The, 13
Siodmak, Robert, 215, 222
Sirk, Douglas, 242, 259
Skelly, Hal, 8–11, 13, 27
Small, Edward, 75
Smilin' Through, 83
Smith, Dave, 287
So Big, 29, 41–42, 47, 55, 83
Song of the Lark, The, 68
Sorry, Wrong Number, 211–15
Sothern, Ann, 280
Sparks, Ned, 80
Spelling, Aaron, 271, 313
Stanley, John, 301–4
Stanwyck, Jane, 5
Steiner, Max, 165
Stein, Jules, 181
Stella Dallas, 55, 83, 93–94, 99–110,
   113, 115, 170
Stevens, Byron, 1

Stevens, Catherine McGee, 1
Stevens, George, 75
Stevens, Millie, 1
Stevenson, Houseley, 215
Stevens, Ruby, 1, 5
Stine, Harold E., 288
Stopover, 242
Strand Roof, 1
Strange Love of Martha Ivers, The, 165,
   177, 195–98, 200, 203
Stromberg, Hunt, 169
Sturges, John, 237
Sturges, Preston, 133, 134, 145, 147
Sullivan, Barry, 237, 241, 259, 263
Sutherland, A. Edward, 13
Swerling, Jo, 21, 27, 32, 39, 41

Talbot, Lyle, 47, 68
Talmadge, Norma, 13
Taste of Evil, A, 311–13
Taylor, Robert, 80, 93, 128, 202, 215,
   232, 288
Ten Cents a Dance, 27–29
Tetzlaff, Ted, 134
Thaxter, Phyllis, 222
There's Always Tomorrow, 259
These Three, 83
These Wilder Years, 233, 260
This Above All, 83
This Is My Affair, 93
Thomas, Bob, 293
Three of a Kind, 170
Tiller, Lawrence, 4
Titanic, 242, 247
To a Lonely Boy, 8, 11
Toland, Gregg, 162
Toomey, Regis, 39, 41
To Please a Lady, 229–32
Tourneur, Jacques, 273–79
Tracy, Spencer, 241
Treasure of Sierra Madre, The, 247
Tree Is a Tree, A, 104
Trooper Hook, 263
Tums Hollywood Theatre, 215
Turney, Catherine, 222
TV-Radio Mirror Magazine Award, 304
Two Mrs. Carrolls, The, 181, 185

Union Pacific, 125–28
Untouchables, The, 287

Van, Billy, 4
Van Dyke, W. S., 83
Van Fleet, Jo, 260
Variety Girl, 203
Vidor, King, 93, 94, 99, 100, 104, 109,
   110, 115
Violent Men, The, 255

Vogel, Virgil, 287, 294–301
Von Sternberg, Josef, 169
Vye, Murvyn, 255

Wagner, Robert, 242
Wagon Train, 287
Wald, Jerry, 233
Walker, Joseph, 1, 17, 32–34, 39, 41, 50, 115, 155
Walk On the Wild Side, 265, 280
Wallis, Hal B., 211, 229, 287
Warren, Charles Marquis, 263
Watters, George Manker, 8
Waxman, Franz, 80, 83, 185, 200, 211, 229
Webb, Roy, 115, 233
Wellman, William, 29, 41, 47, 151, 169
Werlé, Dan, 273
Westmore, Wally, 151
White, Pearl, 1, 294
Whorf, Richard, 273
Wilder, Billy, 155, 169–70, 177, 290
William, Warren, 68
Wilson, Lois, 8

Winn, Katherine, 311
Winsten, Archer, 125
Winters, Shelley, 288
Wise, Robert, 248
Witness to Murder, 248
Wolfson, P. J., 77
Woman in Red, The, 68–73
Woman With a Whip, 263
Woodward, Joanne, 260
Woollcott, Alexander, 11
Wuthering Heights, 83, 134
Wyman, Jane, 41

Yordan, Philip, 247
You Belong to Me, 155
Young, Gig, 165
Young, Loretta, 280, 293
Young, Robert, 75
Young, Victor, 222

Zane Grey Theatre, 271
Zanuck, Darryl F., 54, 77
Ziegfeld Follies, 4